Sousveillance, Media and Strategic Political Communication

Iraq, USA, UK

Vian Bakir

continuum

NEW YORK • LONDON

The Continuum International Publishing Group Inc
80 Maiden Lane, New York, NY 10038

The Continuum International Publishing Group Ltd
The Tower Building, 11 York Road, London SE1 7NX

www.continuumbooks.com

Library of Congress Cataloging-in-Publication Data
Bakir, Vian, 1971-
  Sousveillance, media and strategic political communication : Iraq, USA, UK / Vian Bakir.
    p. cm.
  Includes bibliographical references and index.

  ISBN-13: 978-0-8264-3008-3 (hardcover : alk. paper)
  ISBN-10: 0-8264-3008-2 (hardcover : alk. paper)
  ISBN-13: 978-0-8264-3009-0 (pbk. : alk. paper)
  ISBN-10: 0-8264-3009-0 (pbk. : alk. paper)

1. Iraq War, 2003—Mass media and the war. 2. Communication in politics–Iraq.
3. Communication in politics–United States. 4. Communication in politics–Great Britain.
5. Mass media–Political aspects–Iraq. 6. Mass media–Political aspects–United States. 7. Mass media–Political aspects–Great Britain. I. Title.

  DS79.76.B349 2010
  956.7044'31–dc22

                                                        2009049171

ISBN: 978-0-8264-3008-3 (Hardback)
      978-0-8264-3009-0 (Paperback)

Typeset by Newgen Imaging Systems Pvt Ltd, Chennai, India
Printed in the United States of America

CONTENTS

ACKNOWLEDGMENTS

This book was supported by a Research Leave Scheme Award from the Arts and Humanities Research Council (AHRC). The AHRC provides funding from the UK Government to support research and postgraduate study in the arts and humanities, from archaeology and English literature to design and dance. Only applications of the highest quality and excellence are funded and the range of research supported by this investment of public funds not only provides social and cultural benefits but also contributes to the economic success of the UK. Further information on the AHRC is available at: www.ahrc.ac.uk.

The University of Glamorgan, and key staff there, have been supportive of this enterprise – in particular, David Barlow, John Beynon, Philip Mitchell, Gillian Allard, Ruth McElroy, Peter Jachimiak, Diana Brand, Peter Robertson and Brian Hobbs. Thanks also to Sanna Inthorn, for giving me the opportunity to talk to the Media & Politics group at the University of East Anglia, when this book was in its very early stages.

Particular gratitude goes to Andy, for his keen insights on the final draft, and to Ali for his continuous insights on Iraq. Thanks to Basil for all the oral history on Iraq during the 1980s. Others who have helped me out with specific details or ideas include Martin Gibbs, Rob Campbell and Ian Franklin. Several others, who wish to remain anonymous, have contributed insights. Thanks, guys!

And finally, I'd like to extend my appreciation to the neigbourhood mogs – Black-and-White Cat, Fat Cat, Sketched-Out Cat and Yoda – for keeping me sane and warm during many hours of computer time reviewing often grisly material.

Arts & Humanities
Research Council

GLOSSARY

3G	3rd Generation mobiles
320th MP Battalion	320th Military Police Battalion
372nd MP Company	372nd Military Police Company
800th MP BGD	800th Military Police Brigade
ABC	Australian Broadcasting Corporation
ABC	American Broadcasting Company
ACLU	American Civil Liberties Union
Arabsat	Arab Satellite Communications Organisation
AWRAC	Army Web Risk Assessment Cell
CBS	Columbia Broadcasting System
CD	Compact Disc
CENTCOM	Central Command (US)
CIA	Central Intelligence Agency
CID	Criminal Investigation Command
CJTF-7	Combined Joint Task Force-7
CNN	Cable News Network
CPA	Coalition Provisional Authority
CPIC	Combined Press Information Centre
DA	Department of the Army (US)
D News	Director of News (UK)

DoD	Department of Defense (USA)
DVIDS	Digital Video and Imagery Distribution System
fatwa	A non-binding, Islamic legal opinion issued by a competent Islamic authority.
fedayeen	Saddam Hussein's paramilitary force.
FOB	Forward Operating Base
hawza	The Shi'i network of clerics and seminaries based in Najaf (the spiritual centre of about 150 million Shi'i around the world).
IAEA	International Atomic Energy Agency
ICRC	International Committee of the Red Cross
IED	Improvised Explosive Device
IGC	Iraqi Governing Council
IIG	Iraqi Interim Government
imam	Islamic prayer leader, and anyone in a position of religious authority
imamate	A divine Shi'i Islamic institution, leading the Muslim community after the death of the Prophet Mohammed.
IMN	Iraqi Media Network
INA	Iraqi National Accord
INC	Iraqi National Congress
Info Ops	Information Operations
IO	Information Operations
ISF	Iraqi Security Forces
ISP	Internet Service Provider
ITN	Independent Television News
JIC	Joint Intelligence Committee (UK)
KGB	Komitet Gosudarstvennoy Bezopasnosti

khutba	A form of oratory that predates Islam.
LBC	Lebanese Broadcasting Corporation
Media Ops	Media Operations
MI	Military Intelligence
MNF	Multi-National Force
MNF-I	Multi-National Force-Iraq
MoD	Ministry of Defence (UK)
MP	Military Police
MTV	Music Television
mujahideen	A military force of Muslim guerilla warriors engaged in a *jihad* (holy war)
mukhabarat	The intelligence service in Arab regimes
NBC	National Broadcasting Company
NGO	Non-Governmental Organization
OIF	Operation Iraqi Freedom
OPSEC	Operations Security
PA	Public Affairs
Pfc.	Private First Class
PLO	Palestinian Liberation Organization
PR	Public Relations
PSB	Public Service Broadcaster/Broadcasting
Psyops	Psychological Operations
rafida	Refuters: a Sunni derogatory term for Shi'a.
RCC	Revolutionary Command Council
SCIRI	Supreme Council for the Islamic Revolution in Iraq
SERE	Survival, Evasion, Resistance and Escape
shari'a	Islamic law
SIS	Secret Intelligence Service

SMS	Short Messaging Service
Spc.	Specialist
TV	television
UAE	United Arab Emirates
UIA	United Iraqi Alliance
UK	United Kingdom
ulama	Islamic religious scholars.
ummah	The Islamic concept of the community.
UN	United Nations
UNCAT	United Nations Convention against Torture
UNMOVIC	United Nations Monitoring, Verification, and Inspection Commission
UNSCOM	United Nations Special Commission on Disarmament
URL	Uniform Resource Locator
US	United States of America
USA PATRIOT Act	Uniting and Strengthening America by Providing Appropriate Tools Required to Intercept and Obstruct Terrorism
USSR	Union of Soviet Socialist Republics
Web 1.0	World Wide Web
Web 2.0	The Social Web
Web 3.0	The Semantic Web
WMD	Weapons of Mass Destruction
WWI	World War I
WWII	World War II
WWW	World Wide Web

Chapter 1

WEB-BASED PARTICIPATORY MEDIA, STRATEGIC POLITICAL COMMUNICATION AND SOUSVEILLANCE

WEB-BASED PARTICIPATORY MEDIA AND STRATEGIC POLITICAL COMMUNICATION

This book aims to understand the limits of control over strategic political communication in the newly emerged era of web-based participatory media ('Web 2.0') across the first decade of the twenty-first century. It examines the emergence of Web 2.0 (a revolutionary way of remixing, repurposing and managing information online) and its impact on strategic political communication (the careful planning of communication tools to meet very specific political objectives). Normally strategic political communications are developed in media environments where the chosen medium of communication is well established, and therefore understood, by those seeking to manipulate it. However, as this book shall show, the emergence of Web 2.0 created a media environment that, for a while, was poorly understood, allowing challenges to strategic political communication from lay-people going about their everyday lives. These challenges from lay-people are examined through the theoretical lens of sousveillance, a concept developed by Steve Mann to explore the philosophical and techno-social issues arising from human-centred capture, processing and transmission of sensory information (Mann, 1995, 2002, 2004a, 2004b, 2005; Mann et al., 2003, 2006). I posit that sousveillance helps explain why people participate in the social practices that constitute web-based participatory media, focusing on their pleasure and personal empowerment derived from

1

sharing their lives with others, and in taking a stance against the surveillant state. Perhaps uniquely, this book explores these various processes across three countries with different approaches to strategic political communication and surveillance, and which have had their interests publicly intertwined across the first decade of the twenty-first century – namely Iraq, the US and the UK.

'Web 2.0' is a term of contentious origin, but it appears to have emerged between 2002 and 2004 (O'Reilly, 2005; O'Reilly & Battelle, 2009; McStay, 2009). Regardless of its etymology, its principles are agreed. Simply put, Web 2.0 technologies constitute the architecture of mass user participation online. It can be contrasted to the retrospectively named 'Web 1.0' model (the early World Wide Web (WWW)), although it is some way off the futuristic, speculative 'Web 3.0' model, one version of which envisages the Semantic Web where machine-readable metadata (information about information) is attached to web content to enable computers to 'understand' the meanings of the content as they process it (Metz, 2007). Since 1993, Web 1.0 had promised powerful publishing and connectivity capabilities, envisaging a change from old media practices where there were few content producers and many, relatively passive, content receivers or consumers (Castells, 1996; Anderson, 2003). As such, much 'new media' theory coming out of this era focused on the potential impacts of the new media environment upon sociality, community and citizenship, with the internet hailed as having the potential to renew citizens' political engagement and freedom of expression (Rheingold, 1993; Grossman, 1995; Negroponte, 1995; Castells, 1996; Alexander & Pal, 1998; Mosco, 2000). Arguably, however, Web 1.0 failed to live up to its ideals. Rather than becoming a space for politically re-engaging the masses, on the whole, the internet provided new venues for existing political actors, as politicians used the internet for strategic political communication activities like targeting persuasive, unmediated messages to potential voters (Singer, 2005). Furthermore, running websites required expert knowledge, and enthusiastic amateurs were soon largely replaced by professional website designers and information technology managers (Quiggin, 2006). By contrast, Web 2.0 is about the enrichment of online social interaction and communication through more *easily produced* user-generated content and users' collective intelligence (Lévy, 1997).[1] The importance of sociality and community of web-based participatory media is implicit in many authors' expositions (Fuchs, 2009). As such, Web 2.0 has attracted the moniker 'the Social Web'.

Web 2.0 encompasses technologies and social software that enable many-to-many publishing. A range of Web 2.0 technologies and social practices are discussed in this book, but the primary focus is on web logs (blogs) and social network websites. Blogs were initially basic text web pages (although they are now multi-media enabled) that allow writers to correspond directly with their audiences, and to link with other websites. Being easily updateable and time-stamped, they are akin to web diaries (Kerbel & Bloom, 2005). In 1999, blogging software tools like *LiveJournal* and *Blogger* made it possible to post blogs without any technological knowledge, introducing blogging to a wider audience (Blood, 2002; Graves, 2007). Whereas in 1999 there were just 23 blogs (Brown, 2006), by 2008 Technorati tracked over 112.8 million blogs – a figure excluding the 72.82 million Chinese blogs (Helmond, 2008). Social network websites encourage the building of online social networks of members with similar interests, and have proliferated since 2003 (Boulos & Wheeler, 2007; Boyd & Ellison, 2007). In some social network sites, all content is ostensibly provided and regulated by the users themselves – for instance *Flickr* (2004 –) and *YouTube* (2005 –). Users create and share photographs, videos, audio and other files, usually of an aesthetic quality that is 'good enuf,' taking cultural production out of the hands of the professional 'creatives' and corporations (Kinder, 2008, p. 55).

While a web that was as easy to write as it was to read was what the original architects envisaged when the WWW was launched for free public use on 30 April 1993 (Castells, 1996; CERN, 2003; Quiggin, 2006), it was not until the first few years of the twenty-first century that the tools to enable this mass interaction were developed, leading to what has since been called the era of user-generated content, participatory media (Jenkins, 2006a, 2006b), citizen journalism (Rheingold, 2003), social video (Manovich, 2008), mass self-communication (Castells, 2009) and creative commons (Creative commons, n.d.). This proliferation of terminology reflects the varied forms of new media and their social practices within Web 2.0. While there is much definitional contestation in this terrain (Dowmunt & Coyer, 2007), I shall use the term 'web-based participatory media' (interchangeably with 'Web 2.0'), on the basis that it best captures what people are doing with media as they produce and share media content online.

Alongside hopes that Web 2.0 would usher in the mass sociality and community-building that Web 1.0 was supposed to have allowed, there are downsides. Rather than renewing citizens' political engagement, Web 2.0 is seen as replicating the practices of 'politics as usual', which

Dahlberg (2007, p. 130) summarizes as: 'state coercion, strategic bargaining, partisan rhetoric, dogmatic enclaves, activist disruptions, and destabilizing conflict.' Other critics note that Web 2.0's discourses of freedom involve an enticing invitation to produce Lazzarato's (1996) immaterial labour (Fuchs, 2009; McStay, 2009). Here, the data mining of the wealth of information about ourselves that we willingly place online (such as in social networking sites), as well as unwittingly reveal through our online activities (such as e-commerce) is used to better target us as individuals by informing the framing of messages from professional strategic communicators according to the needs, wants, expectations, beliefs, preferences and interests of the audience member, thereby minimizing the potential for communicative deliberation with others and maximizing the probability that the professional communicators' message will be effective (Bennett & Manheim, 2006; McStay & Bakir, 2006; Castells, 2009; McStay, 2009). Other critiques of Web 2.0 query how widespread the production of user-generated content actually is. A 2007 statistic shows, for instance, that only between 0.5 to 1.5 per cent of users of the most popular social media sites (*Flickr, YouTube, Wikipedia*) contributed their own content, the rest remaining consumers of others' user-generated content (Manovich, 2008). There is also scepticism about how much of the user-generated content is produced by users themselves, as opposed to official/commercial content and viral marketing masquerading as user-generated content (Jenkins, 2007; McStay, 2007; Burgess, 2008; Losh, 2008; Manovich, 2008).

As with any new technology, we need to understand its surrounding cultural and political protocols, these emerging from what the technology enables and how it gets used, as well as from its perceived importance. The question of intelligibility of media technologies is linked to that of media literacy (Bakir & McStay, 2008) and has a long history in media and cultural studies (Adorno, 1982 [1938], p. 270), reinvigorated by each new medium that emerges. I suggest that a related question to intelligibility concerns the media literacy of official bodies seeking to control information content and flows. Correspondingly, it is important to ask: what official control of information do new media technologies enable and disable? Both of these questions are ever more important in the era of Web 2.0, particularly its emergent stage. As this book shall show, from 2003–2006, organizations used to supreme control over strategic political communications were caught out by the mass adoption of Web 2.0 technologies. Through key moments of generation and sharing of web-based participatory media–encompassing the Baghdad Blogger's blogs in the 2003 Iraq War, the US military's

Abu Ghraib digital photographs in 2004, the UK military's spoof music video in 2005 and witnesses to Saddam Hussein's execution in 2006 – a series of sousveillant lay challenges confounded the most adept of strategic political communicators.

Thus, to examine the question of what official control of information Web 2.0 enables and disables, I examine the interplay of web-based participatory media and mainstream media in impacting on US, UK and Iraqi strategic political communication about Iraq – three nations that have been intertwined very publicly since 2003. My focus is on *political* communication defined by Manheim (1991, p.7) as 'the creation, distribution, use and control of information as a political resource'. More specifically, my focus is on *strategic* political communication. Strategic communication suggests an end-game in sight, involving the achievement of specified goals. It is redolent of Jurgen Habermas' (1995 [1981]) description of open strategic action (conscious deception, manipulation) where, 'Critical publicity is supplanted by manipulative publicity' (Habermas, 1996 [1962], p.178). Habermas sees this as compromising his ideal of a public sphere in a deliberative democracy where rational deliberation leads to consensus on the common good. Instead, open strategic action helps to engineer public consent on behalf of interest groups – for instance, in order for politicians to win votes or for interest groups to win a bigger slice of the public purse – creating a quasi-public opinion which can be traced back to specific institutions, thereby debasing the public sphere (Habermas, 1995 [1981], 1996 [1962]). Although Habermas' ideal of the public sphere has been much-criticized, it is the most commonly invoked ideal of public involvement in democratic dialogue. However, Habermas' idealized consensus-oriented approach has since been challenged by Chantal Mouffe's (2000, 2005) conflict/compromise-oriented approach. Mouffe points to the unavoidability of political differences, tensions and conflicts of interest between adversaries, as people are deeply embedded in a number of different communities each passionately attached to their own conceptions and interpretations of the common good, leading to contingent subject positions in ever-shifting we–they configurations. Mouffe distinguishes between antagonism, understood as struggle between enemies, and agonism, which is struggle between adversaries (that is, struggle between friendly enemies who agree on the ethico-political principles that inform their political association but disagree about the interpretation of those principles, so forming a conflictual-consensus). As such, Mouffe (2000) argues that the task of a radical democracy of what she calls agonistic pluralism is not Habermasian rational consensus (Mouffe regards consensus as the end of democracy because a consensus implies that there is no possibility for an alternative), but to transform antagonism into agonism and to mobilize passions towards democratic designs. Indeed, whereas Habermas decries the rise of strategic communication within the public sphere as it derails the formation of a rational consensus, Mouffe sees communication in strategic terms as a means by which hegemony and strategic alliances may be formed and challenged.

Whether one sees strategic communication as a debasement of an idealized public sphere, or as a means for mobilizing passions towards democratic designs, its prevalence cannot be denied. As Manheim (1991, p.7) argues:

> What sets *strategic* political communication apart from other types is the way in which those engaged in it use sophisticated knowledge about human behavior to mold information to accomplish very specific, and often very short-term, objectives. Their emphasis is very much on controlling the messages that are sent, the circumstances of their transmission, and the roster of recipients.

Imbued within the notion of strategic political communication is the idea of struggle between different sources over definitional power, leading to battles over information management (Schlesinger, 1990). How strategic political communication differentially manifests in the West and the Middle East is explored below.

STRATEGIC POLITICAL COMMUNICATION IN THE WEST AND THE MIDDLE EAST

Scholarship on strategic political communication in the Middle East is limited given that in this part of the world the political order is oppressive and has long-maintained direct control over its media. Indeed, in much US and Arab public discourse, Arab media have not been regarded as important in forming public opinion, and Arab public opinion was not seen to exist in any recognizable form (Ayish, 2002). Instead, Arab leaders were perceived as monitoring and manipulating a dangerous, unpredictable, irrational, national and international 'Arab street' that might rise up in fury to challenge and overthrow its rulers if sufficiently provoked (Nisbet et al., 2004; Lynch, 2006). Authoritarian Arab rulers have stoked this perception by invoking fear of the Arab street to generate leverage in international bargaining. For instance, in the run-up to the 2003 Iraq War, Arab leaders predicted

Islamist uprisings,[2] should they attempt to force regime change in Iraq, using this to explain their reluctance publicly to support the war. Thus, the Arab street is often invoked by regimes looking for an excuse not to act, as well as by Arab governmental opposition figures looking for a credible source of influence. Certainly, Arab leaders keep an eye on the Arab street, aligning themselves with it where prudent (Lynch, 2003, 2006). Nonetheless, the field of strategic political communication has been delineated largely from a western perspective derived from the practice of massaging the implicit contract between government and the public imbued within western liberal democracies.

Strategic Political Communication in the West

Soft power – or 'getting others to want the outcomes that you want' (Nye, 2004, p.5) – rests on co-optation and the ability to shape others' preferences. It arises in international politics from the values an organization or country expresses in its culture, the examples it sets by its internal policies and institutions, and how it handles its diplomatic relations – comprising a mixture of attraction and agenda-setting behaviours. Importantly, unlike hard power, which has tangible resources, currencies and policies (the use of alliance, war, force, threats, sanctions, payments, bribes and aid), soft power is more intangible. As a result: 'Governments sometimes find it difficult to control and employ soft power, but that does not diminish its importance' (Nye, 2004, p.8). Achieving even partial control over competing framings of meaning in media texts demonstrates significant influence over communications and is a form of soft power. As such, to what extent, and how, policy-makers, the media and the public influence each other's agendas has been extensively researched in the West since the 1960s (Cohen, 1963; Lang & Lang, 1983; Rogers & Dearing, 1988; Robinson, 2002; Feldstein, 2007), as well as how certain 'framings' come into being thereby conveying preferred interpretations to broader audiences (Gamson et al. 1992; Entman, 1993, 2004; Castells, 2009). Consequently, agenda-setting and agenda-building research has developed a myriad of concepts and models for understanding strategic political communication, as outlined below.

In terms of media-centric explanations, technological advances in communication resulting from globalization of electronic journalism have led to suggestions that our governing systems are media-dominated telediplomacies (Gilboa, 2000). Whereas traditionally, diplomacy was secret and formal, exposing diplomacy to the media and public opinion has led to the formulation of the much-disputed *CNN* effect. Inspired by the rise of the first global, 24/7 news channel, Cable News Network (*CNN*), this is the process by which real-time, global, 24/7 media coverage of ongoing strategic decisions and military operations influences foreign policy by evoking immediate, international public awareness and analysis through concentrated and emotionally based coverage. Whether in response to actual or perceived public opinion, governments are pressurized to act quickly, rather than taking time to evaluate their intelligence estimates and diplomatic dispatches (Winseck, 1992; Livingston, 1997; Gilboa, 2002; Robinson, 2002; Bahador, 2007). More recently, others point to the *Fox* effect where 'politically partisan coverage, loud voices, and a preference for opinion over news . . . may prove detrimental to critical public reason' (Lynch, 2006, p.62); and to the *al-Jazeera* effect where graphic coverage of western armed intervention in Muslim countries increases negative Muslim sentiment against the western power, pressurizing Muslim governments to act against that western nation's policy (el-Nawawy & Gher, 2003; Nisbet et al., 2004). However, most research empirically disputes such telediplomacy effects, demonstrating that communicative power flows mainly from governments to the media, although this depends upon the administration's policy objectives and degree of policy certainty, clarity and unity (Livingston, 1997; Mermin, 1999; Robinson, 2002; Bahador, 2007; Bennett et al., 2007).

Reflecting other forces at work within agenda-setting and agenda-building, less media-centric processes abound. At one end of the informational-control continuum are techniques for keeping information out of the media. For instance, to attempt to maintain message control over large, inherently leaky bureaucracies, the Bush administration issued mobile phones to its officials to monitor their calls, thereby preventing anonymous leaks (Suskind, 2006). At the other end of the informational-control continuum are ways of shaping media content through propaganda,[3] psychological operations,[4] information intervention[5] and strategic public diplomacy.[6] Operating with less direct control than these mechanisms, but correspondingly generating more credibility, is the use of news management techniques. Given that journalists tend to rely on information from pro-active official sources (such as the executive branch of government, wider powerful and expert elites and the military) rather than unofficial sources (Sigal, 1973; Tuchman, 1978; Feldstein, 2007), routines of journalistic newsgathering are exploited by those seeking to manipulate reportage

(Molotch & Lester, 1975; Herman & Chomsky, 1988; Bennett et al., 2007). As such, the role of policy entrepreneurs, such as politicians, bureaucrats and independent advocates, in mobilizing public senti- ment has been studied extensively (Manheim, 1991; Bakir, 2006; McNair, 2007; McClellan, 2008; Castells, 2009).

Strategic Political Communication in the Middle East

In contrast to the West, most of the regimes governing the Arab League's 22 states are autocratic (traditional monarchies or single- party states), lacking democratic institutions (Nisbet et al., 2004). Power is maintained in similar ways. Dissent is minimized through employing an extensive *mukhabarat* (intelligence service) with a vast network of informers, and an expansive government bureaucracy that allows the regimes to dispense patronage; and through the co-optation of religion (Mandaville, 2007; The Economist, 2009b). Given the frag- ile legitimacy of most Arab ruling elites, state broadcasting monopo- lies and strict government censorship over media has been the norm since the 1950s, with topics limited to leadership speeches, official vis- its and protocol activities (Alterman, 1998; Sakr, 2001; Ayish, 2002; Lynch, 2003, 2006; Abdulla, 2006, 2007b). There are four taboos in Arab national media coverage: promoting the views of political opposi- tion, particularly Islamic; criticizing a country's rulers or their families; religious writing that might cause undue dissension; and upsetting social and sexual mores (Alterman, 1998). In controlling their media, Arab regimes propagate discourses that they believe will bolster their legitimacy. For example, the royal family of Saud attempts to buy pop- ular legitimacy and unite the region's tribal families while justifying to the *ummah* (the wider Islamic community) their control of Islam's two holiest shrines, Mecca and Medina, by patronizing the fundamentalist Wahhabi sect – the dominant local strain of Sunni Islam (Nakash, 2006; Mandaville, 2007). A fusion of Islamic Wahhabi and traditional tribal discourse is therefore propagated through mosques, state- controlled media and Saudi control of major pan-Arab media outlets (Fandy, 1999; Teitelbaum, 2002; Kraidy, 2006).

Certainly, in Iraq, under Saddam Hussein's regime, information was strictly controlled with minimal access for foreign journalists (Gher & Amin, 1999; Simpson, 2003). Supplementing this, Saddam Hussein created gruesome media events. For instance, on assuming presidency of the Ba'th Party and Iraq in July 1979, Saddam Hussein declared that a plot had been uncovered to topple the regime through the Revolutionary Command Council (RCC). In a special convention of the Ba'th Party on 22 July 1979, where one of the alleged plotters confessed to his own involvement and implicated colleagues, Saddam Hussein denounced over 60 other alleged conspirators who were led out of the convention hall in an atmosphere of increasing terror, while Saddam Hussein occasionally pretended to weep at this betrayal. On Saddam Hussein's instructions the proceedings were filmed for the edification of the Party and country, with copies of the videotape sent to Party organizations throughout Iraq and to Iraqi student groups abroad (Simpson, 2003; interview with Iraqi-UK citizen, January 2009). By 1 August 1979, up to 500 senior members of the Ba'th Party had been democratically executed – a method whereby senior Party members took part in the firing squads, so spreading the responsibility (Hamza, 2000; Simpson, 2003; Tripp, 2007). Nonetheless, control breeds resistance. For instance, using the media technologies of the day, Iraq saw the underground use of audio-cassette sermons by al-Da'wa Party leader, Ayatollah Sayyid Mohammed Baqir al-Sadr,[7] while under house arrest in Iraq in 1979, denouncing the Iraqi regime (Tripp, 2007).

Given strict state control over their media, Arabs have long turned to the transnational level for political debate (Lynch, 2003). From the 1950s, the main forum was the pan-Arab newspaper – such as Saudi-financed *al-Hayat* and Palestinian Liberation Organization (PLO)-financed *al-Quds al-Arabi* – edited in London, and printed remotely in world capitals using satellite communications. Arguably they have significant agenda-building roles, being read by opinion leaders (newspaper editors, university professors, businessmen and expatriate Arabs) (Alterman, 1998, 2004; Lynch, 2003; Mellor, 2007). The arrival of the internet in the 1990s meant that the European-based pan-Arab press became more readily available online (Lynch, 2006), swiftly followed by major daily and all state news services by 2003 (Anderson, 2003). However, internet penetration was low and pan-Arab newspapers had small combined sales (400,000 copies a day worldwide in 2004) (Alterman, 1998, 2004). Having much greater impact in countering Arab governments' control over their media in the 1990s was the growth of around 100 Arab satellite TV channels (Cherribi, 2006), led by Saudi-owned Middle East Broadcasting Centre. Exceptionally, Iraq did not join this explosion of satellite TV consumption. Although it had an initial 8.3 per cent share in Arabsat, its membership was suspended after invading Kuwait in 1990 (although in 1998, Egypt's *Nilesat* rented a transponder to Iraq). Pan-Arab satellite channels were less concerned about the political repercussions that might deter domestic media organizations, bypassing national restrictions on information and influencing the output of state monopoly broadcasters by forcing them to face unwanted competition (Seib, 2005; Abdulla, 2006, 2007b). Given their content, the development of satellite TV channels exercised Arab regimes because of their scope to reach the illiterate masses: illiteracy across Arab countries was 39 per cent in 2000 (Sakr, 2001). Indeed, by 1998 between 10 and 15 per cent of Arabs in the Middle East regularly watched satellite broadcasts (Alterman, 1998, 2000; Abdulla, 2007b). As well as introducing Arab audiences to new content, satellite TV introduced them to new broadcasting forms. While most satellite channels were entertainment focused, Qatar-based *al-Jazeera*, broadcasting since 1996, became the first to be dedicated to political news, with a credo of non-censorship based on the *BBC* model of objective reporting (Sakr, 2001; Aday et al., 2005; Miles, 2005a, 2005b). It ushered in open, contentious, public politics, providing opposition groups with a high-profile platform, giving it credibility among many Arab viewers as well as earning it accusations of sensationalism in official Arab circles. After '9/11' *al-Jazeera* became even more central to Arab politics with its exclusive access to al-Qaeda leaders and its refusal to adopt America's perspective (el-Nawawy & Iskandar, 2002; Lynch, 2003, 2006; Miles, 2005b; Zayani & Ayish, 2006). *Al-Jazeera* created a more demanding audience that came to expect no less from other news stations (Nisbet et al., 2004; Lynch, 2006; Fahmy & Johnson, 2007).

Middle Eastern governments have long proven adept at developing new mechanisms of surveillance and control over emerging communication technologies – such as licensing fax machines and domestic and foreign publications, finding compliant owners for satellite TV stations, and jamming short-wave and television signals (Alterman, 1998; Fandy, 1999; Teitelbaum, 2002; Seib, 2005; Miles, 2005b). The internet is also subject to control, given that its networked nature creates structural choke points that are vulnerable to state policing (McNair, 2006). Web censorship is attempted through state-controlled Internet Service Providers (ISPs) where the state filters internet content manually and through commercial filterware products to block certain search terms, Uniform Resource Locators (URLs), and search engines themselves. Web censorship includes giving internet café proprietors lists of people banned from using their services; limiting private users and internet cafés to slow connection speeds, so making data transmission difficult; and publicized arrests of objectionable internet users to encourage self-censorship (Teitelbaum, 2002; Alterman, 2004; Reporters without borders, 2005; Lynch, 2006; Abdulla, 2007b).

However, satellite jamming is technically difficult and almost impossible to do over a large area for long (Miles, 2005b), and internet penetration is rising. Although internet access in the Middle East is low compared to other countries, estimated in 2000 at only 3,284,800 (3 per cent of the Arab population), globally the Middle East experienced the greatest growth rate in internet access across 2000–2008 (1,296 per cent compared to an average world total of 342 per cent) (Internet World Stats, 2009). Thus, Arab state's control over media to which their populations have access is likely to further weaken, and as such, Arab regimes may increasingly perceive the need for the wider range of strategic political communication techniques developed in the West. However, the rapid rise of Web 2.0 across the first decade of the twenty-first century along with convergence of media means that rules of strategic political communication may need to be re-written. As such, the following section considers how Web 2.0 technologies, together with convergence cultures, have affected the struggle over strategic political communication in both the West and the Middle East.

Web-Based Participatory Media, Convergence and the Struggle for Control Over Strategic Political Communication

In the era of top-down media (pre Web 1.0), challenging elite control over strategic political communication through the media was difficult practically, due to the technical expertise needed; the high costs of producing and distributing media content nationally and globally; and the fact that organized resistance attracts state attention and retaliation. Correspondingly, resistance tended to be limited to groups who relied on (and therefore understood) the mass media to propagate their demands and stances to the wider public, thereby exerting pressure on decision-makers. Such groups ranged from media-aware Non-Governmental Organizations (NGOs) like Greenpeace (Anderson, 1991; Bakir, 2005, 2006, 2007) to terrorists (Schmid & de Graaf, 1982; McNair, 2007). However, as the media environment rapidly changes in the era of Web 2.0, the ability of governments to control information is being strongly and continuously challenged through the 'digitally active masses' rather than momentarily subverted at the margins by the few. Globally, by 2002 there were over 500 million internet users – compared to 16 million in 1995 (Haythornthwaite & Wellman, 2002). Of course internet penetration remains uneven. For instance, in 2006, 60 per cent of UK households had internet access (Ofcom, 2006b) whereas in the Middle East, most internet users were to be found in Iran (39 per cent internet penetration), followed by Israel (19 per cent) and Saudi Arabia (13 per cent) (Hendelman-Baavur, 2007). Furthermore, there is a 'digital divide' regarding internet awareness, access and use between the rich and poor, urban and rural, male and female and young and old (Chen et al., 2002; Mudhai, 2006; Abdulla, 2007b). Nonetheless, it is fitting that as the internet became more widely used, producing content for it also became easier.

What are the implications of web-based participatory media practices for control over strategic political communication? On the celebratory side, as early as 1991, Manheim noted that in a world characterized by strategic communication efforts: 'there may be some protection afforded to society when the natural diversity of interests is reinforced by a broad distribution of image-making skills or sensibilities' (1991, p. 218). A decade later, McNair (2003) hails the infinite possibilities arising from the internet's evolution for horizontal communication, demystification and deprofessionalization of journalism, and endless information choice. Certainly, the implications for democracy of web-based participatory media are much debated (Rheingold, 2002; Jenkins & Thorburn, 2003; Dean et al., 2006; Carpentier et al., 2007; Castells et al., 2007; Dahlberg & Siapera, 2007). Questions raised include: Who controls production and distribution of political discourse? Does the corresponding media content foster rational discourse and expand the volume and diversity of civic discourse? Are people mobilized to participate more fully?

In terms of the earliest form of web-based participatory media – blogs – their importance in diversifying the public sphere has been evident since 9/11 which produced an explosion of personal, public testimony in the US, comprising links to materials like web-cam stills and witness accounts (Allan, 2004; Andrews, 2006). Blogging technology became available across the Middle East in 2001 and 2002 where it was embraced by the few who could access it, taking off particularly in Iran with the birth of 'Weblogistan' in late 2001 (Hendelman-Baavur, 2007). The popularity of blogs in Arab and Asian countries arises partly because the internet is often subject to less stringent control than print newspapers and broadcasting; partly because of the option to publish anonymously (Haugbolle, 2007; Hendelman-Baavur, 2007; Kulikova & Perlmutter, 2007); and partly because of their use of the Arabic colloquial language, as opposed to the more formal Arabic used in mainstream media (Eid, 2007; Mellor, 2007). Arab political blogs engage in three principle types of activity: bridge-blogging, public sphere engagement and activism. Bridge-bloggers primarily address western audiences, usually writing in English with the intention of explaining their societies. Public-sphere bloggers tend to engage in public arguments about domestic (often Arabic or Islamic) politics. Activist bloggers are directly involved in political movements, coordinating political action and spreading information (Lynch, 2007). The use of Web 2.0 by Arab and Asian citizens as a basis for international campaigning ranges from liberals such as women's rights campaigners, to traditionalists, with a significant Muslim presence on the internet comprising traditional Islamic establishments as well as activist, oppositional and militant Islamic organizations (Anderson, 2001, 2003; Abdel-Latif, 2004; Alterman, 2004; Hendelman-Baavur, 2007; Lynch, 2007).

However, Habermas himself has speculated that blogs (and by extension, other web-based participatory media forms) can only constitute a public sphere when they 'link up' to the mass media (Lynch, 2007). Such 'linking up' is part of the technological and social phenomenon of convergence. The transition from scarcity to plenty in terms of broadcast channel choice and the rise of domestic internet access has produced an active, volatile audience, eroding audiences for older media technologies like television broadcasting and print newspapers since the mid-1990s (Department for Culture, Media and Sport, 2005; Project for Excellence in Journalism, 2006, 2008). In response, media companies embraced convergence/multiple-platform publishing as a tool for increased productivity and marketing (Quinn, 2005). In the UK, for instance, the *BBC* – which needs audience volume to demonstrate value-for-money as a Public Service Broadcaster (PSB) – pioneered convergence activities. These included proliferating *BBC* digital television, radio and *YouTube* channels (the latter in March 2007),[8] and creating *BBC* i-player (launched December 2007). The *BBC* hoped that its *YouTube* channels would drive traffic to its own website where it could point users to the BBC's downloadable programmes, while also getting a share of the advertising revenue generated by traffic to the *YouTube* channels (Weber, 2007). It further hoped that given access, people would mash up and forward clips of quality *BBC* content, and in this way, *BBC* content (and brand values) would be spread virally, while also creating brand loyalty given the time that co-creators would have invested in the mash-ups (Hayes, 2009). This illustrates how value in cultural production and consumption in Web

2.0 is generated by 'spreadability' (Jenkins, 2007), as opposed to the 'stickiness' sought by pull media (such as broadcasting or Web 1.0, which aims to retain audiences). Convergence cultures can also be witnessed in the Middle East. An early example is Beirut-based *Lebanese Broadcasting Corporation* (LBC) joint venture with London-based newspaper *al-Hayat* in 2003, with the newspaper's correspondents supplying news to LBC International (Quinn, 2005). However, for Jenkins, convergence is more than just a business model. Rather, convergence represents, 'a cultural shift as consumers are encouraged to seek out new information and make connections among dispersed media content' (Jenkins, 2006a, p. 3), allowing them to bring media flows more fully under their control and to interact with other users (Jenkins, 2004). From this perspective, convergence in the Middle East can be seen in the use of widespread technologies like photocopiers combined with rarer technologies like the internet to widely disseminate web content (Alterman, 2000).As the democratization of media production has become more actualized in Web 2.0, and as convergence causes more 'linking up' between web-based participatory media and mainstream media, we enter a media environment of complexity, chaos and populism, taxing the control exercised by strategic political communicators. In the mid-1990s, Castells (1996, p. 70) argued that we were living in the 'network society' where: 'the power of flows takes precedence over the flows of power. Presence or absence in the network and the dynamics of each network *vis-à-vis* others are critical sources of domination and change in our society' (Castells, 1996, p. 500). A decade later, McNair (2006, p. 3) describes the turbulent communicative environment with its proliferation of media channels, volume of information and speed of circulation as a shift from a 'control paradigm' to a 'chaos paradigm,' with elite groups having less effective power (although no less desire and no less attempt) to influence news agendas, and traditional media monoliths less able to uphold the status quo. McNair is careful not to reduce the causes of this chaos paradigm to techno-determinism, citing, among other things, global democratization processes and the associated influence on political decision-making of global and domestic public opinion and public relations (PR). Nonetheless, for McNair, new information and communication technologies such as satellite TV and the internet help generate the chaos paradigm, which stresses: 'contingency (sensitive dependence on initial conditions) at all phases of the communication process' (McNair, 2006, p. 48). The unruliness that Web 2.0 introduces into the process of strategic political communication has been noted by various authors (Kraidy, 2006; Kalb & Saivetz, 2007; Christensen, 2008), and referred to as the '*YouTube* effect' (Naim, 2007, p. 103; Christensen, 2008, p. 157). Agenda-building now seems to be a more open field. As such, understanding the limits of control over strategic political communication in the newly emerged era of web-based participatory media is a central aim of this book.

So far, various debates have been explored in order to facilitate our understanding of strategic political communication in the contemporary era. However, these academic debates have neglected a highly relevant concept – that of sousveillance (although see Losh, 2008). Yet, sousveillance is a concept that encapsulates key political and social practices to be found in Web 2.0.

FROM SURVEILLANCE TO SOUSVEILLANCE

Sousveillance comes from the French words for 'sous' (below) and 'veiller' to watch (Mann et al., 2003 p. 332), as opposed to 'surveillance' – 'to watch from above' by a God-like, or higher, authority (Mann, 2004b, p. 620), or 'to watch over' (Lyon, 2001, p. 3). In short, sousveillance entails 'watchful vigilance from underneath' (Mann, 2002). The concept was coined by Steve Mann, a Canadian inventor and academic, in conjunction with his pioneering research on wearable computing and wearable cameras that he conceived from the 1980s, before hand-held computers and digital cameras were commonplace. His aim in developing such technologies, usable for sousveillance, is to promote personal empowerment in human technology interactions by restoring complete control to individuals over the technologies that they use (Mann, 1997, 2001). His inventions include WearCam (wearable camera) and WearComp (wearable computer) (Mann, 2001, 2003a). An example of a wearable camera is a camera mounted on an individual's front, connected to a large separate screen displaying what the camera views, mounted on the individual's back or projected on the floor. Mann's wearable computing allows the wearer to automatically watch, record and perhaps broadcast his/her surroundings. Mann coined the concept of 'sousveillance' to describe the effect a wearer of his devices has on others – an effect that he investigated using Harold Garfinkel's (1967) ethno-methodological approach to breaching norms. Primarily, for Mann, sousveillance was a technique to enable people to take a stance against the surveillant state. Thus, before expanding on this concept of sousveillance, it is useful first to delineate the nature of the surveillance that sousveillance aims to counter.

Mann (2004b, p. 620) defines surveillance (given its God-like nature) as: 'the capture of multimedia content (audio, video or the like), by a higher entity that is not a peer of, or a party to, the activity being recorded'. Surveillance can be defined further as the 'routine ways in which focused attention is paid to personal details by organizations that want to influence, manage, or control certain persons or population groups' (Lyon, 2003, p. 5). Surveillance societies, then, emerge 'wherever such practices begin to touch daily life at every point – whether we are working, shopping, voting, travelling, being entertained, or communicating with others' (Lyon, 2003, p.5).

The academic literature on surveillance harks back to the publication of *Panopticon* in 1791 by social reformer, Jeremy Bentham, who envisioned a novel architecture based on implied, or potential, surveillance that could be used in places like prisons, schools and workplaces. In the example of a prison, a central tower would be placed at the hub of a circular building, with individual prison cells fanning out. The tower's visual supremacy meant that it could see into every cell and all inmates could see the tower, but inmates would never know whether anyone was in the tower or whether they were actually watching. Bentham suggested that this constant actual or potential surveillance would prevent the Panopticon's inmates from misbehaving, in a form of self-regulation. This idea of the exercise of power in the form of self-discipline under the eye of authority was highlighted in the 1970s by Michel Foucault. He invoked the Panopticon as a symbol for contemporary methods of social control, where human beings regulate their own individual behaviour by conforming to normalizing social rules exercised under the gaze of the powerful (Foucault, 1977). For Foucault, the Panopticon ensures:

> that the surveillance is permanent in its effects, even if it is discontinuous in its action; that the perfection of power should tend to render its actual exercise unnecessary; that this architectural apparatus should be a machine for creating and sustaining a power relation independent of the person who exercises it; in short, that the inmates should be caught up in a power situation of which they are themselves the bearers. (Foucault, 1977, p. 201)

Interestingly, while a Panopticon was never built in Bentham's lifetime, Panopticon-inspired buildings have since been built. For instance, in Saddam Hussein's Iraq – a highly surveillant state – in order to keep tabs on the Shi'a in Karbala, the Hassan mosque was built with a minaret much higher than the norm, and acted as a security and surveillance outpost, complete with binoculars and recording devices. The mosque's location offered a clear view of the pedestrian esplanade between two of the holiest mosques/tombs for all Shi'a (and therefore a site of regular pilgrimage) (Engel, 2008). Indeed, under Saddam Hussein's regime (1979–2003), which created an authoritarian (and some suggest, totalitarian) state (Dodge, 2005; Kets de Vries, 2006; Jabar, 2007), Iraq's intelligence and security effort became so large and permeating that it gave Saddam Hussein control over every aspect of Iraqi life – penetrating security, military and civilian structures inside Iraq and abroad (Cordesman, 1999).[9] For instance, by 1994, dissidents and deviants became publicly surveilled as Law 109 ordered that anyone repeating the crimes of theft and desertion would be branded on the forehead, 'with a mark in the shape of an X. Each intersecting line will be one centimeter in length and one millimeter in width' (Makiya, 1998, p. ix). This law came about because army desertion was rife after the 1991 Gulf War (when Iraq was driven out of Kuwait by Coalition forces), and the previous punishment of instant recourse to a firing squad ineffective (Makiya, 1998). In terms of civilian surveillance, scores of journalists throughout the Middle East and Europe were on Saddam Hussein's payroll (Lynch, 2006), and Iraq relied on its strong internal intelligence apparatus to keep other journalists at bay (Alterman, 1998). Ordinary people were co-opted or forced into complicity with state surveillance. Organized along the lines of the KGB's Marxist–Leninist system,[10] every citizen was supposed to tell the Ba'th Party *mukhabarat* of the slightest sign of criticism against the regime or non-conformity, and anyone who failed to do so would share in the guilt of the person they should have turned in. Children were used to inform on their parents, and teachers were instructed to question children in class to uncover irregularities in their parents' lives (Simpson, 2003). In this situation of intense surveillance, self-control exercised by the citizens was paramount. Meanwhile, sousveillance was discouraged: from the 1970s, while cameras were sold in Iraq, photography was suspect without the written authorization of the Ministry of the Interior (Makiya, 1998).

Although not the only theoretical framework available for understanding surveillance,[11] the Panopticon is a motif that has been most taken up and critiqued (Deleuze, 1992, 1995; Mathiesen, 1997; Poster, 1997), including by Mann himself. Perhaps the strongest critique of the Panopticon comes from Deleuze and Guattari who posit that disciplinary societies are being replaced by 'societies of control' (Deleuze,

1992, p. 4) where, rather than a centralized panoptic apparatus (such as state forms of surveillance) regulated by 'watchwords' (Deleuze, 1992, p. 5), surveillance is rhizomatic (Deleuze & Guattari, 1987). Here, control operates through data banks and 'modulation, like a self-deforming cast that will continuously change from one moment to the other' (Deleuze, 1992, p. 4) and in a dispersed manner, regulated by the 'password' (Deleuze, 1992, p. 5) or the code, leading to 'ceaseless control in open sites' (Deleuze 1995, p. 175). This conceptualization leads Haggerty & Ericson (2000) to suggest the notion of a 'surveillant assemblage' (or loosely linked systems). The surveillant assemblage is emergent, unstable and operates across state institutions and others that have nothing (directly) to do with the state, such as supermarket and credit card transactions. In the assemblage, rather than individuals passing through spaces of panoptic enclosure, surveillance works by computers tracking persons, abstracting bodies from places and splitting them into data flows to be reassembled as virtual data-doubles (Lyon, 2003). Data from the surveillant assemblage is increasingly sophisticated, driven by online commercial data-mining and Customer Relationship Management (CRM) practices that classify, cluster, forecast and profile our behaviours – so that we are each reconfigured as (security) risks or (commercial) opportunities (Lyon, 2001, 2003; Gandy, 2003; McStay & Bakir, 2006; McStay, 2009). Yet, rather than the surveillant assemblage replacing the panoptic apparatus, Lyon (2003) sees the assemblage and apparatus as mutually informing systems, with the assemblage producing a routine stock of analysable material that the apparatus can appropriate – as in 9/11, when, after the terroristic act, governments were able to trace the terrorists' activities through their data trails (Suskind, 2006).

While risk management regimes such as the Cold War involved suspicion and surveillance of enemies within as well as massive development of computer power, Lyon (2003) sees a further intensification of these processes since 9/11 and the Global War on Terror. 9/11 required the US military to fundamentally re-examine how it collected intelligence, concluding that: 'Many of the terrorists and insurgents are geographically dispersed non-state actors who move across national boundaries and operate in small cells that are difficult to surveil and penetrate' (Schlesinger, 2004, p. 64). Such assessments generated the political will to impose sweeping new surveillance legislation upon civilians in order to maintain security bringing, as Lyon (2003, p.80) puts it, 'the apparatus and the assemblage into closer coordination with each other'. For instance, six weeks after 9/11, on 25 October

2001, the US Congress passed, by a huge majority, the USA PATRIOT Act (an ingenious acronym for 'Uniting and Strengthening America by Providing Appropriate Tools Required to Intercept and Obstruct Terrorism').[12] This allowed a vast increase in surveillance within the US, including the ability to search financial and personal records, and the monitoring of US citizens without their knowledge through telephone wiretaps and e-mail and internet surveillance. A year later, the federal Department of Homeland Security was created (Lyon, 2003; McLaren & Martin, 2004). Such measures sat alongside existing automated governmental surveillance systems like Echelon and Carnivore which monitor all forms of electronic information from other countries for keywords in order to identify behaviour patterns that are deemed potentially threatening (Lyon, 2001, 2003; Suskind, 2006). Thus, to try to pre-empt future terrorist attacks, the US surveillance state generated 'data' from terror suspects in camps like Guantánamo, and combined this with data mined from across the assemblage. Similarly, in the UK, there were changes in practice and law to deal with terrorists. The UK's Anti-terrorism, Crime and Security Act (December 2001) brought down the barrier to information sharing among organizations (Raab, 2003). While the Regulation of Investigatory Powers Act already had sweeping capacities to obtain communications data without a court order, soon after 9/11, anti-terrorist legislation allowed these to be retained for longer (Lyon, 2003), while the providers of communication services were to retain personal data beyond their own requirements, to be available for national security and law enforcement purposes. Meanwhile, the discourse of War on Terror, propagated at length by the US media in particular (Zelizer & Allan, 2002) turned us into compliantly surveilled, risk-averse subjects, giving away our civic rights of privacy to the state to alleviate our fear of homegrown terrorists, and the like (Furedi, 1997; Altheide, 2006).

Competing with these social practices and discourses of surveillance are those oriented towards civic freedom through personal empowerment. Although Fernandez & Huey (2009) argue that surveillance scholars have paid relatively little attention to the issues of resistance to surveillance technologies, Steve Mann has been developing the idea of sousveillance since at least 1995. Taking a stance against the Panoptic surveillance society where organizations routinely observe people without their permission, Mann envisages *sous*veillant individuals using tools (such as wearable cameras) to observe the organizational observer, enhancing the ability of people to access and collect data about their surveillance in order to neutralize it, and violating prohibitions stating that ordinary people should not use recording devices to record official acts (Mann, 2001; Mann et al., 2003). Expanding on this idea, Mann sees sousveillance as a form of 'reflectionism' – Mann's term for the philosophy and procedures of using technology to 'mirror and confront bureaucratic organizations' (Mann, 2001, 2003b ; Mann et al., 2003, p. 333) by creating a nonsensical but nearly symmetrical construct of the way we understand the relationship between technology and the body (Mann, 2001).[13] Sousveillance is a technique for 'uncovering the Panopticon and undercutting its primacy and privilege' and so seeking to increase the equality between surveiller and surveillee, including enabling the surveillee to surveil the surveiller (Mann et al., 2003, p. 333). Thus, while the heart of sousveillance is: 'human-centered capture, processing, storage, recall, and transmission of sensory information' (Mann, 2005, p. 636), this was initially situated in the larger context of democratic social responsibility, aiming to restore 'a traditional balance that the institutionalization of Bentham's Panopticon itself disrupted' (Mann, 1995; Mann et al., 2003, p. 347).

Mann's clearest definition of sousveillance is as follows:

> The term 'sousveillance' refers both to hierarchical sousveillance, e.g. citizens photographing police, shoppers photographing shopkeepers, and taxi-cab passengers photographing cab drivers, as well as personal sousveillance (bringing cameras from the lamp posts and ceilings, down to eye-level, for human-centered recording of personal experience). (Mann, 2004b)

As such, the term 'hierarchical sousveillance' (Mann, 2004b) refers specifically to politically or legally motivated sousveillance. This is an activity undertaken by those who are generally the subject of surveillance and involves the recording of surveillance systems, proponents of surveillance, authority figures and their actions. Meanwhile, sousveillance that typically involves community-based recording from first-person perspectives without necessarily involving a political agenda, is referred to by Mann (2004b) as 'personal sousveillance.' Mann (2005, p. 636) sees the social value of personal sousveillance as follows:

> Surveillance tends to objectify or subjectify people as objects or subjects (or suspects) of scrutiny, whereas sousveillance allows people to be creators of data. Sousveillance allows people to be lifelong photographic artists rather than merely subjects. It is this 'human-centric' rather than architecture-centric view that gives sousveillance much of its humanistic value.

Thus, whereas Foucault's surveillant Panopticon tends to isolate individuals from one another while setting up a one-way visibility to authority figures, Mann's personal sousveillance tends to bring individuals together – as when personal electronic diaries are made public on the web – as well as giving people control over the recorded moment and greater insight into their own personal epistemology (Mann, 2001, 2004b, 2005).

As alluded to earlier, Mann invents sousveillant devices. These include CyborgLogs whereby an individual can use technology to effortlessly and unconsciously capture information in real-time (for instance, Mann's EyeTap[14] technology or a camera-phone programme called 'cyborglogger'[15]), which is automatically stored to a time-stamped log-file, which, if placed on the web, can make serendipitous personal experience recordings available to the world (Mann, 2003a; Mann et al., 2006). In such cases, the individual becomes a cyborg experiencing a technological synergy that requires no conscious thought or effort (Mann, 2004b). Indeed, from 1994 to 1996, while a student at Massachusetts Institute of Technology, Mann continuously transmitted every waking moment of his life in real-time to his website for others to experience and respond to (Mann, 2001, 2003a). His CyborgLogs ('glogs), such as the spontaneous reporting of news as everyday experience, were an early predecessor of blogs: Japan's Joi Ito puts Mann's 'glog of February 1995 (entitled *wearcam.org as roving reporter*)[16] as the first example of moblogging – blogging using camera or video phones (Ito, 2004).

Mann's focus on the science and technology (if not his focus on the art, or related philosophical and technosocial issues) of capturing, storing and transmitting personal experiences has since been capitalized upon by the growing sousveillance industry in the development of mobile phones, pagers, and digital cameras with wireless communications, and applications (Mann, 2001; Fiorina, 2002). For instance, Nokia's, *Lifeblog* is a mobile phone and PC application launched in December 2004 that gathers pictures, Short Messaging Service (SMS) communications, video clips, audio clips and notes from the mobile and arranges them on a timeline in various ways.[17] In March 2006, Samsung released a camera phone in Korea that had sharing built into its logic, allowing almost instantaneous uploading to a blog (compared to a digital camera that would need to be taken to a computer and then uploaded). With the release of the iPhone 3GS on 19 June 2009 – the first iPhone with the ability to record video and easily, wirelessly upload it directly to the internet – sousveillance went mainstream. One week after the launch, *YouTube* reported that mobile uploads had increased by 400 per cent (Sousveillance Network, 2009). Such mainstreaming is welcomed by Mann who suggests that the purest form of sousveillance is 'not merely the carrying around of a hand-held camera, but, rather, must include elements of incidentalist imaging to succeed'. He gives examples of camera phones and pocket organizers containing cameras, and suggests that this 'backgrounding' by another socially justifiable function is essential for sousveillance to take root in most societies (Mann, 2005; Mann et al., 2006). Mann (2001) also sees sousveillance as working best when human-centred (decentralized, adaptable to the individual) technology proliferates and diffuses as widely as possible.

It is the widespread, everyday nature of sousveillance that distinguishes it from other more established practices of observing and challenging power structures – such as investigative journalism – the hallmarks of which are, as Goddard (2006) notes, long camera lenses, hidden recording devices and concealed identities to access material outside the public domain, and painstaking research of not easily-accessible evidence within the public domain. While Lyon (2001) was sceptical that placing camcorders in the hands of bystanders in the street can ever amount to anything more than brief moments of resistant activity in a surveillance society, Web 2.0 generates an *intensification* of sousveillance and the rise of '*sousveillance cultures*'.

The Case Studies

This analysis so far has highlighted the potential of Web 2.0 in sousveillantly resisting strategic political communication in an era of convergence cultures. While the book's empirical analysis as a whole broadly covers the period 2001–2009, the next three chapters will pause at a number of significant moments across 2002–2006, to examine Web 2.0's resistive potential to strategic political communication in a politically differentiated global environment and within a media environment of increasing convergence, itself differentially achieved across the globe. Specifically, this book examines the interplay between web-based participatory media, mainstream media and official attempts at strategic political communication, in the period before certain Web 2.0 media forms become normalized – when they were still in their *emergent* state. I posit that it is during these emergent periods that official attempts at strategic political communication suffer from lack of understanding of the digital cultures they are seeking to emulate or infiltrate. It is therefore at these moments that web-based participatory media can be at its most resistive and impactful.

I have adopted a comparative case study approach throughout the rest of this book – an appropriate methodology given that my focus is on a contemporary phenomenon within real-life contexts, where the detail is important to eliciting analysis and understanding (Yin, 2003; Kumar, 2005). The case studies all focus on events concerning Iraq, allowing a build-up of contextual knowledge that enables clearer and deeper analysis of how the emergent environment of Web 2.0 impacted on strategic political communication over time. The case studies are drawn from two different political communication environments – war-time and post-war – each with different communicative rules of operation. The uses of a specific set of Web 2.0 technologies are examined – most notably blogs, digital photographs and videos captured on mobile phones and social network sites. These choices were dictated by the case studies examined, as they were the Web 2.0 technologies involved in particular moments of subversion of strategic political communication. Relevant aspects of the political and media environments under which each case study operates will be explained further in the following chapters, but below is a brief outline of key features of these environments leading up the 2003 Iraq War, itself examined in the first two case studies.

In the Middle East's media during the 1980s, the horrors of Saddam Hussein's regime were not widely aired. Instead, Saddam Hussein was generally portrayed as the Arab champion against Persian Shi'i Iran as it mired itself in the 1980–1988 Iran–Iraq War (Lynch, 2006). This war led the West to see Saddam Hussein as a bulwark against Iran's export of its Islamic Revolution following its deposition of the US-backed Shah in 1979 (Tripp, 2007). Given that Saddam Hussein rarely allowed foreign journalists into Iraq, other than for short periods to report on specific events (Simpson, 2003), western media attention to the Iraqi-American relationship in the 1980s was sporadic at best, with the White House managing to keep its support for Saddam Hussein's regime secret (Carruthers, 2000). In the 1990s, little was heard about the country in the British or American media, apart from the period between Iraq's invasion of Kuwait in August 1990 and Kuwait's subsequent liberation by Allied forces in February 1991 (Miskin, 1991; Dorman & Livingston, 1994; Seymour, 2004), and the subsequent plight of the Kurds (Shaw, 1993; Bahador, 2007). In Middle Eastern media, by the 1990s there were intense public arguments rather than consensus in the new pan-Arab satellite TV media and pan-Arab newspapers over the right course of action for Iraq. Here, the suffering of the Iraqi people under post-1991 Gulf War sanctions (1991–2003) became a touchstone for Arab debate, offering a starting point of consensus – to the extent that it was invoked by Osama bin Laden in a tape broadcast by *al-Jazeera* in November 2002 (Lynch, 2006). Unsurprisingly, Saddam Hussein attempted to mobilize transnational Arab public opinion through the release of dramatic footage of Iraqis suffering as the result of sanctions, as well as through direct appeals to the Arab masses to rise up against unsympathetic governments (Lynch, 2003). Of course, he did not promote the fact that the suffering arising from sanctions was greatly compounded by his own networks of patronage and favouritism that determined how the limited imports (after the oil-for-food deals of 1996–1999) were distributed (Tripp, 2007).

As Chapter 2 shows, the West's information vacuum changed after the 9/11 terrorist attacks by al-Qaeda on the US, as the British administration under Prime Minister Tony Blair (1997–2007) and the US administration under George W. Bush (2000–2008) publicly built up their case for war with Iraq. This was the first pre-emptive war in a century and the first waged on the basis of so-called intelligence reports (Butler Report, 2004; Fawn & Hinnebusch, 2006). Thus, the starting point for the time period chosen for analysis here (2002) not only coincides with the explosion into popular discourse of web-based participatory media, but also represents a period where both UK and US governments were geared up towards maximum control of their own, and international, media's agenda in the battle for public opinion during a period of highly controversial warfare. Several key media developments are taken from the 2003 Iraq War to exemplify the authorities' heightened ability to control information (through the proliferation of embedded reporters from mainstream media), and the simultaneous *loss of control* (through sousveillant blogs from an Iraqi civilian, Salam Pax). The Pentagon hoped that embedding would encourage journalists to identify with the military – and so report less critically – but this control over identification was challenged by Salam Pax's blogs. Herein lay the potential for unravelling the West's strategic political communication that aimed to convince domestic audiences that the war was legitimate and necessary, with a clear demarcation of 'enemy' and 'friend' (Bakir & McStay, 2008). As such, Chapter 2 discusses the inter-relationship between identification, authenticity and trust generated by the use of two different ways of bearing witness – embedded reporting and ordinary, civilian blogging.

Four case studies focus on post-war Iraq, across Chapters 3 and 4. This balance of attention is deliberate. While we have a detailed understanding of strategic political communication under conditions of

mass-mediated war under different media environments, our understanding of strategic political communication under civil war conflict
situations and turbulent post-war periods of nation-building is much
less developed (Knightley, 2003; Bloch-Elkon; 2007; Kyrke-Smith,
2007). The UK and US administrations' desire for control over strategic political communication continued in the post-war situation (that
is, after the official end of war in May 2003), as Iraq descended into
low-level civil war by 2006–2007, emerging from this in 2008–2009.
Across this period, the UK and US military continued to work towards
implementing their governments' strategic political goals including
counterterrorism and nation-building in the face of the collapse of the
Iraqi state's infrastructure on the ousting of Saddam Hussein (Wright
& Reese, 2008).

Chapter 3 shows how torture photographs from Abu Ghraib (2004)
and the military spoof music video, *Is this the Way to Armadillo* (2005),
illustrate the loss of control through sousveillant media over the military's carefully constructed image. The issue of prisoner torture by US
soldiers at Abu Ghraib prison in Iraq came to public attention in April
2004 through the publication in mainstream news of sousveillant photographs showing prisoner 'abuse', the photographs taken by the 'abusers' themselves. This publicization initiated a massive damage limitation
exercise by the US government as it framed Abu Ghraib as the outcome
of isolated abuse within the military rather than a covert policy of torture to extract intelligence for the War on Terror. While the Bush administration's strategic political communication successfully manipulated
mainstream US media for over a year, the Abu Ghraib images resonated
across the Middle East, fuelling the insurgency in Iraq. Presenting a very
different image of the military than Abu Ghraib, also through user-
generated content, and commanding popular attention in 2005 was a
spoof music video shot by a UK military unit in Iraq and e-mailed to so
many that it crashed the Ministry of Defence's (MoD) server. *Is This the
Way to Armadillo*, although not 'official' military communication, was
subsequently approved of by military authorities on the grounds of its
morale-boosting qualities. These two different examples of military sousveillance lead to a discussion about the extent to which control over
institutional image is possible or desirable in Web 2.0.

Exploring the impact of Web 2.0 on strategic political communication during a post-war period of nation-building in a country as ethnically
and religiously divided as Iraq is particularly instructive, as ethno-religious sentiment emerged with force after decades of Saddam Hussein's
repression. When Britain granted independence to Iraq in 1932, it

established the Hashemite King Faisal as their client ruler, and selected Sunni Arab minority elites from the region for appointment to government and ministry office, despite the fact that most of the population were Shi'a (Cordesman, 1999; Nakash, 2006).[18] In 1958, the monarchy was overthrown by a coup d'état of the Iraqi Army, leading to a series of nationalistic and authoritarian Iraqi leaders, ending with Saddam Hussein. Continuing the pattern of ethno-religious Sunni domination of Iraq's state, Saddam Hussein and his supporters drew from a relatively small mix of Sunni tribal and clan elites centred around his home town of Tikrit (Tripp, 2007). So here we have a country, ruled for its entire existence by a Sunni minority, and never having known democratic representation. Within the context of democratic state-building activities going on in Iraq after the end of major combat activities in May 2003, in a political environment of increasing insurgency and sectarian slaughter, two case studies are examined in Chapter 4, highlighting the extremes of totally controlled strategic political communication and hierarchical sousveillance. The first case study is the internationally televised inspection of a dishevelled Saddam Hussein on his capture in December 2003 where, for the first time, he was presented as disempowered and humiliated. This presentation was important to US and UK governments in quelling thoughts among Saddam Hussein's supporters that he could return to reinstate his regime, thereby also reassuring ordinary Iraqis of the new political order. The sousveillant photographs of his capture that subsequently emerged supported this official framing. This highly controlled image of Saddam Hussein's disempowerment is contrasted with the lack of control surrounding images of his execution in December 2006, where, two versions of reality stood in stark contrast to each other – the official Iraqi government version and unofficial mobile phone footage captured by a witness at the execution and disseminated online. It was imperative that Saddam Hussein's execution convey the appropriate political message, with multiple governments needing to balance a complex mesh of volatile political forces: yet, the official version of the execution was compromised by the mobile phone footage which showed a highly sectarian execution. This leads to a discussion about the political intent behind sousveillance and its relationship to democratic social responsibility.

In Chapter 5, major political developments in Iraq, the US and UK across 2007–2009 are outlined – assessing the success of the nation-building project in Iraq. Major media developments are delineated, illustrating the mainstreaming of sousveillant web-based participatory media in the West, but also that Iraq remains on the wrong side of the digital divide. However, with the intensification of convergence, sous-veillant activity in Iraq can find a global audience. Against this backdrop the case studies are considered together to tease out the characteristics of sousveillance in the era of web-based participatory media, and the implications for strategic political communication. Finally, the future of sousveillance given the likely technological developments of web-based participatory media, are assessed.

In writing this book, I have deliberately sought various points of views. Ordinary people's views were garnered through their blogs, postings on *YouTube* and comments online. Journalists' accounts of their time covering Iraq came from books written by freelance journal-ists, mainstream media institutions' embedded and non-embedded journalists and investigative journalists. The military's perspective came from a range of leaked military investigations, publicly available memoranda, Field Manuals and analytical reports. Non-governmental organizations' views came from their published reports. Perspectives from politicians and their spin doctors involved in the political devel-opments came from their memoirs. Governmental views came from their speeches, postings on government websites and government inquiries into various aspects of the war. To supplement these, I have conducted a small number of informal interviews with a range of people – Iraqis living in the UK, UK military experts and ex-PR officers in the UK military. While none of these informants are key protago-nists, they have provided me with background knowledge of the cul-ture of the organizations and nations in question, and a sense that my analysis was on course rather than off-beam. As such, while I anony-mized all of these sources, in fact they rarely appear directly in this book. Additionally, I have examined a wide range of US and UK main-stream news media websites, being fortunate enough to have con-ducted this research before most mainstream news outlets decided to monetize and restrict access to their web content. Broadcast news texts examined include a range of mainstream UK and US network and cable television news and radio broadcasts from 2003–2006. All news content has been sampled and examined qualitatively, sometimes as discursive texts in themselves, and at other times as offering fragments of information to help construct the overall analytical picture. Given that the operation of strategic political communication was uppermost in my mind throughout, efforts were made to triangulate, as much as possible, information derived from all texts examined, while remain-ing critically aware of their sources, framing and ideological and com-mercial persuasion.

At the time of writing, a UK committee of Privy Counsellors was conducting an Inquiry into Iraq chaired by Sir John Chilcot, considering the period from the summer of 2001 to July 2009. It is considering the UK's involvement in Iraq, including the way decisions were made and actions taken, to identify lessons that can be learned (Chilcot, 2009). It is expected that it will be published after summer 2010. It will be interesting to compare that account with the analysis in this book, given their comparable time period and subject matter. Certainly, delving into extended analysis about strategic political communication concerning the Middle East is always going to be a complex affair due to the multiple post-colonial interests involved and the chronic, interconnected causes of conflict. Attempting to unpick the mutual agenda-building influence of Web 2.0 and older media technologies on strategic political communication is also complex. That this book attempts to broach two types of complexities is therefore an ambitious project. Yet, I felt such an exploration necessary as it results from my twin fascinations with governments' ability and desire to pick Iraq up, only to put it down again, and their seemingly decreasing ability to control the story-tellers – the mass media – in the era of web-based participatory media.

NOTES

[1] Collective intelligence invokes open-ended, inter-disciplinary, combined knowledge of diverse experiential, insider or expert communities with disorderly rules governing data access and processing.

[2] Islamism is the kind of Muslim politics that seeks to create a political order defined in terms of Islam, usually a *shari'a*-based state (Mandaville, 2007).

[3] Lasswell (1971 [1927], p. 9) defines propaganda as 'concerned with the management of opinions and attitudes by the direct manipulation of social suggestion rather than by altering other conditions in the environment or in the organism'. Propaganda aims to: mobilize hatred against enemies; preserve allies' friendship; preserve the friendship and procure the co-operation of neutrals; and demoralize enemies.

[4] Psychological operations (psyops) are designed to influence attitudes and behaviour affecting the achievement of political and military objectives (Ministry of Defence, 2001).

[5] Information intervention is 'the extensive external management, manipulation, or seizure of information space in conflict zones' (Price & Thompson, 2002, p. 8), condoned in Chapter VII of the UN Charter as a measure against threats to international peace and security (Blinderman, 2002).

6 Public diplomacy constitutes the building of long-term relationships that create an enabling environment for government policies. It consists of day-to-day communication, strategic communication of key messages, and development of lasting relationships with key individuals through practices like scholarships and exchanges (Leonard, 2002; Nye, 2004).

7 The honorific title 'sayyid' is bestowed on males who claim direct descent from the Prophet Mohammed (primarily used by Shi'a Muslims).

8 http://www.youtube.com/BBC

9 Authoritarian regimes aim to keep the privileges that come with retaining power, exerting repression to achieve this. Totalitarian regimes strive to invade and control their citizenry's social, economic, political and personal life, repressing individual rights, exercising thought-control and controlling moral education to ensure loyalty to the regime's ideology (Kets de Vries, 2006).

10 The KGB was the national security agency of the USSR.

11 For summaries of other approaches see Lyon (2001) and Ball & Webster (2003).

12 See The USA Patriot 107–56, II5 Stat. 272 (26 October 2001).

13 Mann's reflectionist philosophy draws on the Situationist movement from 1950s France, itself a response to increasingly alienating technological change, where situations were designed to provoke recognition of alienation. With reflectionism, the aim 'is not momentary disruptions of everyday life (situations) but rather ongoing projects that constantly confront hidden biases' (Mann, 2001, p. 104). Reflectionism is related to 'detournement' – the tactic of appropriating tools of social controllers and resituating these tools in a disorienting manner (Mann et al., 2003, p. 333).

14 The EyeTap device is equivalent to putting both a camera and a display inside the eye (Mann, 2001, 2004b). It is the primary input/output device into WearComp. The WearComp user 'sees' through miniature cameras, with the image filtered into the computer system before being projected into the eye (Mann, 2005).

15 This is downloadable from http://glogger.eyetap.org. It aims to create real-time and personal narratives – features that photo-sharing websites do not emphasize (Mann et al., 2006).

16 http://wearcam.org/eastcampusfire.htm

17 www.nokia.com/lifeblog

18 Shi'ism grew out of a quarrel among Arab Muslims over the question of succession to the Prophet Mohammed, following his death in AD 632. The Shi'a (a term derived from the Arabic phrase 'shi'at Ali,' which means the partisans or party of Ali – the cousin and son-in-law of the Prophet Mohammed) believe that Sunni Muslims stole Islam's sacred leadership of the caliphate from the Prophet Mohammed's family. Thus, the Shi'a do not recognize the caliphate, but hold that the *imamate* holds an analogous function, reflecting the Shi'i belief that the qualities of spiritual leadership are

vested in the Prophet's descendants. While the Sunni (a term derived from the Arabic phrase 'ahl al-sunnah wa-l-jamaa' meaning the people of the custom of the Prophet and community) tend to recognize authority as residing within a canonical textual tradition, the Shi'a tend to emphasize the authority of a living, spiritual guide, hence the tendency in Shi'i Islam to choose and follow the jurisprudential practice of a particular living cleric (Mandaville, 2007). The Sunnis believe that the Shi'a have long been rebels and heretics. Sunni purists, like Wahhabis and Salafists (the orientation of the religious establishment in Saudi Arabia) and Sunni radicals like al-Qaeda, view the Shi'a as the *rafida,* or refuters, because they refuse to accept what Sunnis consider the basic tenets of Islam and the historic progression of power through the caliphs, so corrupting Islam from within (Nakash, 2006).

Chapter 2

BEARING WITNESS DURING
THE 2003 IRAQ WAR
Embeds and Bloggers

If you do not wrap your arms around the media, then you will no longer be able to influ-
ence the media. I am a firm believer that if you don't control the media it will control you.

(Colonel Michael Tucker, brigade commander of 1st Brigade Combat Team,
1st Armoured Division, interviewed in 2006, cited in
Wright & Reese, 2008, p. 293).

INTRODUCTION

In the 2003 Iraq War, the US Pentagon and the UK Ministry of Defence
(MoD) exercised maximum control over western mainstream news
media by incorporating them into the national war effort, most visibly
through the use of around 800 media representatives embedded with
military units as war correspondents (embeds) (Ministry of Defence,
2003b; Wright & Reese, 2008). The US military presented embedding
as a form of giving up message control by giving journalists 'unparal-
leled access to the battlefield' and allowing them 'to file uncensored
views of the action as it happened' (Wright & Reese, 2008, p. 292).[1]
However, I shall show how embedded reporting was, in fact, part of psychological operations (psyops), this defined by the MoD as designed
'to influence attitudes and behaviour affecting the achievement of
political and military objectives' (Ministry of Defence, 2001, p. 1–3),
and usually operating by offering 'only part of the facts or a particular
slant on reality' (Schleifer, 2007, p. 156). Whereas embedding offered
privileged access to the troops and encouraged journalistic identification with the troops, I will then show how this control over strategic

political communication was partially compromised by sousveillant use of web-based participatory media in 2003 that offered us alternative points of identification – notably through blogs from an Iraqi civilian, Salam Pax. In demonstrating this, I shall explore the inter-relationship between identification, authenticity and, ultimately, trust.

Certainly, by the first decade of the twenty-first century, trust in politicians and journalists appeared permanently low given the professionalization of strategic communications which effaces genuinely debating publics (Bakir & Barlow, 2007a, 2007b), thereby compromising ideals of the public sphere (Habermas, 1995 [1981], 1996 [1962]; Mouffe, 2000, 2005). In terms of distrust of the UK Blair government in particular, British people's concerns included pro-active government news management strategies which, since at least the mid-1990s, had generated challenging and adversarial media responses, leading the public to expect the worst of politicians, even when evidence supported the government's position (Phillis, 2003; Duffy et al., 2004; McNair, 2006). As this chapter shall show, UK and US governments did nothing to engender trust in their judgement to go to war. Polls indicate that we do, however, trust the military (The Harris Poll, 2005; Saad, 2006). In this context, from the UK and US administrations' perspective, being able to present the military's perspective (via embeds) could work to neutralize adversarial journalism. Trust in media is differentially bestowed not only according to specific events, actors and institutions but also according to media forms (Bakir & Barlow, 2007a, 2007b). Television news retains higher trust levels compared to other sources of news information, partly because words are often followed by moving images that verify claims, making them more convincing (Taylor, 1997, p. 85; BBC/Reuters/Media Center Poll, 2006). Blogs, on the other hand, are the least trusted of media. For instance, by 2006 after about six years of mainstream blogging, whereas 86 per cent of the British trusted national TV as a news source, and 81 per cent of Americans trusted local newspapers, blogs were trusted by only 25 per cent of Americans and 24 per cent of the British (BBC/Reuters/Media Center Poll, 2006). Note, however, that these figures are significant in that they show that a quarter of the population *do* invest trust in this new media form. Certainly, direct testimony online has an attractive indexical quality with certain audiences (Gumpert & Drucker, 2007; Ibrahim, 2007; Jones, 2007).

Before progressing to discuss the two case studies – embeds' reportage and blogs from an Iraqi civilian – this chapter explores the political environment and the media environment during the 2003 Iraq War.

POLITICAL ENVIRONMENT

The US' decision to go to war with Iraq on 19 March 2003 must be seen in the light of the Bush administration's policy commitments to long-term transformation of the Middle East, following al-Qaeda's terrorist attacks on American soil of 11 September 2001 – 9/11. Here, four airplanes were spectacularly transformed into Weapons of Mass Destruction (WMD) (Nye, 2004; Hill, 2009), killing nearly 3,000 people and forming a terroristic media event (Dayan & Katz, 1992) as they brought down the Twin Towers in New York. Al-Qaeda ('the base') consisted of a union of embittered Arab veterans of 'holy wars' in Afghanistan and elsewhere, its world-view a hybridization of hostility to US global hegemony combined with Sunni Muslim fundamentalist opposition to western cultural hegemony, with the mission of changing the world to make it safer for Islam (Louw, 2003; Nakash, 2006; Mandaville, 2007).

The aims of the US in launching the 2003 Iraq War have been much debated in terms of their ideological and realist foundations (Rowell, 2004; Dodge, 2005; Fawn & Hinnebusch, 2006; Suskind, 2006; Klein, 2007). Fundamentally, however, the war resulted from the Bush doctrine (Bush, 2001, 2002; White House, 2002, 2006). This was formulated from the fear generated by 9/11 (and the subsequent anthrax attacks) and the realization that the US homeland was vulnerable to terrorist attacks from non-state actors who could be exploited by rogue states to attack the US surreptitiously, thereby rendering Cold War doctrines of deterrence (the promise of massive retaliation against nations) and containment lacking. The Bush doctrine announced the US' right to use its military might pre-emptively anywhere in the world against any perceived enemy that it believed may at some point become a threat to American interests (McLaren & Martin, 2004; Fawn, 2006; Suskind, 2006; McClellan, 2008). Accordingly, if there was any chance that Saddam Hussein had WMD, then he needed to be prevented from deploying them or giving them to a terrorist (Suskind, 2006). Certainly since the 1991 Gulf War, Saddam Hussein had not cooperated with UN Special Commission (UNSCOM) inspections of its dismantling of its WMD programme (Lynch, 2006; Tripp, 2007). Waging pre-emptive war is illegal, contravening Chapter VII, Article 51, of the UN charter, under which the US could make war on Iraq legally only if there were a direct attack by Iraq against the US and only until the UN Security Council were to convene and formulate a response (Zunes, 2006). However, a successful attack on Iraq could inaugurate, and even normalize, the Bush doctrine (Kellner, 2004), while making an example of Iraq could deter other states harbouring WMD or terrorist intentions towards the US (Suskind, 2006).

Indeed, others suggest that the specific WMD threat posed by Iraq was never the main reason for the war. After the war, Paul Wolfowitz (US Deputy Secretary for Defense) emphasized that Bush saw himself in an epochal struggle against evil and wanted to reorder the Middle East towards democracy, this perhaps, a reflection of the Protestant fundamentalism embraced by Bush and others in his administration who saw the world in simplistic good versus evil terms, believing that freedom was everyone's most basic desire (Ricks, 2006; Zunes, 2006; McClellan, 2008). Certainly, 9/11 persuaded the Bush administration's neoconservative ideologues that terrorism carried out in Islam's name was bred partly by the Arab world's lack of democracy (Engel, 2008; The Economist, 2009a). Thus, by February 2003, Bush publicly justified war in Iraq as necessary for democracy: 'The world has a clear interest in the spread of democratic values, because stable and free nations do not breed ideologies of murder. They encourage the peaceful pursuit of a better life' (Bush, 2003). The US' stated strategic goal transcended mere regime change to include establishing a stable, secure, prosperous, peaceful and democratic Iraqi nation that was a fully functioning member of the community of nations (Bush, 2003; Fontenot et al., 2004; Wright & Reese, 2008). The neoconservatives in the Bush Administration, including Bush and Vice President Dick Cheney, Defense Secretary, Donald Rumsfeld, and Deputy Secretary of Defense, Paul Wolfowitz, believed that Saddam Hussein's regime could be removed easily (Suskind, 2006), and that democracy would then spread to neighbouring countries, domino-theory-style, thereby changing the dynamics in the Middle East and establishing a new Pax Americana (Hersh, 2004d; Hinnebusch, 2006; Zunes, 2006; McClellan, 2008).[2]

Regardless of the precise reasons for the war, it was still a war of choice rather than a war for national survival. As such, key audiences had to be persuaded of its merits. As Chapter VII, Article 51, of the UN charter did not apply to Iraq, the US invoked Article 42, which says the Security Council may 'take such action by air, sea or land forces as may be necessary to maintain or restore international peace and security'. As such, discursive links between Iraq, WMD and al-Qaeda were forged in a psyops media campaign under the White House Iraq Group (WHIG) (Kull et al., 2003–2004; Miller et al., 2004; Kellner, 2007; McClellan, 2008), despite analysis from the CIA that cast doubts on any solid link given the unreliability of sources (Cook, 2004; Hinnebusch, 2006; Suskind, 2006; Zunes, 2006; Bennett et al., 2007).

Accordingly, a largely unsceptical US press reported dramatic accounts of advances in WMD or ties to terrorist groups, often through directly reporting Bush's and Cheney's major speeches, and interviews with Donald Rumsfeld, and National Security Advisor, Condoleezza Rice, and through right-wing media commentators like Rush Limbaugh (Cirincione et al., 2004; Hersh, 2004d; Kellner, 2004; Rampton & Stauber, 2004; Altheide & Grimes, 2005; Ravi, 2005). Here, the Goebbels-Hitler strategy of the Big Lie was practiced, assuming that if you repeat an idea enough times, the public would eventually believe it (Kellner, 2007). Another agenda-building tactic used was to trade on the press' reputation for objectivity to confer credibility on suspect 'intelligence'. Misleading stories that overstated the threat of Iraq's WMD were channelled from US military and intelligence agencies and sources (such as the Iraqi National Congress (INC)[3]) to western reporters – most infamously, Judith Miller of *The New York Times* – forming the basis of many front-page stories concerning WMD (Boyd-Barrett, 2004; Hartnett & Stengrim, 2004; Lynch, 2006).[4] Rand Beers, who served on the staff of the US National Security Council (NSC) during the run-up to the war noted: 'As they embellished what the intelligence community was prepared to say, and as the press reported that information, it began to acquire its own sense of truth and reality' (Ricks, 2006, p. 56).

This psyops campaign appeared to be effective. Whereas by the end of Summer 2002, only a slim majority of the US public supported war, on 11 October 2002 the US' Republican-controlled Congress voted to authorize the President to go to war against Iraq if he deemed it necessary (Hartnett & Stengrim, 2004; McClellan, 2008). On 12 January 2003, a poll in the US for Knight-Ridder newspapers found that only one-sixth of the respondents knew that none of the 9/11 terrorist hijackers were Iraqi whereas 44 per cent said that some or most of them were from Iraq. Almost two-thirds thought that Iraq and al-Qaeda were 'allied and working together to plan new acts of terrorism'. Two-thirds said that the US should 'take military action to disarm Iraq and ensure that it cannot threaten other countries with nuclear, chemical, or biological weapons' (Brady et al., 2003). A month later, a poll showed that 72 per cent of Americans believed it was likely that Saddam Hussein was personally involved in 9/11 (Hersh, 2004d).

While key US domestic audiences had been convinced, the US' main ally in waging the 2003 Iraq War was the UK, and her domestic audience also needed convincing. The UK's policy on Iraq, closely tied to that of the US since the 1991 Gulf War, intensified after 9/11 with similar fears to the US about the 'creeping tide' of WMD proliferation (Butler Report, 2004, pp. 70, 105) and the UK's vulnerability to terrorist attacks from non-state actors (Blair, 2004; Butler Report, 2004; Jervis, 2008). As Tony Blair stated in a policy paper: 'What has changed is not the pace of Saddam Hussein's WMD programmes but our tolerance of them post 11 September' (Butler Report, 2004, p. 70), and Iraq's continuing challenge to the UN's authority was no longer acceptable (Butler Report, 2004, p. 105). Blair aspired to combine the UK's 'special relationship' with the US with a leading role in Europe, thereby acting as bridge across the Atlantic (Cook, 2004; Hollis, 2006). Blair appeared convinced that broad international support for war could be built at the UN, and that he could persuade Bush to follow the UN route rather than acting unilaterally (Simpson, 2003; Cook, 2004). Demonstrably going down the UN route was critical domestically for Blair, as his Labour Party was a pacifist party at heart (Cook, 2004; Woodward, 2004). Eventually persuaded by Blair to seek UN approval for war by making a case that Saddam Hussein had WMD, Colin Powell (US Secretary of State, January 2001–2005), secured unanimous approval for UN Security Council Resolution 1441 on 8 November 2002. The Resolution insisted that Iraq produce official documents proving that her WMD had been destroyed. It created a tougher UN inspections regime, requiring Iraq to re-admit inspectors of the UN Monitoring, Verification and Inspection Commission (UNMOVIC) (inspectors left Iraq in 1998), and offered Iraq a last chance to comply fully, immediately and unconditionally with its disarmament obligations or face serious consequences (Ministry of Defence, 2003b; Tripp, 2007). The allies differed on the key question of whether or not this Resolution also gave UN approval for use of force against Iraq, as the Americans contended. The majority of the UN Security Council, including the British, conceded that a second resolution authorizing military action would be required. Yet this proved impossible to achieve, as on 9 February 2003, Russia joined France and Germany in what became known as 'non-nyet-nein' alliance (Ramesh, 2003, p. 35; Fawn, 2006).

Meanwhile, the UK administration tailored its strategic political communication to convince its public of the threat posed by Iraq. Alastair Campbell, communications chief at No. 10 Downing Street, chaired a cross-departmental committee – the Iraq Communication Group – directing the campaign to mislead the media about the existence of WMD (Miller, 2004a). The now infamous example of Campbell's influence is the retrospectively dubbed 'sexed-up' dossier derived from the British Joint Intelligence Committee (JIC). As UK public opinion across summer 2002 remained stubbornly anti-war, in a historically unprecedented move, the government made the dossier public on 24 September 2002 in an attempt to persuade public opinion (Butler Report, 2004; Ipsos MORI, 2007; Jackson, Jervis & Johnson, 2008). Its most controversial claim was that Iraq was able to deploy WMD 'within 45 minutes of a decision to do so' (JIC, 2002, p. 17; The Hutton Inquiry, 2004) – a claim that, six months later, was revealed to have come from an uncorroborated source (Cook, 2004). Senior intelligence officials outraged at the abuse of their work told the *BBC's Newsnight* programme after the war (4 June 2003) that the original mention of a 45-minute response time referred to how long it might take the Iraqis to fuel and fire a Scud missile. The original intelligence said nothing about whether Iraq possessed the chemical or biological weapons to use in such missiles. Indeed, the Butler Report (2004, p. 107) cast doubt on a 'high proportion' of human intelligence sources used in the Secret Intelligence Service's (SIS) intelligence assessments and how these were presented to ministers and officials; and pronounced that there was 'no recent intelligence' (p. 105) to suggest that Iraq was of more immediate concern than other countries. Thus, the government had transformed a hypothetical risk based on unreliable intelligence into an immediate, deadly threat (Edwards & Cromwell, 2004).

Unsurprisingly given this emphasis, the WMD issue was perceived as important by the UK public. For instance, in an Ipsos-Mori poll (28 February–2 March 2003), only 24 per cent supported war without UN approval or proof that Iraq had WMD; but the number approving if there was proof of WMD rose to 42 per cent even without UN approval for war, with 75 per cent supporting war if there was both proof of WMD and UN approval (Ipsos MORI, 2007). Yet, UN Weapons Inspector, Hans Blix, had found no evidence of WMD in Iraq since UNMOVIC's return there on 18 November 2002. Iraq's 12,000-page document on its WMD programme, handed to UN weapons' inspectors on 7 December 2002, said she had not possessed chemical, nuclear or biological weapons or missiles for over 10 years (Blix, 2004; Zunes, 2006; Tripp, 2007). While across summer 2002, Labour Party ministers maintained public silence about their concerns over war, as Parliament was recalled for an emergency debate on 24 September 2002, the system of parliamentary democracy made for a vigorous debate, reflected in the UK press (Couldry & Downey, 2004). Opposing the war was a minority of the UK mainstream press: the *Daily Mirror*, *The Guardian* and *The Independent* (Petley, 2004; Stanyer, 2004; Goddard et al., 2008).

While much of the mainstream UK press – particularly those belonging to Rupert Murdoch and Conrad Black – supported the build up to war, their readers remained sceptical (Cook, 2004). Months of public opinion polls and large anti-war demonstrations across autumn 2002 and spring 2003 showed consistent UK support for an anti-war platform (BBC, 2003b; Cunningham & Lavalette, 2004). On 27 February 2003, 121 Labour MPs rebelled against their own government, backing a motion that the case for war was unproven. However, the Blair government ultimately won parliamentary support for war on 18 March 2003 (Ramesh, 2003; Cook, 2004).

While opinion polls showed that a majority of Americans supported war in Iraq, with the UK divided, most showed minimal support abroad (Lynch, 2006, p. 14). In the weeks preceding war, Gallup International polled people in 40 countries. Less than 9 per cent supported a US-led war without UN approval (Hiebert, 2003). Knowing that they lacked the votes for the second UN resolution, the US and UK did not put it to the test. Instead, they spun the report from Blix and Mohammed el-Baradei (Director General of the International Atomic Energy Agency (IAEA)) on 7 March 2003 that Iraqi cooperation had increased since January but that full inspections would require several months. Powell took this as evidence of Iraq's breach of Resolution 1441 in that Iraq had refused 'immediate, active and unconditional cooperation' (Fawn, 2006, p. 6). Thus Operation Iraqi Freedom (OIF), as the Americans called it,[5] was initiated on 19 March 2003 – a US-led 'Coalition of the Willing' with substantial contribution from UK forces.[6] Its invasion stage comprised a 'shock and awe' air campaign combined with the pouring of US and UK troops into southern Iraq from Kuwait (Fawn, 2006).

Whilst liberal proponents of the press' democratic function suggest that the quality of news coverage is most important when society is pondering waging war (Carruthers, 2000), governments who have already decided on war desire no such public engagement. Given the divisiveness of this war, careful control of media coverage of the war's operations was vital if domestic and international populations were to be mobilized – or at least, not further disaffected. Before moving to examine how this was achieved, and compromised, the media environment will be explained.

MEDIA ENVIRONMENT

Saddam Hussein's regime controlled Iraq's media tightly, as outlined in Chapter 1. In the build-up to war, Iraqi media stressed the unjustness of the imminent war and that the US was the aggressor (Falah et al., 2006). As the war started, Saddam Hussein called on Iraqis to fight a jihad against the invading US forces. To incentivize a reluctant population, Iraqi state radio publicized substantial cash rewards for killing the enemy. During the initial days of fighting, Iraqi newspapers – especially *Babil* – printed colour photographs of gruesome civilian casualties, hoping to galvanize Iraqis and disprove the US' promise of a precise war of liberation. The gory pictures, however, demoralized Iraqi armed forces, triggering surrenders and after two weeks, the images stopped being printed. Instead, Iraqi media exaggerated American and British casualties, displaying American Prisoners of War (POW) on television to demoralize her enemy, these then shown on *al-Jazeera* and many European TV networks (Engel, 2004; Kellner, 2004; Hirji, 2006). While satellite news was banned in Iraq, some Iraqis picked up Arab satellite news broadcasts on their illegal satellite dishes – although risking a $350 fine and six months imprisonment (Pax, 2003a; 2003c; Riverbend, 2005).

Saddam Hussein had long been demonstrably attuned to the importance of the foreign press (Manheim, 1991). Perhaps hoping that international journalists would document the horrors of the war's impact on civilians thereby turning international public opinion further against the war, in the run-up to OIF there were about 1,500 foreign journalists in Baghdad – compared to around 30 in the 1991 Gulf War (Simpson, 2003; Engel, 2004). Control was maintained by confining journalists to three state-run hotels and the Ministry of Information Centre in Baghdad; ordering that their satellite phones be stored at the press centre (a rule that many flouted); and assigning them government minders (Iraqi Intelligence officers) to control what ordinary Iraqis said in interview and, ultimately, the flow of information leaving Iraq (Engel, 2004; Tatham, 2006). *Fox* cable news network was expelled from Iraq before the war, apparently for being too supportive of US military action. *CNN* was evicted two days into the war for, in the eyes of the Iraqi regime, warmongering (Simpson, 2003; Engel, 2004). Given *al-Jazeera*'s large international audience, it had been allowed to maintain a Baghdad bureau since 1997 and was the only international news agency with permission to operate an uplink from Iraq (Miles, 2005b). In the run-up to war, *al-Jazeera*'s staff in Iraq increased from 3 to over 30 – far more than any other news organization (Ridley, 2004; Miles, 2005b). However, *al-Jazeera* pulled out of Iraq in the third week of war, after its Baghdad bureau was blasted by US missiles (Solomon 2003; Knightley, 2004; Miles, 2005b). Other Arabic satellite channels, *al-Arabiya* and *Abu Dhabi TV*, and a Sudanese TV crew also had correspondents inside Iraq during the war (Engel, 2004; Riegert & Johansson, 2005).

As noted in the previous section, strategic political communication played a central role in US and UK efforts to mobilize domestic support for invasion. Once war started, these political and military elites were able to move into a more controlled informational environment. It is important to distinguish between two concepts regarding information that are used by the military – Information Operations (IO in American parlance and 'Info Ops' or 'I Ops' in British parlance) and Public Affairs (PA in American parlance or 'Media Ops' in British parlance). The UK MoD defines Information Operations as:

> actions undertaken to influence an adversary or potential adversary in support of political and military objectives by undermining his will, cohesion and decision-making ability, including his information based processes and systems while protecting one's own decision makers and decision-making processes. (Ministry of Defence, 2001, p.1–2)

There are many examples of IO in the 2003 Iraq War. E-mails were sent to internet users in Iraq (Pax, 2003a) and 36 million leaflets were air-dropped over Iraq to persuade Iraqis that the war was against the government, not the people; to persuade the Iraqi military to surrender; and to prevent use of WMD or oil field sabotage (O'Rourke, 2003; Clark & Christie, 2005; Tatham, 2006). Within the first week of OIF, Iraqi TV offices in Baghdad were hit by a US missile strike, taking Iraqi television temporarily off air (FAIR, 2003). The day after Saddam Hussein's government collapsed (10 April 2003), UK and US psyops operatives took over Iraqi state television, using Baghdad's Channel 3 for Pentagon-controlled programming to persuade Iraqis that their country was being liberated, not occupied (Hiebert, 2003; Miller, 2004a, 2004b).

Running parallel with IO/Info Ops was Army PA/Media Ops. The UK military defines Media Ops as: 'That line of activity developed to ensure timely, accurate, and effective provision of Public Information (P Info) and implementation of Public Relations (PR) policy within the operational environment, whilst maintaining Operational Security (OPSEC)' (Ministry of Defence, 2001, p.1–1; 2007, p.1–3).[7] The MoD notes that Media Ops are always based on 'absolute and demonstrable truth' (Ministry of Defence, 2001, p.1–1). Yet, the dividing line between PA/Media Ops and IO/Info Ops is increasingly muddied, with a convergence of public diplomacy and deception cultures within military interventions, under the banner of perception management (Taylor,

2002). The Pentagon's PA strategies included DoD briefings from Central Command (CENTCOM) in the million dollar media centre in Doha, Qatar (Miller, 2004a; Stanyer, 2004); direct interaction with news media organizations with Rumsfeld himself making frequent appearances (Johnson, 2005), and an abundance of military images from Joint Combat Camera Program (actively engaged on the battlefield for the first time on a 24/7 basis) made available online (Hiebert, 2003); and media embedding.

'Embedding' entailed reporters operating in close proximity to military units – eating, sleeping and travelling with soldiers in specifically assigned troop units for weeks or months (Department of Defense, 2003; Ministry of Defence, n.d.). In OIF, embeds agreed to give up most of their autonomy in exchange for military protection from physical harm, access to the fighting on military terms and unprecedented access to military information and plans including mission preparation and debriefing as long as OPSEC was not compromised (Department of Defense, 2003; Fontenot, et al., 2004). Although embedding was not a new practice (Morrison & Tumber, 1988; Knightley, 2003, 2004; Paul & Kim, 2004), the extent of its deployment in OIF was unprecedented. British troops allowed about 128 embeds from British media (over 160 embeds overall) covering terrestrial, cable and satellite broadcasters, broadsheet, mid-market, tabloid and regional press, and media agency, *Reuters* (Ministry of Defence 2004; Paul & Kim, 2004; Hall, 2007). US troops allowed more than 600 US and foreign journalists selected from the top 100 media markets in the country, giving 100 of its embedded placements to non-American media, including *al-Jazeera* (Project for Excellence in Journalism, 2003; Paul & Kim, 2004). However, the DoD had the right to determine which reporters received the choicest embed slots. Given that their prime audience was the US public, priority was given to the 50 largest circulation media with Washington bureaus, while *al-Jazeera*'s embeds were attached to 'rear area' units assigned to Kuwait (Paul & Kim, 2004). Furthermore, *al-Jazeera*'s embeds left within days, believing themselves to have been cut out of briefing processes. Although *al-Arabiya* secured a place with US forces, its correspondents became detached from their unit and were captured by Iraqi troops. Due to lack of space and concerns over operational security, no Arab correspondents embedded with UK troops. As such Arab journalists became totally absent in the Coalition's embedding (Tatham, 2006).

Military control over information was paramount, as audiences are demonstrably interested in war. The first few weeks of coverage of OIF showed sharp increases in the number of average daily viewers for US and UK satellite and cable news channels (Sharkey, 2003; Stanyer, 2004; McNair, 2006). *Al-Jazeera*'s audience is estimated to have risen from 35 million in February 2003 to 50 million in March and April, and during the war, was considered the most credible news source and remained the most-watched station in the Middle East – with considerable regional variations (Miles, 2005b; Lynch, 2006; McNair, 2006). Of all media outlets, US and UK outlets that relied on embeds were the most controllable by the Coalition. While embeds sometimes provided documentation of war's brutal aspects (such as civilian deaths) (Knightley, 2004; Ravi, 2005), and also provided a more balanced and independent (from military briefings) account than some non-embedded reporters (Lewis & Brookes, 2004; Lewis et al., 2004; Aday et al., 2005), embeds' accounts that questioned official versions of events were rare. As such, it was the 1,440 independent, 'unilateral', journalists who provided the most accurate accounts of the war's horrors (Kellner, 2004; Paul & Kim, 2004; Pfau et al., 2004, 2005; Stanyer, 2004). However, they were unevenly distributed. Coalition governments (such as the US, UK and Australia) had publicly pressurized journalists to leave Baghdad on safety grounds, and as a result, by the eve of war there were only about 150 journalists left there – about a fifth of the number embedded with military forces – with big US institutions like *ABC*, *NBC* and *CBS* absent (Miskin, et al., 2003; Engel, 2004; Tumber & Palmer, 2004). Furthermore, the death through American 'friendly fire' of a senior *Independent Television News (ITN)* unilateral correspondent early in the war led to the immediate withdrawal, or reattachment to Coalition troops as surrogate embeds, of unilateral journalists from South Iraq. Consequently, embeds became the primary source of information from the theatre of operations (Gopsill, 2004; Threadgold & Mosdell, 2004; Tatham, 2006). Furthermore, the American news networks mostly decided against broadcasting reports filed by the independent correspondents in Baghdad (Lewis et al., 2004; Threadgold & Mosdell, 2004). Correspondingly, US TV media coverage was highly partial to US interests, showing a bloodless game of shock and awe, with *CBS* and *Fox* particularly pro-war and pro-US military in tone (Andersen, 2003; Media Monitor, 2003; Pfau et al., 2005). The US TV networks tended to ignore Iraqi casualties, Arab outrage about the war, and global anti-war and anti-US protests (Kellner, 2004; Williams, 2004). Although UK news outlets were less reliant on embeds given their Baghdad-based unilateral correspondents, embeds in UK mainstream TV evening news helped make the main narrative a simple story about the war's progress (Lewis & Brookes, 2004). Furthermore, across these news broadcasts (*BBC, ITV, Channel 4* and *Sky*), twice as many news reports came from embeds and reporters at CENTCOM in Qatar (13 per cent) as came from reporters in Baghdad and unilaterals (7 per cent) (Lewis et al., 2004), therefore privileging accounts from the Coalition military over other accounts. However, as observed in Chapter 1, the global news environment in 2003 presented a severe challenge to strategic political communicators' ability to control the news agenda, as news organizations with different stances on the war emerged. This was largely the result of the proliferation of Arab satellite TV stations and the internet, each of which shall be examined below.

The 2003 Iraq War coincided with a shift in the market structure of Arab satellite television news media, as *al-Jazeera* faced intense competition for the same audience (Lynch, 2006). *Al-Arabiya* launched in February 2003, and *Abu Dhabi TV* changed into a news channel format on the war's outbreak, as did *al-Jazeera* (Miles, 2005b; Lynch, 2006). Together, these Arab satellite television stations portrayed the fall of Baghdad as a narrative about subduing Iraq rather than liberating it (Zayani & Ayish, 2006). They depicted Iraqi soldiers putting up fierce, heroic resistance against 'invading forces,' and bloody victims of Anglo-American bombardment brought, screaming, to operation rooms, keeping a running count of Iraqi civilian casualties at the bottom of the screen (Kellner, 2004; Riegert & Johansson, 2005; Zayani & Ayish, 2006). Arguably, outrage over the deaths of Iraqi civilians is a consensus builder in a region split over the political and economic treatment of Iraq (Lynch, 2003). These alternative viewpoints filtered through to western audiences as all the big US networks that had left Iraq had sharing agreements with *al-Jazeera* (Miles, 2005b). Additionally, *al-Jazeera* was available for the first time to satellite subscribers in the UK, with 87 per cent of UK Arab households having access through BSkyB (Stanyer, 2004).

Alongside the proliferation of 24/7 satellite TV news channels, the other important feature of the media environment, disrupting strategic political control over information, was the ubiquity of the internet. By 2003, over 60 per cent of US households had a computer, with nearly 90 per cent of them connected to the internet (US Department of Commerce, 2004); and 46 per cent of UK households had internet access (Stanyer, 2004). That high-speed, broadband internet access was available meant that news sites were able to offer users live video and audio reports, multimedia slideshows and animated graphics (Hiebert, 2003; Allan, 2004). As such, the 2003 Iraq War was the first military conflict in which online journalism played a significant role. Traditional news organizations from around the world provided extensive coverage of the conflict on their websites, with non-US online media more likely to discuss issues like blame and responsibility, while US sites focussed on details of military action and its human interest angle (Dimitrova et al., 2005; Dimitrova & Neznanski, 2006). In the run-up to war, mainstream online Arab newspapers (most under direct government surveillance and censorship) were also largely anti-war, this reflecting the views of Arab populations (Bodi, 2004; Stanyer, 2004; Falah et al., 2006). To cater for news-hungry readers looking for new perspectives on the Iraq War, some mainstream and online media invited their own journalists to keep blogs. For instance, *The Guardian*, housed embedded reporter Audrey Gillan's war diary and *MSNBC* had three warblogs (Allan, 2004; Dimitrova et al., 2005; Matheson & Allan, 2007).[8] Others worked as solo journalist bloggers, such as Christopher Allbritton's blog '*Back to Iraq 2.0*'[9] (Allan, 2004). Some kept a blog for their friends and family, such as *BBC*'s Stuart Hughes' blog, '*Beyond Northern Iraq*'.[10] These blogs varied widely in style and claims to authoritativeness (Matheson & Allan, 2007). Mainstream media's blogs were scrutinized by editors for accuracy, fairness and balance while others had no such restrictions (Allan, 2004). Yet, users willingly participated in these blogs as consumers or producers, knowing in advance their potential for one-sided, emotive and partial representations of reality.

In contrast to the West, since the destruction of its infrastructure by Coalition forces in the 1991 Gulf War and the post-1991 sanctions, Iraq was one of the world's most telecoms-poor countries, making it hard for anyone to access the internet there (McCarthy, 2003a). In 1996, Iraq's state-run *al-Jumhuriyah Bulletin* newspaper denounced the internet as a tool of American imperialism (Stockman, 2005), and across 1997–1998, it was illegal to access the internet in Iraq (Abdulla, 2007a, 2007b). Saddam Hussein removed the internet ban in 1999, but ensured that all traffic was run through a single government-run service – Uruklink.net – with access limited to official Iraqi press, some ministries and business centres (Alterman, 1998, 2000; Balnaves et al., 2001; Engel, 2004). In 2000, the first state-operated internet centre was opened, and the following year, the internet was domestically accessible, although censored (Pax, 2003b; Engel, 2004). In the north of Iraq, the Kurds had set up their own system free from Baghdad's control by riding on the back of satellite feeds for Turkey. Both systems were costly (Chen et al., 2002; McCarthy, 2003a). As such, in 2002, Iraq had only 25,000 internet users, representing 0.1 per cent of its population (Internet World Stats, 2009). Given such restrictions, the voice of Iraqi civilian blogger, Salam Pax was a rare but vital addition to the public sphere.

IDENTIFYING WITH THE EMBEDS

Virilio (2002 [1991]) argues that in the 1991 Gulf War, military, cinematic and techno-scientific logistics of perception had melded, forming the military-industrial-media-entertainment network. Here, Virilio was referring to the specific television news aesthetics of the 1991 Gulf War, where, for the first time, satellite technology enabled real-time, high-resolution media feeds, while video game computer imagery aesthetically enabled impersonal, targeted, military depictions of the enemy. Often, these were framed by the military camera's optic, looking through a grainy, green or grey-hued telescopic viewfinder that was also a gun barrel trained on the enemy (Kellner, 1992; Beier, 2007). As such, the idea of 'Nintendo War' entered popular consciousness in 1991 (Beier, 2007). However, such presentational styles arguably engendered emotional *distance* between the audience at home and its military, presented in all its impersonal, technological sophistication and effectiveness. This distance could have been replicated in OIF, 12 years later. Here, the intensive bombing of Baghdad was depicted in US and UK mainstream TV coverage via hotel rooftop cameras linked to satellites which beamed long shots of explosions and fires while TV networks supplemented these visuals with graphics of weapons in the US arsenal (Knightley, 2000; Sharkey, 2003). Indeed, Shock and Awe three nights into the war, was described by Engel, a US freelancer for *ABC* in Baghdad, as 'furious and spectacular, but also distant and oddly cinemagraphic' (Engel, 2004, p. 175). However, in OIF, while technological supremacy remained a focus in western television news reportage (Bakir & McStay, 2008), this problem of engendering distance through depictions of the Coalition military's technological sophistication and effectiveness was circumvented by the close-up portrayal of its personnel via the embeds – as this section will show.

Rather than being a wholly planned component of the US military's informational operations, the use of embeds in OIF was partly the result of journalistic pressure not to repeat their experience of reporting the 1991 Gulf War (Katovsky & Carlson, 2003; Fontenot, et al.,

2004). Then, following the perception generated in the Vietnam War (1957–1975) that military victories and TV wars were mutually exclusive, journalists had been formed into a Press Pool, where a small number of pre-selected reporters were allowed access to otherwise unavailable information sources, in exchange for reporters pooling their resources with each other (Carruthers, 2000; Hersh, 2004d; Paul & Kim, 2004). Pool journalists followed the war from afar, in a briefing room in Kuwait, and were allowed on battle sites only long after the slaughter had been cleared away, preventing them from discerning the extent of civilian deaths and the invasion's destructiveness (Kellner, 1992; Taylor, 1992; Miskin et al., 2003; Simpson, 2003). Having lobbied the US government for months prior to OIF for something different to 1991 (Ricchiardi, 2003), in January 2002, 50 bureau chiefs of major news agencies met with DoD representatives to discuss ground rules for an embedded press system, resulting in the *Coalition Forces Land Component Command Ground Rules Agreement* (Paul & Kim, 2004). Similarly in the UK, some of the planning for the media operation in the 2003 Iraq War arose as a response to media dissatisfaction with the news gathering opportunities in operations, such as Kosovo (1999) and Afghanistan (2001), as well as the 1991 Gulf War (Threadgold & Mosdell, 2004).

In addition to pressure from journalists for something different to the Press Pool, pressure came from US Army officers, many of whom argued that the 1991 Press Pool caused a dearth of stories about its well-trained and well-equipped soldiers' skill and heroism in battle (Miracle, 2003; Sylvester & Huffman, 2004; Tumber & Palmer, 2004; Wright & Reese, 2008). Meanwhile, analysis of US media coverage of the 1991 Gulf War showed that interviews with US soldiers had humanized the coverage, while human interest stories of the troops' families suffering from divided families created bonds of sympathy with the public, ultimately feeding into the construction of public support for war (Kellner, 1992). Furthermore, the UK military knew from long experience in Northern Ireland that the best spokespeople for its forces are the sergeants, corporals and privates who talk from their experiences and emotions rather than a script prepared in army headquarters (Simpson, 2003). Embedding the media with Coalition ground troops, therefore, would allow the media to further showcase the military's efforts and create empathetic public support for the war. Indeed, in the 2003 Iraq War, US regional newspapers were allocated embedded slots with the geographically closest troop unit, so they could give as much of a human face to their region as possible (Sylvester & Huffman, 2004;

Tumber & Palmer, 2004); and US troop units could nominate local and regional media to be embedded with them (Lewis et al., 2004). Furthermore, the Pentagon perceived embedding as an advert for American democratic values, believing that OIF would be a swift campaign of liberation rather than a long, hard-fought war against insurgents (Simpson, 2003). As such, the Pentagon focused on the need to influence global opinion as well as US domestic opinion, with 20 per cent of its embeds consisting of foreign media (Lewis et al., 2004). The US DoD Public Affairs Guidance on embedding in CENTCOM's area of responsibility explained its policy:

> Our ultimate strategic success in bringing peace and security to this region will come in our long-term commitment to supporting our democratic ideals. We need to tell the factual story – good or bad – before others seed the media with disinformation and distortions, as they most certainly will continue to do so. (Department of Defense, 2003)

Thus, embedding would act as a corrective to enemy disinformation (Iraq was well-known for her propaganda, from the 1991 Gulf War), circumventing journalists' need to seek information from unofficial sources such as disaffected military members, the enemy (as in Kosovo (1999), where Milosovic ensured that the press had access to sites of collateral damage from Allied bombs) or indeed Arab media (Hersh, 2004d; Paul & Kim, 2004; Sylvester & Huffman, 2004; Tumber & Palmer, 2004). Given that a prime feature of OIF was its propensity for transmitting live images across a plethora of 24/7 news channels (Hiebert, 2003; Lewis et al., 2005), making censorship more difficult, the military public affairs officials realized that the media will get their story somehow, and so it was better that they heard the Army's side directly through embeds (Ministry of Defence, 2001; Wright & Reese, 2008).

Limiting embeds' freedom of movement to their assigned troop unit, of course, acted as a form of censorship, and given the US and UK news media's aversion to screening particularly violent or graphic images on grounds of taste and decency (Lewis et al., 2004; BBC editorial guidelines, 2009), embeds were unlikely ever to reveal the true costs of war in terms of enemy military deaths. These, going on recent wars, were likely to be substantial. The 1991 Gulf War saw 20,000 enemy military deaths, the 1999 Kosovo war saw 1,000 and the 2001 Afghanistan War is estimated as causing thousands or tens of thousands (Shaw, 2002). Furthermore, based on data from recent wars, the likelihood of embedded journalists witnessing Coalition military casualties was slight. The 1991 Gulf War saw 250 deaths of western military at the hands of the enemy; the 1999 Kosovo war resulted in no such deaths; and the 2001 Afghanistan war resulted in only 1 such death. Meanwhile, in recent wars, while civilian deaths are far fewer than in the big wars of the twentieth century (World War I (WWI), World War II (WWII), Vietnam), the *comparative* risks of military action have shifted from the West's military to the civilian population, particularly in the Middle East. 3,200 civilians were killed directly by the West in the 1991 Gulf War and tens of thousands are estimated to have died indirectly as a result of western action in the war's immediate aftermath; and up to 1,300 civilians were killed directly in the 2001 Afghanistan war with over 3,200 killed indirectly (Shaw, 2002, p. 347). This distribution of death is the product of western military strategy (high altitude airpower) and weapons (bombs, Cruise missiles) that enable the West to fight wars at little human cost to itself (Shaw, 2002, 2007). As such, encouraging embeds with the Coalition military and discouraging independent reporters among the civilian body would have been seen as the best way to avoid coverage of the true costs of war to the civilian population and the enemy military.

Allowing privileged access to Coalition troops, while encouraging journalistic identification with the troops was therefore the main formula for exercising control over the news agenda. Correspondingly, embedding can be seen as part of the military's planned psyops activity, and explains most anecdotal evidence from embeds and the military that the intrinsic nature of embedding may undermine impartiality (Miskin et al., 2003; Paul & Kim, 2004; Tumber & Palmer, 2004; Pfau et al., 2005).

What follows is an analysis of points of identification offered from several typical 'everyday' moments from the war, as presented by embeds across two UK mainstream, national television news channels (*BBC News 24, ITV News Channel*)[11] and one US regional outlet (*The Detroit News*),[12] as well as accounts from embeds themselves, and from the military troops with which they embedded.

Exposing Humanity: Our Boys Have Feelings Too

Depersonalization of 'our' troops when killing the enemy is a feature of war reporting. In OIF, extensive reference is made in mainstream US and UK news to the machinery of war – the hard bodies of the planes and tanks, but not to the individual members of the Coalition military operating them (Chouliaraki, 2006b; Bakir & McStay, 2008). Chouliaraki (2006b) suggests, with reference to the *BBC's* televised reportage of the bombardment of Baghdad in the Shock and Awe phase of the war, that this avoidance of human agency also avoids evoking the spectator's emotional potential to take a denunciatory attitude toward the bombardment. The danger of such depersonalization, from the military's perspective, is that it breaks 'the ties of sentiment between the soldiers in the field and the home front' (Hallin and Gitlin, 1994, p. 161). The troops therefore had to be rehumanized for domestic consumption.

In preparation for being embedded, prior to the start of invasion, embeds received some military training preparing them with basic survival skills. As well as helping soldiers feel more comfortable with media in their ranks, it was appreciated by most reporters, generating feelings of gratefulness and awareness that they were a security liability to the troops (Poole, 2003; Ayres, 2005; Wright & Reese, 2008). This feeling of obligation towards the military for that most basic of needs – preservation of one's own life – no doubt set up a frame of reference for embeds to dwell upon the humanity of the military. For instance, on the eve of war, *BBC News 24* (19 March 2003) broadcast a report from embed, Ben Brown, in Kuwait with the US 101st Airborne Division. Alongside numerous 'pack shots' of military equipment, Brown repeatedly describes and asks front line troops how they feel. An extreme close-up of one such young, white American soldier overhears him saying on the mobile telephone: 'I love you – I told you I'm not going to die, so don't worry' (Bakir & McStay, 2008, p. 169). As the study of embeds by the Project for Excellence in Journalism (2003, p. 5) puts it, through the embeds:

> We have seen what it looks and sounds like to be on a military convoy, to be stuck in a sandstorm, and have sensed the vastness of the desert and the real meaning of hurry up and wait. We have seen what it takes to put on a chemical suit, to sweat and shiver on the same day, to sleep in the shade of a tank or the seat of an armored personnel carrier.
>
> We also have heard soldiers reflect on what it feels like to decide whether to shoot at someone who is dressed as a civilian.

As the embeds expanded on the troops' feelings, so it is likely that audiences would have felt an emotional bond, too. Lieutenant General William Wallace, commander of the US Army V Corps in 2003, observes that: 'embedded media told the story of the Soldier to the nation. Otherwise it would not have been told. The stories filed by the embedded media gave the public something to hold onto at the "mom and pop" level' (Starnes, 2004, cited in Wright & Reese, 2008, p. 294).

The military have long sought to rehumanize their troops for home consumption. Indeed, as early as WWI, the propaganda film, *Battle of the Somme*, which realistically showed the actions and suffering of soldiers at the Front, appeared to increase identification between the home and fighting fronts (Carruthers, 2000). In the 2001 Afghanistan war, 'low-tech' humanized images of the tanks, soldiers and cavalry of the US' local allies, the Afghan Northern Alliance, (occasionally accompanied by US special forces) were presented to the media (Louw, 2003). In OIF, countering the standard depersonalization of the Coalition's hard military body, embeds exposed the humanity of the troops. Embedding must therefore be seen as the latest version of a long-standing strategic aim to increase identification processes for domestic audiences, rather than as an entirely new phenomenon.

Patriotism and Pride: We Are as One

During war-time, states often rhetorically identify the ends for which war is waged as indivisible from the national interest, with wars of choice dressed up as wars for national survival (Williams, 1992; Carruthers, 2000) – not unlike the emphasis in the run-up to OIF on Saddam Hussein's WMD and terrorist links. As such, criticism of the war – its ends or means – becomes an act of treachery, with patriotism used as a mechanism for ensuring media compliance (Carruthers, 2000). Certainly, with OIF, any news outlet's perceived lack of patriotism was quickly pointed out by those news outlets whose editorial policy echoed the Bush administration's official stance, such as Rupert Murdoch's Fox News – the US televisual ratings leader during the war. *Fox*'s success in attracting the large and receptive American audience ensured that it became the model for other US commercial networks which then shifted toward *Fox*'s patriotic terrain (Sharkey, 2003; Calabrese, 2005). So patriotic was *Fox* that it became the adopted TV station of the US military, with plasma screens in the cafeteria of the US Navy's Fifth Fleet headquarters in Bahrain constantly tuned to *Fox*, when not showing films and sport (Tatham, 2006). Willing, and perhaps unconscious, submission to patriotism was nurtured through the embeds, by setting up conditions of identification of reporters with the troops (Tumber & Palmer, 2004).

Identification with the military's aims is illustrated in the following extract from the official war blog of John Bebow, embedded with the US Marines (reporting for *The Detroit News*, on 26 April 2003). For him, the Iraqis were depersonalized – referred to only as a collection of dead bodies and dog food – whereas his admiration for the US military's bravery and patriotic spirit is palpable:

> My hubris soon disappeared when I saw the rotting bodies of Iraqi soldiers raked by Cobra fire. . . .
>
> One day I spotted a stray dog sitting comfortably on a mound above a smoldering Iraqi soldier trench. As the trucks rolled by the destruction, the dog panted and wagged his tail as if he smelled his next U.S.-military-issued doggy bag of meatloaf, or other rubbery meat, 'chunked and formed.'
>
> The dog seemed to share the Marines' power of positive thinking.
>
> 'Bloom where you're planted,' they would say in spots of adversity. 'Adapt. Improvise. Overcome.' (Bebow, 2003)

Identification of the embedded reporters with their regiment, as illustrated above, is now well documented, and by embeds themselves (Larson, 2004; Tumber, 2004; Tumber & Palmer, 2004; Robinson, 2006; Engel, 2008). For instance, *NBC*'s reporter, David Bloom, who died on 5 April 2003 while embedded with soldiers of the 3rd Battalion, 15th 'Can Do' Infantry Regiment, reportedly 'felt honored to be reporting on TF 3–15 IN [Task Force 3–15 Infantry],' according to a US Army report (Fontenot et al., 2004, chapter 4). Indeed, President Bush, in a ceremony on 27 April 2003, honouring journalists from around the world who died covering the war, noted that Bloom was 'the perfect man to carry viewers along on the charge to Baghdad' (Hamilton, 2004, p. 41). Bloom became the friend of those he reported on: 'Bloom was a "real guy" and would just sit down and talk to soldiers. Bloom also allowed (with permission from the chain of command) soldiers to use *NBC*'s satellite phones and Internet connection to call and e-mail home' (Fontenot et al., 2004, chapter 4). The power of friendship has long been recognized in military and policy-making circles. As far back as WWI, the military discovered that by 'stationing the reporters at the various army headquarters, and by making them personal friends, they became apologists for the British cause' (Peterson, 1939, cited in Carruthers, 2000, p. 66), rendering the need for censorship redundant as the reporters willingly self-censored. Reporters in WWI were given notional status as officers, dressed in appropriate uniforms, and billeted in luxurious accommodation, escorted everywhere by military minders who lived and ate with them

(Knightley, 2000). The parallels with embeds in OIF are striking. Arguably, identification with the military was increased still further by embeds sharing the troops' harsh and dangerous living conditions, rather than being housed in luxury accommodation. This is exemplified by an account from *The Times*' reporter, Chris Ayres, embedded with the US Marines. Ayres recounts an incident when his unit came across an Iraqi man, apparently a civilian, gesticulating and shouting in Arabic, and standing on a steep berm so making it impossible to tell if he was alone, or part of an ambush:

> 'Shall I take him out, sir?' asked Murphy, hopefully. . . .
>
> 'Negative,' said Buck. 'Do *not* take the dude with the robe out.'
>
> *Shoot him,* said a voice in my head. *Just shoot him.* I felt disgusted with myself. The Iraqi was probably terrified; we'd probably just turned his family into 'arms and legs and pink mist', as the faceless infantry commander had boasted. What I *should* have been thinking was, *Interview him; get out and interview him.* But I was more interested in staying alive than staying objective. The trouble was, I felt like a Marine. (Ayres, 2005, p. 226)

It is the emotional connection between media audience and portrayed soldiers that is so prized by both military and media. Indeed, during OIF, the US soldier's story became so compelling that *Time* magazine named 'The American Soldier' as the 2003 person of the year, after following a single platoon from the army's 1st armored Division. It stated that its choice of the American soldier for person of the year was based on their: 'uncommon skills and service, for the choices each one of them has made and the ones still ahead, for the challenge of defending not only our freedoms but those barely stirring half a world away' (Gibbs, 2003, p. 1). Such active identification with the troops as a result of embedding shows journalists' loyalty to have shifted to their military unit and away from their audience – a predictable outcome, given analysis of the (limited) use of embeds in the 1982 Falklands War (Morrison & Tumber, 1988; Tumber, 2004).

Western mainstream news media's standard patriotic framing of war illustrates the discursive power of facilitating journalistic access to Coalition troops during war-time, increasing the identification of journalists and domestic audiences with the troops. However, for that part of the audience who tired of mainstream media's reportage, alternative voices with their own processes of identification were available. The rest of this chapter will explore those generated by the world of Iraqi civilian blogging.

IDENTIFYING WITH THE IRAQIS: SALAM PAX, THE BAGHDAD BLOGGER

Analysis of western media coverage of the invasion stage of OIF shows that it largely erased the agency of ordinary Iraqis. While embedded reporting resulted in more imagery of Iraqi civilians than in the 1991 Gulf War, US and UK news' visual depiction tended to show them cheering US troops or receiving humanitarian aid from Coalition soldiers, adhering to the narrative of the Coalition's war aims. Periodically, we also saw graphic visuals of Iraqis as wounded or dying victims of collateral damage (Griffin, 2004; Stanyer, 2004; Hill, 2008). UK mainstream television evening news rarely used Iraqi citizens as on-screen sources (only 6 per cent of sources used were Iraqi citizens), allowing others to speak for them: official Iraqi sources from Saddam Hussein's Ministry of Information comprised 30 per cent of on-screen sources, and Red Cross and ordinary service personnel comprised 12 per cent. Indeed, UK TV news viewers felt that what was missing was a broader analysis of the war – especially in relation to the Iraqi people themselves (Lewis et al. 2004). Certainly, the Iraqi regime was not a legitimate spokesman for Iraqis' interests, and the Iraqi opposition exile groups favoured by Washington were discredited within Arab public spheres by their association with the US and the fact that they had long escaped the hardships of Saddam Hussein's regime. A small number of exiled Iraqi dissidents who maintained their independence from those groups were published in the Arab press and appeared on Arab television, but even these individuals could not claim to speak for the Iraqi people living under Saddam Hussein's rule (Lynch, 2006). As Lynch (2006, p. 18) observes, the Iraqi people were endlessly invoked by all sides in the debate, 'but they remained objects rather than subjects in the great debates about their own future'. For the first time, however, we saw the reclamation of some agency through Salam Pax's blog, *Where is Raed?*[13] This became famous for its accounts of life in Iraq during the last months of Saddam Hussein's rule. Written by an Iraqi architect in his late twenties, who had spent lengthy spells living in Vienna, since 2002 he posted anonymously from the Lebanese architecture firm in Baghdad where he worked, or from his bedroom in his parents' house in Baghdad (Katz, 2003; Zalewski, 2003).[14] Although Salam Pax was not the average 'man in the street,' as he was the son of a high-ranking politician (Haugbolle, 2007), nonetheless, he provided an independent and authentic Iraqi view (as opposed to the dominant voice of the Iraqi regime and the NGOs heard on western news). Salam Pax himself, a number of times, warned on his blog that he was but one lone voice and could not speak for the Iraqi people, yet as the lone voice that westerners could relate to, this is what he came to do. Several months after the war, as one reader of his blog put it: 'I wonder whether you can really concieve how well-known and vital you have become as a "voice"?' (Vicky, 2003).[15]

Salam Pax wrote in *The Guardian* in September 2003 about his own motivations to blog. Personal sousveillance ranked highly here, and initially with a strictly limited audience, namely:

> . . . Raed, my Jordanian friend who went to Amman after we finished architecture school in Baghdad. He is a lousy email writer; you just don't expect any answers from him. He will answer the next time you see him. So instead of writing emails and then having to dig them up later it would all be there on the blog. So Where is Raed? started. (Pax, 2003b)

As the war drew nearer, and Salam Pax's blog became more popular, his sousveillance became targeted more at the outside world:

> I just felt that it was important that among all the weblogs about Iraq and the war there should be at least one Iraqi blog, one single voice . . . I was sometimes really angry at the various articles in the press telling the world about how Iraqis feel and what they were doing when they were living in an isolated world. The journalists could not talk to people in the street without a Mukhabarat man standing beside them. (Pax, 2003b)

On indexing his site under 'Iraq', it was linked, first to the *Legendary Monkey* and then *Instapundit*, causing Salam Pax's site counter jump from the usual 20 hits a day to 3,000 (Pax, 2003b). In the week ending 23 March 2003, Blogspot.com – one of the largest blog hosts – saw 86 per cent of its traffic going to Salam Pax's blog (Alexander, 2004). During the war, 20,000 people were regularly reading the blog and his writing became the most linked-to diary on the internet (McCarthy, 2003b). As the internet went down in Iraq on 24 March 2003, four days into the war, Salam Pax maintained his diary offline and e-mailed entries to a fellow blogger, Diana Moon, on 7 May 2003 as a Word attachment, who posted them online that day, from her e-mail at work (Pax, 2003a). At this point, Salam Pax started posting again. On 30 May 2003, after Salam Pax met with a Guardian reporter in Baghdad, *The Guardian* announced that the Baghdad Blogger would write a biweekly column for the newspaper (Katz, 2003; McCarthy, 2003b).

So why did the Baghdad Blog appeal to wider audiences? To find out, I trawled the entirety of Salam Pax's blogs, which he wrote consecutively, if intermittently, (*Where is Raed, Shut Up You Fat Whiner* and *Salam Pax: the Baghdad Blogger*), from September 2002 to April 2009.[16] His first two blogs did not allow comments, but his photosite (*Where is Raed? the photographic supplement [I am working my way up to Pax TV]*), which he contributed to across June and July 2003, did. As this was the first opportunity people had to publicly post to Salam Pax, I examined all the comments (466 between 26 June 2003 to 29 June 2009) on this photosite over this period.[17]

This blog was impactful, perhaps, in its unusualness for a western audience. By 2003, most blogs were still written by individuals in the US (Cohen, 2005), but here was a blog coming out of internet-poor Iraq, and moreover, in the run-up to war with that country. As one reader commented: 'I'm a 50 something grandma, whos been reading you since before the war started. You are a voice in the wilderness, all the more captivating for its aloneness' (nana, 27 June 2003, 02:45). Furthermore, for westerners, Salam Pax was very different to the standard portrayal of Iraqis as poor, anti-western and often hysterical (Katz, 2003). Instead, he addressed us in good idiomatic English, peppered with references to western popular culture – such as alcohol, the SIMS, WWF smackdown videos, David Bowie, the Deftones and Massive Attack – and framed with a dry sense of humour. For instance, a post on 7 September 2002 reads:

> I'm preparing my emergency lists these days – any suggestions are welcome. At the moment I have:
>
> Candles
>
> Alcohol (maybe red wine?)
>
> Good books
>
> Crunchy munchies
>
> I think that will get me thru the bombing quite nicely. (Pax, 2003a, p. 1)

Throughout the blog, there are hints, some more obvious than others, that Salam Pax is gay – again confounding stereotypes of the homophobia of Arabs (homosexuality is prohibited across the Middle East). In a post on 15 October 2002, Salam Pax writes: 'Last night, while wondering whether to watch semi-naked muscle-men wrestle or tell "whisper of the night" what the man of my dreams looks like, I realized that I really needed to get loaded' (Pax, 2003a, p. 16). Indeed, users' comments on Salam Pax's photosite indicated that dispelling stereotypical images of Iraq and Iraqi attitudes towards the US was one reason why readers found the posts compelling. This post came from an American:

For years, the only face of Iraq (actually, pretty much anything in that part of the world) I have been able to see was the ugly side – the endless loops of Saddam firing guns into the air in front of a madly cheering mob, the US flag on fire while people cheer, and of course the inevitable litany of how awful my country is.

It's more than just nice to read your perspective on things. (Yet another American, June 2003)

Others enjoyed the personablility of Salam Pax: 'Salam, Your words and pictures are incredible. You're better (and a whole lot more personable) than the evening news' (Rob, 26 June 2003, 18:08). The personable tone of his blog came from the fact that it was addressed to his friend, Raed. There are also numerous references to his small circle of net-friends (such as Diana at *Letter from Gotham* and the *Legendary Monkey*)[18], as well as familiar references to internet culture – not least the narcissistic phenomenon of 'googling' oneself. For instance a pre-war post on 6 October 2002 reads:

Googlefight! Googlefight! Googlefight!

Raed vs Salam.

Salam wins with a whopping 268,000 hits compared to Raed's weak 17,700. Thank you, ladies and gentlemen and goodnight. (Pax, 2003a, p. 11)

Yet the normality and shared cultural frame of reference of such postings are punctuated regularly with sharp contrasts of everyday vignettes under Saddam Hussein's sanctions-beleaguered regime. For instance, on 10 October 2002, Salam Pax posted:

For how much would you sell your kidney?

Salah sold his for $250. His fiancée sold hers as well, for the same price. They've been engaged for a while and they needed the $500 (that's equivalent to a million Iraqi dinars) to build two extra rooms in his parents' house for them to live in. I know this because a relative of mine was the buyer. (Pax, 2003a, p. 12)

On 20 March 2003, as war began, Salam Pax provided us with what was to be studiously absent from western television coverage: the humanized face of the enemy. After a series of posts that day describing the interminable waiting for war to start, he posted:

Today the Ba'ath party people started taking their places in the trenches and main squares and intersections, fully armed and freshly shaven. They looked too clean and well groomed to defend anything. And the most shocking thing was the number of kids. They couldn't be older than 20, sitting in trenches sipping Miranda fizzy drinks and eating chocolate (that was at the end of our street) other places you would see them sitting bored in the sun. (Pax, 2003k)

He also provided us with more nuanced Iraqi civilian reactions to the 'liberators' than that promulgated by Coalition policy makers:

> People (and I bet 'allied forces') were expecting things to be mush easier. There are no waving masses of people welcoming the Americans nor are they surrendering by the thousands. People are oing what all of us are, sitting in their homes hoping that a bomb doesn't fall on them and keeping their doors shut. (Pax, 2003i)

In short, Salam Pax offered English-speaking audiences a bridge to understanding his Iraqi perspective. As Lynch (2007) notes, Salam Pax was one of the first major bridge-bloggers (that is, Arabs writing in English as interpreters of their communities, less engaged in local politics than in building bridges to western audiences), becoming so because of the attention he received in the English language blogosphere. As Salam Pax was westernized, he was able to explain the minutiae of different cultural practices to us, these much appreciated by his fans:

> Would it be possible for you to expand your coverage of 'Baghdad by Night.' Has the curfew eradicated night life? Are there any public swimming pools (this admittedly an inane question). Where would one go if one wanted to check out an Iraqi in his speedos? Can we please have more sex/drugs/rock and roll coverage especially if it involves hunky Iraqi soap opera stars or any Baywatch-like situations? Are there any Iraqi Soap opera stars? Can you highlight the most recent fashion thingy in Baghdad? Please don't turn your back on the trivialities of daily life. There is too much high-mindedness going around as it is . . . (Gill in London, 2003)

As the war started, Salam Pax corrected in detail some of the inaccuracies he heard reported on media like the *BBC* and *al-Jazeera*:

> I watched al sahaf[19] on Al-Jazeera. he said that the US has bombed the Iraqi sattelite channel, but while he was saying that the ISC was broadcasting and if it really did hit the ISC headquarters it would have been right in the middle of baghdad. what was probably hirt were transmiters or something. all TV stations are still working. (Pax, 2003l)

> On BBC a couple of hours earlier I heard Rageh Omar say that he saw a lot of people buying antennas, he said that people told him that is because they want to watch the Iraqi TV broadcast, not entirely true. Since the war started an Iranian news channel called Al-Alam (the world) started broadcasting in Arabic and if you have a good anntena you can get it, actually quite informative considering the only thing you would get otherwise is Al-Sahaf on Iraqi TV telling us that the US army has been crushed and defeated. (Pax, 2003h)

As one of the only uncensored voices heard from inside Iraq, and in the absence of a substantial foreign news corps on the ground, Salam Pax's regular dispatches with their insights and corrections were appreciated by his followers, many of whom were suspicious of media spin and inaccuracy and preferred the authentic, experiential voice of Salam Pax:

> I have been reading your accounts just prior to the start of the war, and your input really helps me understand the reality of what you and fellow Iraqi's are going through. Your words express the emotions that people are feeling. The media here in the US isn't even touching on what is still going on over there. (Luana in Washington State, 26 June 2003, 23:38)

Others, however, doubted Salam Pax's authenticity, and his identity – and even his existence – was debated on the internet in the run up to, and during, the war. Some felt his colloquial fluency in English, his familiarity with western pop culture, and his use of the palindrome 'Dear Raed' marked him out as a hoax; others thought he was an agent for Mossad, the Central Intelligence Agency (CIA) or the Ba'th Party (Katz, 2003; McCarthy, 2003b). Yet, the question of authenticity was crucial. Given their lack of trust in mainstream media, people wanted other information sources on Iraq, but given that Salam Pax was anonymous, people had no way of verifying the truth of his statements – although some web commentators conducted technical checks on his e-mails to establish where he was posting from, and others cited their own contacts with him as evidence of his authenticity (Katz, 2003). Despite this lack of positive proof, for many, Salam Pax offered unmediated access to the real, derived from the first-hand, experiential, eye-witness perspective:

> Seems like the only people who are trustworthy with the news are the ones who are living it. CNN got it all wrong about a couple of US Marines and how they died. CNN made them out to be heros. Turned out they were in my brother's unit and they died of their own stupidity. Drowned while trying to swim a canal in their chem suits (CNN said they drove their Humvee into the canal). Keep up the reports, please. (Crickett in LA, 2003)

In speaking from first hand experience and providing original material, Salam Pax's blog was close to the original blog form based on the guiding principal of traditional personal journals and self-documentation (Hendelman-Baavur, 2007). As Wall (2005) suggests, in such blogs, the more personal and more open about opinions a site is, the more trustworthy and credible it will be. As Matheson (2004) observes, the authority of blogs emerges from bloggers' explicit articulations of what matters to them, rather than traditional journalism's disembodied discourse. Indeed, outbursts of anger and sarcasm over the lack of control over his own life as a result of politicians' machinations – both Iraqi and US/UK – are regular features of Salam Pax's blog. For instance, on 22 December 2002, Salam Pax railed against the machinations of the exiled Iraqi opposition groups as detailed in *The New York Times*' 18 December online edition:

> . . . According to **opposition members**, Washington wants the opposition to enhance its credibility without growing too independent, so that the United States controls Iraq's political future yet has a legitimizing Iraqi partner ready in the wings in case one is needed after any invasion.
>
> man this is way too funny, the way everyone is so blatant about it. at least try to be a bit discreet. No need for that eh?, just a bunch of stupid arabs there, they won't notice the threads moving these puppets. (Pax, 2002)

While the expression of real feeling, anger and suffering no doubt contributed to his authenticity, and therefore appeal, it is important to stress that these were not the over-riding themes of the blogs, which were much more oriented to elucidating the incongruous cultural minutiae of everyday life in Baghdad. Salam Pax's personal sousveillance of his everyday daily life stands in particular contrast to the type of imagery increasingly commonplace in both western and Arab television news, which Chouliaraki (2006a, p. 161) observes (in reference to western news), has moved towards a more intensive visualisation of suffering. Here, Chouliaraki (2006b, p. 263) – in particular reference to the Shock and Awe coverage – argues that TV news creates a regime of the 'sublime'. This suppresses pity by rendering the identities of the sufferers and the perpetrators on screen irrelevant through the phantasmagoria of the spectacle that aestheticizes the humanitarian quality of suffering through appreciation of its horror from a position of safety and distance. This regime cancels the potential for emotion and engagement with the sufferer that the spectator may have otherwise felt (Chouliaraki, 2006b). By contrast, Salam Pax's blogs negate the regime of the sublime. Where mediatized suffering was referred to, it was always personalized and contextualized. For instance, in one of his last posts on the war before the internet went down, he blogged:

> The images we saw on TV last night (not Iraqi, jazeera-BBC-Arabiya) were terrible. The whole city looked as if it were on fire. The only thing I could think of was 'why does this have to happen to Baghdad'. As one of the buildings I really love went up in a huge explosion I was close to tears. (Pax, 2003j)

Importantly, therefore, Salam Pax reinstated not only the voice of the Iraqi civilian, but an Iraqi civilian's interpretation on the mediations of Iraq by the West and the Middle East. In this sense, some agency was reclaimed, and an emotional, engaging connection was forged between an Iraqi civilian and his global audience based on shared cultural resources, in the example above, 24/7 news. This was evidenced by the many comments expressing concern for Salam Pax's safety, such as: 'Good luck – I so want you and your family to survive' (Rachel, 2003).

CONCLUSION

By 9 April 2003, Coalition forces captured Baghdad, and toppled the Ba'thist regime. That day, Saddam Hussein made his last public appearance in Baghdad's Sunni-dominated al-Azamiya neighbourhood, a Saddamist stronghold, before fleeing into hiding (Engel, 2004; Tripp, 2007). On 1 May 2003, President Bush declared the end of major combat operations (Ministry of Defence, 2003b), visually underlining this with a dramatic photo opportunity by landing in a jet on aircraft carrier, USS Abraham Lincoln, in front of a banner declaring 'Mission Accomplished' on 2 May 2003 (Altheide & Grimes, 2005; Fawn, 2006).

This chapter showed that psyops was used extensively to build and maintain support for the war. The psyops actions of the UK and US used in the build-up to war (notably the false claims about Iraq's WMD and terrorist links) ultimately worked to engender further distrust of politicians, although the deceptions remained hidden until after the war's official end. Lack of trust in Tony Blair's leadership and his reputation for probity became an issue in the subsequent 2004 general election, and contributed to the significant reduction in Labour's majority in Parliament from 161 to 67 (Cook, 2004; Danner, 2005b; Hollis, 2006). Indeed, five years later, a survey, conducted by ComRes for *BBC Radio 5 Live* in March 2009, found 72 per cent of those questioned believed there should be an official inquiry into the UK's role in the invasion of Iraq in 2003 (BBC Radio 5 Live, 2009). Yet, in 2008, the Labour government defeated Conservative attempts to force a public inquiry, saying it would be a 'diversion' for UK troops still serving in Iraq. In February 2009, Justice Secretary Jack Straw vetoed the publication of minutes of cabinet meetings discussing the legality of the war in the run-up to the invasion. Such machinations do nothing to rebuild trust in government. The need to address this trust deficit can be seen as a reason behind the Iraq Inquiry, finally launched by Chilcot in July 2009, which is to be held in public as far as possible without compromising national security (see Chapter 1).

In the US, post-war polls suggested a still credulous public. Polls conducted from June–September 2003 found that 60 per cent of Americans had at least one of the following three misperceptions: clear evidence that Saddam Hussein was working closely with al-Qaeda had been found; WMD had been found in Iraq; and world public opinion favored the US going to war with Iraq (Kull et al., 2003–2004). While by September 2003, the White House conceded that Saddam Hussein had no connection to 9/11, this reaffirmed by the 9/11 Commission report of 16 June 2004 (Kean, 2004), nonetheless, Bush was re-elected for a second term in 2004, on a platform that included strong commitment to the ongoing wars in Afghanistan and Iraq and support for the USA PATRIOT Act. The Democrats had been unable to use the deteriorating post-war security situation in Iraq (detailed in Chapters 3 and 4) as a pawn in the race for the 2004 presidential campaign. This was because, in response to a president who had gained popularity by wrapping himself and his war in the symbolism of patriotism, in an environment where Americans, concerned about future terrorist attacks, supported a tougher national security approach, Democrats had conceded the need for war so thoroughly that when cracks in the administration's popularity finally appeared, there was little left to say that did not sound duplicitous. Bush administration spin reminded everyone that the Democrats, too, had bought what was now described as 'faulty' intelligence about WMD (Bennett et al., 2007; McClellan, 2008). Meanwhile, a large core of people who had been misinformed about the war held onto their misperceptions, as their mental frames would not accept information that contradicted their views (Castells, 2009). This is despite the fact that the search for WMD officially ended on 12 January 2005 (Altheide & Grimes, 2005), their absence corroborated by the US military's 75th Exploitation Task Force (Fontenot et al., 2004).

During the course of OIF, media audiences were left to sift whose version of events to believe – as represented by the continuum of news from embeds to bloggers, each with different claims to authenticity. For the 'seeing is believing' brigade, if trust in politicians' statements and motives was suspect, at least they could trust what embeds depicted on the ground. Yet, that both the US and UK militaries regarded the embed programme as a success (Lewis et al., 2004) should give us pause for thought. Indeed, this chapter has shown that embedding reporters was a successful psyops technique, disingenuous in that it appeared to give journalists unprecedented access to the war and the troops. Embedding was desired by the military: to act as an advert for American democratic values; and to present the Army's side directly, thereby showcasing the military's efforts, correcting enemy disinformation and counteracting other easily accessible sources given the mobility and liveness inherent in broadcasting technologies of 2003. It predictably diverted journalists from revealing war's true costs in terms of enemy military and civilian deaths: an estimated 3,200–7,000 Iraqi civilians were killed during the invasion, as well as 7,000–15,000 members of Iraq's security forces, compared to some 140 US and 33 UK service personnel (Conetta, 2003; Larson & Savych, 2006; Tripp, 2007). As such, embedding influenced the West's mainstream news agenda by allowing privileged access to the troops, enabling journalists to bear witness within the confines of OPSEC thereby increasing their credibility, while simultaneously encouraging journalistic identification with the troops, by exploring the troops' humanity and feelings, and taking pride in their patriotism.

After the war, 35 per cent of UK audiences felt that action from the front lines was excessive, with 41 per cent wanting to hear more about the views of Iraqis. Given that UK broadcasters and publics believe that multiple sources and perspectives are necessary for objective and balanced war reporting (Lewis et al., 2004), this makes the existence of the truly independent, if also partial, voices that bridge the country being invaded and the invaders' countries – such as Salam Pax's blog – even more vital. Certainly, among some audiences, blogs are seen as more credible and trusted than traditional media (Johnson & Kaye, 2004; Wall, 2005). This chapter has explored why Salam Pax's blog was trusted as authentic and why people wanted to read it. It was trusted as authentic because of its first-hand experiential nature, its personal tone, its openness in expressing its opinion and feeling (anger, pain), establishing a connection with the reader over time. As well as offering unmediated access to the real (events on the ground in Baghdad and his feelings), Salam Pax offered commentary on global 24/7 news media, sometimes noting its inaccuracies, and at other times, personally contextualizing the suffering that resulted from the military's actions. This helped generate a shared cultural frame of reference for his non-Iraqi audience. Beyond this, it was attractive to read because of its humour and personable tone, its unusual status as a blog from Iraq and its bridge-blogging, acting as an interpreter of his community and culture for western audiences. Bridge-blogging, here, included confounding western stereotypes of Iraqis; furnishing insights into every-day life under war-time conditions and under Saddam Hussein's regime itself, often sharply different to western life; humanizing the enemy's face; providing a nuanced Iraqi civilian reaction to the 'liberators'; and ultimately articulating a (if not *the*) so far absent voice of the Iraqi people. In glimpsing Salam Pax's hopes, desires, fears and daily life, western audiences could establish that this Iraqi was 'just like us.' While Salam Pax did not dwell on the suffering generated by the war, it inevitably crept into his blogs about his daily existence, thereby reminding the western audience that the techno-drama of war involves personal suffering and loss of people just like us, thus implicitly raising the question: is this war morally defensible?

In Salam Pax's blogs, sousveillance married with web-based participatory media technologies went some way to re-humanizing the enemy for the West, and acted as a partial corrective to identification with the embeds. However, despite the importance of the internet in allowing a vastly expanded range of voices to be heard during this war, it is instructive to remember that even in the US, the world's most connected nation, 89 per cent of people were getting most of their news from TV, with only 17 per cent of those on the internet using it as their primary news source. Moreover, on the web it is the established offline news providers that dominated. According to Nielsen/NetRatings, the number one site in the US during the 2003 Iraq War was CNN.com with 26 million unique users in March 2003. *CNN* was joined in the top five by *MSNBC*, Yahoo!News, *The New York Times* and *Fox News* respectively. In the UK the picture is similar. After years of massive investment, the *BBC* dominated the ratings with 3 million users, according to Nielsen/NetRatings, followed by Guardian Unlimited, with 1.3 million users, then *Sky*, *CNN* and the Telegraph (Alexander, 2004).

With President Bush's declaration of 'mission accomplished', most news organizations withdrew their correspondents from Iraq, given the prohibitive expense of accommodating an embedded news team to cover peacekeeping operations (Threadgold & Mosdell, 2004). Yet, given the deterioration in security in Iraq after the declared end of major combat operations, few independent journalists could operate, and the reduced number of embeds remained a significant conduit of information. For instance, as Palmer & Fontan (2007) note, during the American assault upon the city of Fallujah in November 2004, the danger level was so high that few journalists stayed within the city, and most reporting was done by embeds reporting under military restrictions. Only two Iraqi nationals working for western media managed to file from inside the city during the assault.

Bloggers were also to remain an important voice for post-war Iraq. Given the post-war deterioration in security in Iraq and the result of a lifetime surviving, and in some cases, benefiting from, Saddam Hussein's regime, the operation of Panoptic power meant that mainstream media journalists were unlikely to get at what an Iraqi citizen really felt about their liberation/occupation. An Iraqi blogger called G (a friend of Salam Pax's who blogged from June to October 2003) posted in June 2003, reflecting on what sort of truth mainstream media journalists would get if they interviewed an Iraqi citizen looking for the Iraqi perspective:

> Once during the days of the regime I met a very nice BBC correspondent – (it was my first and last exposure to a western journalist during the days of the regime, I spent one week after that half hour chat waiting for the mukhabarat guys to come and pick me) – she told me that Iraq was the most difficult country for a journalist to be in with all the minders, security service people and the ministry of information officials – who demonstrated last week demanding to return to their old jobs – now she is back in the country walking freely interviewing whomever she wants, but but but what she doesn't know is that every one of us here in Iraq has this small plug in police officer back in his mined which will monitor all our movements and talking even now almost 3 month after the American tanks roared into Baghdad. (G, 2003)

Thus, blogging in Iraq, given its anonymity, remained a significant way of generating insights into ordinary Iraqi's experience of the US-led occupation. Salam Pax's blog was the start of a trend towards greater personal sousveillance in Iraq after the end of major combat operations, as internet access became a little more widespread and affordable, and as he encouraged others to take part. For instance, Riverbend,[20] having occasionally guest posted on Salam Pax' blog just before the war (Pax, 2003a), blogged on *Baghdad Burning* from August 2003 to October 2007, ending a month after she became a refugee in Syria. Another female Iraqi blogger from Basra, *Ishtar talking*, personally encouraged by Salam Pax to blog (he translated her Arabic into English), blogged intermittently for several months (July–September 2003).[21] A third Iraqi blogger, introduced by Salam Pax on October 2003 (Pax, 2003e), Zayed, who posted to *Healing Iraq*, blogged more regularly (when I checked in October 2009, his last post was in September 2009).[22] A fourth Iraqi blogger, Faiza, writing, *A Family In Baghdad*,[23] was introduced by Salam Pax in December 2003 (Pax, 2003d). He introduced us to *The Wacky Iraqi*[24] in January 2004 (Pax, 2004).

This personal sousveillance of Iraqi bloggers, as well as reportage by embeds remains accessible online to anyone interested to look.

Which one the audience chooses to access and believe will depend, undoubtedly, on whose perspective they want to relive – both perspectives strongly marshalling feelings of identification, not least by conveying authentic feeling and the minutiae of lived experience. The search for alternative perspectives will also depend upon audiences' trust in mainstream media and its sources. As the UK Government attempts to rebuild its citizens' trust in their elected leaders through a public inquiry into the Iraq War from 2001–2009 (Chilcot, 2009), this may well be too little too late. Trust, once squandered, is hard to rebuild.

NOTES

[1] Wright & Reese's (2008) 696-page account, *On Point II,* begins to establish the historical record of the US Army in OIF between May 2003 and January 2005. It is informed by extensive interviews with those who participated in OIF, and analysis of military documentation.

[2] The famous 'domino theory' was part of the doctrine of US foreign policy during the Cold War. It is the belief that events, once set in motion, have an inevitable conclusion, symbolized by the effect of one toppling domino in a row of dominoes. Obviously, it ignores country-specific factors.

[3] The INC is an umbrella, secular Iraqi opposition group, formed with US government aid by the Washington DC-based PR firm, the Rendon Group following the 1991 Gulf War, to foment Saddam Hussein's overthrow (Ramesh, 2003; Miller et al., 2004).

[4] The US's most influential newspapers, including *The New York Times* and *The Washington Post,* in an unprecedented step, later apologised for their pre-war reporting (Boyd-Barrett, 2004; Bennett et al., 2007).

[5] Unlike the US, the UK MoD use computer generated terms for their operations, calling the 2003 Iraq campaign 'Operation Telic' (Lewis et al., 2004).

[6] The UK contributed about 46,000 personnel out of a total of around 467,000 Coalition forces. Around 20 countries offered to provide military forces or use of military bases, with others providing intelligence and logistics (Ministry of Defence, 2003a).

[7] UK military definitions of I Ops and Media Ops are close to those of its US counterparts.

[8] http://www.iraqandahardplace.org/ [Accessed 2 November 2009].

[9] www.back-to-iraq.com [Accessed 2 November 2009].

[10] stuarthughes.blogspot.com [Accessed 2 November 2009].

[11] This selection is based on my own surfing between each news channel available to me on my *Sky* box, recording half-hour-long segments of news across

seven 24/7 news channels on a rolling basis from 18 March 2003 to 30 May 2003. Channels captured were *Sky News 24, BBC News 24, ITV News Channel, CNBC News, Fox News, Euronews* and *CNN*. While not claiming to be a representative sample, it generated a database of 60 hours of 24/7 broadcast news, all of which I watched. My selection of clips for analysis here are, in my qualitative opinion, fairly typical of embeds' reports.

[12] An example of the regional US press is used illustratively, as this reveals the phenomenon of 'identification' the most intensely.

[13] Most of the posts can be found, archived, at http://dear_raed.blogspot.com/ [Accessed 2 November 2009].

[14] Although Salam is his real first name, Salam Pax is a pseudonym, playing on the word for 'peace' in Arabic and Latin.

[15] I have kept all extracts from blogs and comments true to their online version, complete with typographical errors and spelling mistakes.

[16] He maintained *Where is Raed?* regularly until April 2004, after which there was a break until August 2004, when he started *Shut Up You Fat Whiner*.

[17] This comprises an archive of the previous two blogs from December 2002 as well as his new posts up until April 2009. Unlike his other blogs, this one allows comments, but there are far fewer here than on the photosite.

[18] http://letterfromgotham.blogspot.com/ [Accessed 2 November 2009].

[19] Mohammed Said al-Sahaf was the Iraqi Information Minister during OIF.

[20] http://riverbendblog.blogspot.com/ [Accessed 2 November 2009].

[21] http://ishtartalking.blogspot.com/ [Accessed 2 November 2009].

[22] http://healingiraq.blogspot.com/ [Accessed 2 November 2009].

[23] http://afamilyinbaghdad.blogspot.com/ [Accessed 2 November 2009].

[24] http://wackyiraqi.com/home/ [Accessed 2 November 2009].

Chapter 3

CONTROLLING THE MILITARY'S IMAGE
Abu Ghraib (2004) and **Is This the Way to Armadillo** *(2005)*

We're functioning in a — with peacetime restraints, with legal requirements in a war-time situation, in the information age, where people are running around with digital cameras and taking these unbelievable photographs and then passing them off, against the law, to the media, to our surprise, when they had not even arrived in the Pentagon.

–(Donald Rumsfeld's testimony on Abu Ghraib to US Congress on 7 May 2004, FDCH E-Media, 2004)

INTRODUCTION

In opinion polls, the US and UK public consistently rank their military as among their most trusted institutions (The Harris Poll, 2005; Saad, 2006). Concomitantly, both militaries go to great lengths to ensure that an appropriate image is projected through various media platforms (Kellner, 1992; UK Defence Communications Strategy, 2007). For instance, as part of the US Army's vast campaign of popular cultural saturation, there have been attempts to seed the web with appropriate gaming and community-building areas to widen the US military's recruitment base and inculcate military values – as in the US military's massively multiplayer game, *America's Army*, launched in 2002 (Jenkins, 2006a; Machin & Suleiman, 2006).[1] Beyond perpetuating its own base of recruitment, the US Army undergoes a continual Public Affairs (PA) mission to inform the American public of army operations. For example, to help portray US combat efforts in Iraq and Afghanistan in a favourable light to a global audience from a 'boots on the ground' perspective, the US DoD launched its own channel on *YouTube* – Multi-National Force Iraq (MNF-Iraq) on 7 March

2007, enabling it to upload official videos to the web.[2] This move was followed by the UK military on 10 May 2007,[3] in recognition that the media landscape had fragmented and that with fewer shared experiences, generic communication strategies targeted at traditional media were unlikely to succeed, requiring segmentation and targeted communications (UK Defence Communications Strategy, 2007).

However, as Christensen (2008) observes, such videos are propagandistic, showing sanitized, victimless depictions of soldiers in situations like combat successes and aiding Iraqi citizens. They avoid 'Profanity, Sexual content, Overly graphic, disturbing or offensive material' and 'Footage that mocks Coalition Forces, Iraqi Security Forces or the citizens of Iraq' (Multi-National Force – Iraq, 2007). Such constructions are rejected by audiences with access to alterative discourses, be these sustained by experience or trust in alternative information sources. For instance, Larson & Savych (2006) find that foreign audiences are far less inclined to believe that the US makes enough of an effort to avoid civilian casualties and are far more likely to view incidents involving civilian deaths as resulting from disregard for human life, or something more malign. Web-based participatory media play a part in circumventing the military's projected image, no matter how carefully constructed over multiple media platforms it may be. For example, photographs of dead American soldiers returning from battle in flag-draped coffins, although banned on US television news since the 1991 Gulf War until February 2009 (The National Security Archive, 2005; *Associated Press*, 2009), entered the mainstream media on 18 April 2004 as digital photographs, shot and circulated outside official military channels, through channels such as user-generated tribute videos to fallen soldiers distributed on *YouTube* and photographs e-mailed to friends (Jenkins, 2006a; Robertson, 2008; Andén-Papadopoulos, 2009).

A landmark instance of user-generated content undoing military and political efforts at image control emerged a year after the declared end of major combat operations, as the issue of prisoner torture by US soldiers at Abu Ghraib prison in Iraq came to public attention in April 2004 through the publication in mainstream news of sousveillant photographs showing prisoner 'abuse', the photographs taken by the 'abusers' themselves. This chapter explores how political and military elites attempted to control this story, and with what media, political and military impacts. It then considers the impact on the military's image of other web-based participatory media content – namely a popular, spoof music video made by the troops for their own entertainment and circulated online. These two case studies illustrate the loss of control over the military's carefully constructed image from within through sousveillant media. These different examples of military sousveillance generate a discussion about the extent to which control over institutional image is possible in Web 2.0, and a critical assessment of the efficacy of the military's subsequent tightening of control over military user-generated content in 2007, one outcome of which is the sanitized, official military images online, already referred to.

Before progressing to these case studies, some explanation of the political environment and the media environment is necessary.

POLITICAL ENVIRONMENT

Following the debacle over the legality of the 2003 Iraq War, keen to avoid further tension with Washington and persuaded that no alternative options were available, in May 2003, UN Security Council resolution 1483 recognized the US and UK as 'occupying authorities' (Paul & Nahory, 2007). The US and UK governed Iraq initially through the Coalition Provisional Authority (CPA). This was created in May 2003 and was headed for most of its existence by Presidential Envoy L. Paul Bremer III (a career diplomat and anti-terror specialist). From July 2003 to June 2004, the CPA was assisted by the US-appointed Iraqi Governing Council (IGC) – a semi-autonomous entity designed to help the CPA transfer full political sovereignty to Iraq (explained further in Chapter 4). In October 2003, UN Security Council Resolution 1511 gave an official UN mandate to the occupation, making the Coalition a US-led Multi-National Force (MNF), in exchange for US–UK promises that a political process would soon lead to elections and a turnover of authority to Iraqis (Paul & Nahory, 2007). June 2004 saw the transfer of power from the CPA to an appointed (unelected) Iraqi Interim Government (IIG) charged with organizing elections for an Iraqi parliament by January 2005 (Fawn, 2006).

In the US' planning for invading Iraq, fierce personal and ideological rivalry had ensued between US government agencies regarding what would happen post-invasion. The DoD, headed by Donald Rumsfeld, prevailed, ignoring the considerable planning undertaken by the State Department and advice from his generals regarding the need for significant post-war troop numbers (Fawn, 2006; Ricks, 2006; Wright & Reese, 2008). Rumsfeld expected that transition to stability would require limited military commitment and would be relatively peaceful as Iraqis would quickly resume responsibility – a scenario resembling the US military's recent experiences in Bosnia and Kosovo (Ministry of Defence, 2003b; Schlesinger, 2004; House of Commons Defence Committee, 2005). Yet, by July 2003, Coalition armed forces were asked to engage in 'full spectrum operations', a doctrinal term that directed military forces to conduct combat and stability operations simultaneously in support of the CPA (Wright & Reese, 2008, pp. 30–31). This covered activities like training Iraq's new security forces, rebuilding Iraq's infrastructure, destroying remnants of Saddam Hussein's regime and responding to increasing attacks on Coalition forces (House of Commons Defence Committee, 2005; Wright & Reese, 2008). As such, Coalition armed forces were under-resourced to meet the size and complexity of their mission (Schlesinger, 2004; The Aitken Report, 2008; Wright & Reese, 2008).

Early in the occupation, a series of poor decisions planted further seeds for the chaos that quickly engulfed Iraq. On 16 May 2003, Bremer issued CPA Order No. 1, *De-Ba'thification of Iraqi Society*, removing from public life those Iraqis who had held the top four ranks in the Ba'th Party. On 23 May 2003, CPA Order No. 2, *Dissolution of Entities*, disbanded Iraq's military and intelligence institutions (Coalition Provisional Authority, n.d.). These orders were designed to signal the end of Saddam Hussein's regime, and were seen as crucial in winning the support of Shi'a and Kurds for a democratic Iraq. Instead, these orders led to the collapse of Iraq's state structures, already weakened by drastically reduced state resources following post-1991 sanctions (Lynch, 2006; Ricks, 2006; Klein, 2007). During the sanctions era, Saddam Hussein had hollowed out the state's bureaucracies, concentrating on keeping alive informal networks of patronage and security services (based on common regional background, tribal affiliation, and tried-and-tested loyalty) that underpinned his rule. De-Ba'thification of Iraq's fragile state structures, therefore, meant that Iraq's institutions went without technical leadership, delaying the restoration of basic services to Iraqis, and reinforcing an image of American ineffectiveness (Barakat, 2005; Dodge, 2005, 2006; Tripp, 2007). The two orders purged the government ministries of about 30,000 people, stopped the pensions of thousands of ex-officers and put some 300,000 armed young men out of work, creating a huge unemployment problem – especially among the Sunni Arabs (the main beneficiaries of Saddam Hussein's regime) who would now be susceptible to recruitment by the insurgency that grew throughout 2003 (Engel, 2004, 2008; Ricks, 2006; Klein, 2007; Tripp, 2007). Meanwhile, neo-Conservatives in the Bush administration exploited the absolutist power of the CPA to introduce free market ideology to the Middle East, moving Iraq from a non-transparent centrally planned economy to a market economy (Cook, 2004). For instance, from June 2003, for the duration of the CPA's governance, Order No. 12, *Trade Liberalization Policy*, followed in February 2004 by Order No. 54, *Trade Liberalization Policy 2004*, suspended all 'tariffs, customs duties, import taxes, licensing fees and similar surcharges for goods entering or leaving Iraq' (Coalition Provisional Authority, n.d.). This led to a dramatic inflow of cheap foreign consumer products, devastating local producers and sellers who were thoroughly unprepared to meet the challenge of their global competitors Cook, 2004; Klein, 2007; Jamail, 2007). Free market competition also undermined the patronage system of tribal *sheikhs*, weakening their ability to maintain the fealty of their subordinates by providing for them financially, and thereby losing a major method of control over their people, making yet more people susceptible to recruitment by foreign insurgents (McCary, 2009).

Ironically, despite claims of terror links that had been used to justify the 2003 Iraq War, Iraq had not been a hotbed of terrorism under Saddam Hussein's rule, but was rapidly becoming so afterwards. As Iraq's civic institutions collapsed, long-suppressed political, religious and ethnic conflicts brutally surfaced, and violent Islamist groups like al-Qaeda began targeting Coalition forces in Iraq as part of their wider terrorist campaign against the West (Zunes, 2006; Jabar, 2007; Tripp, 2007). Yet foreign terrorists were the minority of trouble-makers. Of greater concern was Iraq's own resistance to US-led occupation (Cook, 2004; Jamail, 2007). As early as 2001, Saddam Hussein had drawn up plans for widespread insurgency, soon after Bush's presidential election in January 2001 had brought into office officials who had directed the 1991 Gulf War. Three insurgency divisions were set up, each containing two to four thousand members, their mission being to operate independently in small cells. Large amounts of small arms and other weapons were stockpiled around Iraq for insurgents' use (Hersh, 2004d; Dodge, 2006). Furthermore, criminals were among the thousands of prisoners freed during the previous autumn (2002) by Saddam Hussein as part of a pre-war amnesty (Tripp, 2007), making them easy recruits for the insurgency (Hersh, 2004c).

Accordingly, in late April 2003, as Saddam Hussein's administration melted away, there was an escalation of looting across Iraq, targeting government buildings, weapons caches, the electricity system, libraries, archives, museums and other facilities on such a large scale that Coalition forces were unable to protect most sites (Ministry of Defence, 2003b;

Seymour, 2004; Paul & Nahory, 2007; Wright & Reese, 2008). This chaos was referred to by Rumsfeld as commonplace for countries experiencing significant social upheaval – summed up in his infamous phrase on US television demonstrating his denial of accountability, 'Stuff happens' (Loughlin, 2003; Seymour, 2004; Woodward, 2008). Yet the US had taken care to secure the Ministry of Oil, its neoconservatives believing that oil revenue would pay for Iraq's post-war reconstruction (Cook, 2004; Fawn, 2006; Wright & Reese, 2008). This chaos damaged the image of the military in the expectant eyes of the Iraqis who believed that a force that could rid them of their dictator could surely transform their country, and that failure to do so was a sign of weakness or bad intentions on the Coalition's part (Engel, 2004; Lynch, 2006; Ricks, 2006).

As the CPA set up the IGC in July 2003, US casualties in Iraq spiked, and General John Abizaid (Commander of US CENTCOM) publicly declared the situation an insurgency – a term that US government officials had delayed using (Schlesinger, 2004). US military doctrine defined insurgencies more broadly than traditional definitions, characterizing them as organized movements 'aimed at the overthrow of a constituted government through use of subversion and armed conflict' (Wright & Reese, 2008, p. 99).[4] This description could be applied to the wide variety of groups that made up the insurgency in Iraq – former Ba'thists, secular nationalist organizations, Islamist terrorists (Shi'i and Sunni variations including al-Qaeda in Iraq), sectarian militias and criminal gangs, largely concentrated in the Sunni Arab populations of al-Anbar, Ninawah, Salah al-Din and Diyala provinces as well as in the more ethnically diverse Baghdad. While many of the insurgent groups sought to convey that Iraq could not be governed without their cooperation, their fragmentation meant that there was no unified national leadership with which to deal and only fitful political demands. The insurgency, spectacularly marked with bombings of the Jordanian embassy and UN headquarters in August 2003, then gained momentum (Dodge, 2006; Jabar, 2007; Tripp, 2007). Despite Iraq's long history of resistance to foreign occupation, US troops dispatched there had not been trained in counter-insurgency operations (Cook, 2004). Unwisely, to break the still-existing Ba'thist networks in the Sunni heartland, Lieutenant General Sanchez, the officer in charge of American forces in Iraq, conducted large, indiscriminate cordon and sweep operations following the declared end of major combat operations, primarily intended to humiliate Iraqi men and insult their personal dignity. This resulted in large numbers of Iraqi detainees, most of whom were not insurgents (Ricks, 2006). By August 2003, these sweeps largely were curtailed in favour of more targeted raids, not least because they had massively alienated Iraqis (Wright & Reese, 2008). As Danner documents, when he inquired of a young Iraqi man why people from the city of Fallujah were attacking Americans, the man responded:

> For Fallujans it is a *shame* to have foreigners break down their doors. It is a *shame* for them to have foreigners stop and search their women. It is a *shame* for the foreigners to put a bag over their heads, to make a man lie on the ground with your shoe on his neck. This is a great *shame*, you understand? This is a great *shame* for the whole tribe.
>
> It is the *duty* of that man, and of that tribe, to get revenge on this soldier – to kill that man. . . . The Americans . . . *provoke* the people. They don't *respect* the people. (2004, p. 1)

This sort of testimony was borne out by a report by the International Committee of the Red Cross (ICRC)[5] into treatment of detainees in Iraq between March and November 2003 (ICRC, 2004, pp. 7–8). With increasing insurgency activity, large numbers of Iraqis were detained. In May 2003 there were around 600 detainees and by November 2003, Coalition forces had processed over 30,000 Iraqi detainees with roughly 10,000 still in custody (Wright & Reese, 2008). Yet, in its February 2004 report to Coalition forces, the ICRC reported that military intelligence had told them that 70 to 90 per cent of those in custody in Iraq in 2003 had been arrested by mistake (ICRC, 2004).

Insurgents placed the outnumbered, overworked, US troops under constant fear and stress through ambushing US convoys with Improvised Explosive Devices (IEDs) placed in urban areas so that the US would respond by killing civilians, or by imprisoning them in prisons like Abu Ghraib. This put Coalition troops in a position where they would mistreat Iraqis on a broad scale that would make them hated by Iraqis (Danner, 2004). As Salam Pax dryly observed in June 2003:

> Think of it for a moment. If I wanted to instigate anti-american sentiments in a neighborhood which was until now indifferent towards the Americans what would be the best thing to do?
>
> I would find a way to get the Americans to do bad things in that neighborhood, for example shoot indiscriminately at houses and shops . . . make them go on house to house searches, tie up the men and put sacks on their heads and scare all the children.
>
> this would tilt your American-o-meter from the 'I-don't-really-care' position to the 'what-the-fuck-do-they-think-they-are-doing?' position. (Pax, 2003g)

One such example of insurgent activity occurred on 31 March 2004, when four American private military contractors from Blackwater

Security team were ambushed and killed by Sunni militants in Fallujah, with images of their mutilated bodies hanging off a bridge broadcast around the world (Ricks, 2006; Engel, 2008). Within days of these gruesome images, on 5 April 2004, US Marine Corps forces launched Operation Vigilant Resolve to take back control of Fallujah from insurgent forces (Ricks, 2006; Engel, 2008). However, this was cut short on 28 April 2004 so as not to alienate the Iraqi politicians in the IGC – who had threatened to resign over the marines' invasion of Fallujah and their infliction of collective punishment on its residents. Iraqi politicians' support was crucial at this point as Bremer's scheduled transfer of authority to the US-appointed Iraqi Interim Government was only two months away, and the White House needed this as a concrete sign of democratic progress in Iraq. Thus, Operation Vigilant Resolve ended with an agreement that the local population (rather than US forces) would keep the insurgents out of the city. However, the Blackwater killers had not been apprehended (Ricks, 2006) and Fallujah was now mythologized as a city of heroes that had stood up to US-led occupation (Jamail, 2007; Engel, 2008). As such, insurgent strength grew, with the support of most of the clerical and civilian population of Fallujah, who were seeking to reassert Sunni dominance in Iraq. By November 2004, the strength of the hardcore Sunni rebels had swelled to more than twenty thousand, and the revolt spread from Fallujah to cities in central, western and northern Iraq, including Ramadi and Mosul. The insurgency was financed partly by kidnappings and partly by wealthy Ba'th Party loyalists who had fled Iraq before the US invasion and now funneled money from Syria and Jordan to rebels (Nakash, 2006; Jamail, 2007).

On 7 November 2004, four days after George Bush was re-elected President, with Fallujah now under complete insurgent control, a joint US–Iraqi offensive (Operation Phantom Fury) was led by US Marine Corps against the city. 6,500 marines, 1,500 Army soldiers and 2,000 Iraqi troops assaulted Fallujah over ten days in a once-and-for-all attack to communicate to other Sunni-dominated cities that insurgents would not be tolerated (Ricks, 2006, p. 398). Electricity, water, food and medicines were cut off, and air bombardments pulverized the city, using weapons that included white phosphorus, despite the fact that 30,000 to 50,000 residents had remained there and the Geneva Conventions ban its use in areas where civilians may be hit. Thus, collective punishment was inflicted on Fallujans (Jamail, 2007; Paul & Nahory, 2007). Undoubtedly, the White House had delayed invading Fallujah so the inevitable dead marines and Iraqi civilians would not impact American voters (Engel, 2008). The US reported that the recapture of the city killed many insurgent fighters and degraded al-Qaeda's foothold in Iraq, although others note that US military operations against insurgents here were ineffective at drawing them out into open battle (Jamail, 2007). This did not stop similar US attacks on other insurgent-held cities (Paul & Nahory, 2007).

Between 20 March 2003 and 19 March 2005, 1,874 civilians in Fallujah were killed (Iraqbodycount, 2009)[6] while 70 to 80 per cent of the population fled, including insurgents, bringing tales of anger and humiliation to large swathes of the Sunni Arab population, so intensifying the feelings on which the insurgency thrived (Jamail, 2007; Tripp, 2007; Engel, 2008). By September 2006 the situation had deteriorated to the point that al-Anbar province (containing Fallujah) was under total insurgent control, with the exception of (only pacified) Fallujah, but now with an insurgent-plagued Ramadi (Ricks, 2006). With the broadening of the insurgency, fighting took on a sectarian aspect with killings in Shi'i quarters triggering reprisals in Sunni areas by Shi'i militia (such as the Badr Brigade affiliated to the SCIRI Party and Muqtada al-Sadr's Mahdi army), and vice versa (elucidated further in Chapter 4) (Tripp, 2007).

As such, Iraqis grew increasingly frustrated with the occupation. By February 2004, a national survey of Iraqis found that the biggest single problem people faced was lack of security/stability (22 per cent) followed by no job (12 per cent) and rising prices (10 per cent) (Oxford Research International, 2004). Following the invasion of Iraq, anti-Americanism in Muslim countries deepened sharply, spreading beyond the Middle East to include Muslim countries such as Indonesia, and the wider world such as Russia and the UK (Kohut, 2003). In this context, controlling the image of the US military (as the senior partner) and the UK military (as the junior partner) (House of Commons Defence Committee, 2005) was a vital aspect of 'soft power,' with the potential to win over, or alienate, the Iraqi people and the international community.[7]

MEDIA ENVIRONMENT

The military's primary goals are the operational success and security of its missions, this subordinating all informational goals, including those involving the press (Paul & Kim, 2004). As Chapter 2 noted, IO/Info Ops and PA/Media Ops are, by doctrine, quite distinct. However, in practice, the distinction between IO/Info Ops, which is focussed on manipulating an enemy or neutral host nation audience, and PA/ Media Ops, which is directed at truthfully informing domestic (and international) audiences, has become increasingly blurred in a globally connected, news-saturated planet. A classified secret report produced by the Pentagon in October 2003, the *Information Operations Roadmap*, noted that 'information intended for foreign audiences, including public diplomacy and PSYOP increasingly is consumed by our domestic audience, and vice-versa' and concluded that psyop messages disseminated to any audience except, perhaps, individual decision-makers will often be 'replayed by the news media for much larger audiences, including the American public' (Bennett et al., 2007, p. 143). This blurring between IO/Info Ops and PA/Media Ops became more marked in the US military since the publication of FM 3–13, *Information Operations: Doctrine, Tactics, Techniques, and Procedures*, in November 2003. This defines IO as: 'a set of activities taken to attack or defend information and information systems to gain information superiority and to affect decisionmaking of *both friendly* and enemy forces' (Wright & Reese, 2008, p. 273 – my emphasis). Thus, IO targets were expanded from conventional enemy and neutral host nation audiences to wider audiences, the rationale being that the military had to compete with its adversaries to get its voice heard and to counter false messages in a media ecology where even the most isolated and technologically primitive target audiences have access to a wide variety of news sources and outlets. Thus, this new IO doctrine held that PA measures could also be used in support of military operations.[8] At times, this blurring 'made for uneasy relations between those Soldiers and units performing these related activities' (Wright & Reese, 2008, p. 276).

Some embeds remained with the US Army in Iraq after the end of major combat operations in May 2003, enabling the Army to get its message out that it was a liberating rather than occupying force. As Chapter 2 demonstrated, during major combat operations, due to forces of identification between journalist and soldier, nothing portrays the military's official perspective like an embed. Given that prior to major assaults on insurgents in cities, Coalition commanders banned all non-embedded media workers from entering the targeted cities for the duration of the battle and usually a long time afterwards, this gave the Coalition almost complete control over international public perceptions of what was happening on the battlefield (Jamail, 2007; Paul & Nahory, 2007). However, compared to the 800 journalists embedded with the military during major combat operations in the invasion phase of the war, afterwards there were far fewer with numbers reflecting the ebb and flow of major events in Iraq. For instance, there were nearly 100 embeds in November 2004 on the eve of the US assault on Fallujah (Pfau et al., 2005), but by December 2004 only 35 remained (Wright & Reese, 2008). Such low numbers were the result of financial pressures, security pressures (insurgency violence and kidnapping) and reasons to do with standard news values (the slow progress towards Iraq's stabilization did not lend itself to sound bites and video clips) (Engel, 2008; Wright & Reese, 2008). Analysis of reportage of Iraq in US mainstream media[9] showed that while reports increased dramatically in the months preceding OIF, peaking to over 5,000 stories in April 2003, this fell dramatically after May to around 1,000–2,000 stories per month across the rest of 2003 to February 2004 (Larson & Savych 2006).

Aware that it could not depend on the embed programme in the post-invasion phase to generate a drip-feed of largely controllable reportage, the Coalition military relied on the extensive PA of the US Army to inform the American public of army operations. For instance, in 2004, new technology allowed the Army to launch the Digital Video and Imagery Distribution System (DVIDS).[10] DVIDS users (civilian media and military personnel) seeking information from the field for ongoing operations in Iraq, Afghanistan, Kuwait, Qatar and Bahrain, acquired real-time, broadcast quality products from a centralized archived database via satellite feeds, helping to quickly publicize soldiers' activities and commanders' objectives (Wright & Reese, 2008). While DVIDS did not have the same aura of objectivity, nor the power of identification, evinced by embeds, it provided a glut of readily available information for media use. Thus, the Army worked hard to project the best possible image in the news. Additionally, by-passing the news media altogether, the 24-hour Pentagon Channel[11] became available to Americans in December 2004 via their satellite and cable-company service providers (Bennett et al., 2007).

Meanwhile, post-war Iraqi media enjoyed a freedom long denied under Saddam Hussein's regime. Now, anyone with money could publish a newspaper, this reflected in the appearance by June 2003 of up to 90 new newspapers and journals, with an estimated 170 by October 2003, many associated with, and supported financially by, emergent or traditional political groups acting as party political mouthpieces, representing an enormous variety of political, critical and tabloid sensationalist perspectives (Engel, 2004, 2008; Library of Congress, 2006; Tripp, 2007). While many of these disappeared routinely, some aspired to be respectable, national dailies and reached significant audiences, such as some Kurdish newspapers and Sa'ad al-Bazzaz's newspaper, *az-Zaman*, and his TV station, *al-Sharqiya*, the first privately owned satellite television station in Iraq. Established Arab media outlets continued to report the deteriorating situation in Iraq, further compromising the US' ability to manage perceptions, particularly as people were now allowed access to satellite TV. After the declared end of major combat operations in May 2003, *al-Jazeera* resumed its talk shows (during the war it had switched to an all-news format), where views expressed by callers, including Iraqis, reflected the diversity and complexity of positions on the US-led occupation of Iraq (Lynch, 2006).

American military officials deeply resented their inability to control information from the battlefield in post-war Iraq. For instance, reports from *al-Jazeera* – the only news operation inside the besieged city of Fallujah in April 2004 – contradicted the Coalition's narrative graphically and dramatically. During the fighting, the Americans claimed most of the dead were insurgents in Fallujah, whereas *al-Jazeera* reported doctors saying 700 civilians were killed (Roy, 2004; Lynch, 2006; Jamail, 2007). Consequently, US forces asked leaders of Fallujah to expel *al-Jazeera* journalists as part of their cease-fire agreement (Jamail & al-Fadhily, 2007). In an attempt to draw Iraqis away from Arab news channels, the Pentagon established *al-Iraqiya*, a state-run radio and television station forming part of the Iraqi Media Network (IMN).[12] This constituted a BBC-styled national forum where all ethnicities could openly and constructively debate, and was funded by the US (at $6 million a month) until April 2005 (Calabrese, 2005; MacDonald, 2005; Miles, 2005b). Yet, as Miles (2005b, p. 284) puts it with regard to the Iraqi people, after: 'thirty-five years of practice, they knew propaganda when they saw it'. It produced dreary output that reminded many Iraqis of television under Saddam Hussein (even the singers that had sung his praises on the old Iraqi television network were now commandeered to sing odes to Iraq's liberation (Miles, 2005b)), ran little news and was largely ignored by Iraqis (Lynch, 2006). By April 2004, *al-Iraqiya* could be received without difficulties at home by 84 per cent of Iraqis, compared to 33 per cent for the satellite stations (Library of Congress, 2006). However, a State Department survey in October 2003 found that of Iraqis with access to a satellite dish, 63 per cent preferred *al-Jazeera* or *al-Arabiya*, and only 12 per cent *al-Iraqiya* (Miles, 2005b). Similarly, the US-government-financed satellite TV station called *al-Hurra* Iraq (a version of *al-Hurra*),[13] by April 2004, was watched by only 6 per cent of respondents to a *CNN/USA Today/Gallup* poll (Lynch, 2006). *Al-Jazeera* and *al-Arabiya*, along with Hezbollah's *al-Manar* and Iran's *al-Alam* (the only foreign station available without a satellite dish), became the most popular sources of information for Iraqis themselves in the Shi'i-dominated south (Lynch, 2006; McNair, 2006) (although *al-Jazeera* was viewed with some reservation as it had been seen by many Iraqi Shi'a as too generous to Saddam Hussein's regime under his dictatorship and over-critical of Arab countries who had allied themselves with the US-led coalition (Miles, 2005b)).

Added to the nascent Iraqi public sphere's challenging of the Coalition military's strategic political communication, other challenges came from the proliferation of military user-generated content – in particular, from digital and video cameras. While war photographs have long served as witness testimony (for instance, in the Crimean War and American Civil War), the use of these photographic technologies required specialist skills and the necessary equipment was far from an everyday item (Robinson & Robinson, 2006). Digital cameras, by comparison, were everyday items for westerners in 2003–2005. Some soldiers also packed camcorders, mailing video cassettes back to their family (Davenport, 2004). E-mail and internet access was part of the MoD's Operational Welfare Package for soldiers during the 2003 Iraq War (Ministry of Defence, 2003b); and by August 2003, the US Army established access to e-mail for the soldiers of Task Force 1–22 Infantry and others across Iraq. Such was the soldiers' desire for an internet link that some units even spent their own funds to set up communications systems in Iraq's primitive infrastructure. Most Forward Operating Bases (FOBs), which comprised logisticians who handle payroll, transport, command and control, maintenance and everything else that runs the military machine, were equipped with a 24-hour internet café and a subsequent army study found that 95 per cent of soldiers used these establishments to send and receive e-mail, with two-thirds using e-mail three or more times a week (Engel, 2008; Wright & Reese, 2008). Soldiers' ability to receive web-cam pictures of family and friends in an environment where a letter sent through the post could take three weeks was a real morale boost ; and by 2004, many relatives of personnel in Iraq said they routinely received photographs by e-mail – usually touristic photographs of smiling sons and daughters (Dao & Lichtblau, 2004; Davenport, 2004; Wright & Reese, 2008).

Meanwhile, video-sharing website *YouTube* was launched in 2005, becoming fully operational just before the end of 2005 to become one of the world's fastest-growing websites (Christensen, 2008). Across 2000–2006, a number of factors contributed to making video production capabilities available to millions. This included the introduction of Apple's software product, Final Cut Pro, the first consumer-grade video-editing program to produce broadcast quality video on a laptop, accompanied by cheaper versions of editing software such as Windows Movie Maker.[14] Other contributing factors included: simple open standards for video production (like MPEG-2 and -4); the availability of consumer products that made MPEG video (like Tivo); increased processing power and decreasing cost of personal computers and digital cameras; and the proliferation of broadband internet access.[15] Accordingly, by 2006 we had witnessed a new level of mass participation in video making (Pantic, 2006).

Thus, while the Coalition forces had finance and structures in place to control their public image, in the post-war environment of Iraq, and the media environment of 2003–2005, control over strategic political communication was challenged – most spectacularly by Abu Ghraib.

Abu Ghraib: The Downward Spiral of the Military's Image

Abu Ghraib was the prison at the centrepiece of Saddam Hussein's regime of fear, featuring torture and executions. Under the CPA, Abu Ghraib became the prison for criminal and security detainees[16] and facilitated the conducting of interrogations (Taguba Report, 2004, p.15). Unknown to the public, across July 2003 to February 2004, these interrogations involved physical and psychological attacks on detainees by US Military Police (MP) and Military Intelligence (MI) personnel, violating the Geneva Conventions governing the treatment of prisoners of war and of civilian non-combatants (Taguba, 2004; Ricks, 2006). A large number of these incidents involved photography, the first time-stamped on 17 October 2003. For instance:

> b. (S) Videotaping and photographing naked male and female detainees;
>
> c. (S) Forcibly arranging detainees in various sexually explicit positions for photographing; . . .
>
> f. (S) Forcing groups of male detainees to masturbate themselves while being photographed and videotaped; . . .
>
> j. (S) Placing a dog chain or strap around a naked detainee's neck and having a female Soldier pose for a picture; . . .
>
> m. (S) Taking photographs of dead Iraqi detainees. (Taguba, 2004 pp. 16–17)

The question that remained unanswered for five years after these activities were publicized in April and May 2004 was whether they were merely criminal abuses, conducted by a few bad apples, as the Bush administration maintained, or whether they were part of a covert interrogation and torture policy to elicit intelligence for the War on Terror. The answer, emerging definitively in 2009, was the latter. This answer was a long time coming. Since 2002 there had been continuing protests by human rights groups about prisoner abuse of terror suspects at Guantánamo, Cuba and at the US military's main interrogation centre at Bagram Air Base in Afghanistan; and since 2003 about US military treatment of Iraqi prisoners. In the absence of photographs, the complaints had little traction (Hersh, 2004d). This case study outlines how, through acts of sousveillance at Abu Ghraib, covert policy was publicly unearthed, and how the Bush administration attempted to regain discursive control over this vital issue.

From Personal Sousveillance to Hierarchical Sousveillance

Exploring how the Abu Ghraib photographs came into being uncovers both personal sousveillance (apolitical life-sharing) and hierarchical sousveillance (politically or legally motivated) impulses.

Soldiers involved in prisoner 'abuse' captured the activities with photographs and movies on their own digital cameras, (CID Report and Statements, 2004). A sworn statement by Matthew C. Wisdom from 372nd MP Company, Abu Ghraib, on 15 January 2004, described how the ring leader, Corporal Charles A. Graner Jr., 372nd MP Company, deliberately posed for the 'abuse' photographs: 'During the time he was hitting the detainees, he posed for a photograph in which it looked like he was going to hit the detainee. After the photo was taken, he continued to hit the detainees' (CID Report and Statements, 2004). The very act of posing for the picture suggests that the soldiers were taking trophy shots and mementos of their time in Iraq (Sontag, 2004; Beier, 2007) – or, as Sante (2004) pithily puts it 'here's-me-at-war.jpeg.' Trophy shots of prisoners and killed enemy combatants were common across the Coalition military in Iraq, although they violated Geneva Conventions (Banbury, 2004; Engel, 2008; Sharrock, 2008).

Personal sousveillance is not just about taking pictures that document one's life, but sharing these with interested others. In an interview with Michael Buerk on BBC Radio 4's The Choice on 7 August 2007, the eventual whistleblower, Joe Darby (US Reserve soldier, of the

320th MP Battalion of the 800th MP Brigade), reveals the moment that Graner first started to share the photos with him, this occurring after Darby had been in Iraq for a month:

> I [pause] had been presented with a picture with, within the first month of taking over the prison. It was 4 o'clock in the morning – 'cos I worked a weird shift. The guys were getting off at the hard site,[17] coming back. Graner walked up to me and said 'Hey Darb, check this out.' He showed me a picture and it had a – uh – prisoner chained to a cell. Naked from the waist down with a – uh – hood on his head and the floor was all wet around him. And he looked at me and he says, 'Darby, now, the Christian in me knows this is wrong, but the corrections officer in me can't help but love to make a grown man piss himself.' [Pause]. And I looked at him and said, 'Graner, you're, you're screwed up.' And he laughed and he went in his room and I went to work. I didn't think anything of it because there was – there was a thing of water there – it could have been something Graner staged, just to – you know – get a little shock factor photo for, to take home with him. (Bryan, 2007)

Darby had been at Abu Ghraib for several months when he was first handed the 'abuse' photographs on 2 computer CDs (CID Report and Statements, 2004). In one account, Darby says that they were lent to him by Graner, in response to Darby's questions about what had happened in a shooting incident in the hard site during November 2003 while he had been on leave (Bryan, 2007). In a later interview, Darby said that the desert heat had warped his own snapshots, so he asked Graner for some pictures, hoping for images of camels and tanks (Sharrock, 2008): 'To this day, I'm not sure why he gave me that CD. He probably just forgot which pictures were on it, or he might have assumed that I wouldn't care' (Darby, n.d.). Most of the discs contained general shots around the city of Hilla, the Green Zone[18] and palaces in Iraq, but also the now infamous photos of 'abuse' (Bryan, 2007).

Before Graner lent Darby the CD, the digital pictures had been circulating among specific in-groups – military friends and family members – as a form of personal sousveillance across, in Hockenberry's (2005, p. 1) phrase 'the digital military netherworld of Iraq'. Graner's ex-wife, Staci Morris, reports how Graner proudly e-mailed his children photos of 'these beat up prisoners and blood and talk about how cool it was – look what daddy gets to do,' (Tanner, 2005). Given the volume of pictures taken by military personnel in Iraq, no one reviewed the photos before they were transmitted across the internet (Kewney, 2004). Reservist, Private First Class (Pfc.) Lynndie R. England, 372nd MP Company, one of those convicted for the 'abuses', later revealed that many military personnel knew about the photos (Brockes, 2009,

p. 19). Those involved in the photographs used colleagues' computers to download the pictures (CID Report and Statements, 2004). Others saw the photos by coming across copies as computer screen-savers (CID Report and Statements, 2004). Specialist (Spc.) Sabrina D. Harman, 372nd MP Company in her sworn statement to US Army Criminal Investigation Command (CID)[19] on 16 January 2004, describes how she took photographs of the detainees back to her home town during her Rest and Recuperation leave, where she showed them to her room mate. She also notes the names of a handful of soldiers at Abu Ghraib who had copies of the pictures, and that: 'I know that people from MI have them because they were swapping pictures' (CID Report and Statements, 2004).

The 'abusers' appeared to be aware that the 'abuses' were wrong, as noted in the sworn statements to the CID investigation of those who participated, and in the secrecy that was part of the in-group. Spc. Jeremy C. Sivits, 372nd MP Company, states in his sworn statement on 14 January 2004 about the abuses he witnessed directly, that Graner: 'pretty much said, "You did not see shit"' (CID Report and Statements, 2004). As the Taguba Report's (2004) psychological assessment of the 'abuses' at Abu Ghraib notes: 'the MI unit seemed to be operating in a conspiracy of silence' (Nelson, 2004). At the same time, these knowingly illicit 'abuses' were, to their participants, fun – which may in turn, explain their impulse to photograph and share them. For instance, Lynndie England, in her sworn statement to CID on 15 January 2004 describes the night they abused and photographed a pile of detainees:

Q. Who was taking pictures that night?

A. I took some with GRAINER's [sic] camera, GRAINER took some, FREDER-ICK had a camera and he took some pictures, and HARMAN had a camera, they both took pictures. I took pictures with their cameras as well. They would be like get me in a picture. I took the pictures from the upper tier looking down at the time that I retrieved the camera from the office.

Q. What was the overall mood of everyone?

A. We would joke around, everyone would laugh at the things we had them do.

(CID Report and Statements, 2004)

Atrocity photographs are not new. For instance, German soldiers in WWII photographed atrocities they committed in Poland and Russia (Sontag, 2004) and Saddam Hussein regularly filmed torture and killings of Iraqis as proof of orders being carried out (Engel, 2004). Furthermore, acts of violence proliferate in web-based participatory media content (Christensen, 2008; Kambouri & Hatzopoulos, 2008).

However, snapshots in which the executioners placed themselves among their victims are exceedingly rare (Hersh, 2004b; Sontag, 2004), but this was a feature of the published Abu Ghraib photos. As Hersh (2004a, p. 2) describes:

> In one, Private England, a cigarette dangling from her mouth, is giving a jaunty thumbs-up sign and pointing at the genitals of a young Iraqi, who is naked except for a sandbag over his head, as he masturbates. Three other hooded and naked Iraqi prisoners are shown, hands reflexively crossed over their genitals. A fifth prisoner has his hands at his sides. In another, England stands arm in arm with Specialist Graner; both are grinning and giving the thumbs-up behind a cluster of perhaps seven naked Iraqis, knees bent, piled clumsily on top of each other in a pyramid. There is another photograph of a cluster of naked prisoners, again piled in a pyramid. Near them stands Graner, smiling, his arms crossed; a woman soldier stands in front of him, bending over, and she, too, is smiling. Then, there is another cluster of hooded bodies, with a female soldier standing in front, taking photographs.

Sontag suggests that the Abu Ghraib photos are akin to photographs of black victims of lynching taken between the 1880s and 1930s, which show small-town Americans grinning, beneath the naked mutilated body of a black person hanging behind them from a tree: 'The lynching photographs were souvenirs of a collective action whose participants felt perfectly justified in what they had done. So are the pictures from Abu Ghraib' (Sontag, 2004).

What would lead to participants feeling justified in what they had done? A culturalist explanation is that the soldiers were culturally immersed in porn (Sabatino, 2004), voyeuristic, exhibitionist reality TV shows like *Big Brother* and degradation-of-others shows like *Bumfights* (Hume, 2004) and thereby saw little wrong with their actions. Donald Winslow, photojournalist and editor of *News Photographer* magazine, was not the only journalist to note that the soldiers were using new technology to: 'basically create homemade porn with their digital cameras . . . They assembled them into galleries and e-mailed them to people' (cited in Manjoo, 2004). The popular, right wing, American talk-show host, Rush Limbaugh[20] saw the Abu Ghraib photographs as 'emotional release' for combat-weary US soldiers (Limbaugh, 2004). As one caller to Rush Limbaugh noted, to 'stack naked men' is like a college fraternity prank (Sontag, 2004).

Another, more powerful, explanation for the participants feeling justified in committing and documenting the 'abuses' is that the activities were part of a sanctioned, if secret, policy of interrogation and intelligence-gathering. Indeed, many of the 'abusers' testified that MI personnel at Abu Ghraib approved of the abuse (Hersh, 2004a). The torture policy was long denied by the Bush administration, and also by the military reports into the 'abuses' that proliferated as a result of Darby's whistle-blowing. For instance, The Schlesinger Report – an investigation by the DoD panel concludes that: 'No approved procedures called for or allowed the kinds of abuse that in fact occurred. There is no evidence of a policy of abuse promulgated by senior officials or military authorities' (Schlesinger, 2004, p. 5). Schlesinger (2004) concluded that since the events that took place at Abu Ghraib were an aberration, it was poor leadership and lack of oversight within the prison that had allowed the abuses to occur. However, other evidence existed to the contrary. For instance, a leaked Red Cross report (ICRC, 2004) and evidence of returning special forces soldiers to the UK noted that sexual humiliation of high intelligence value prisoners in Abu Ghraib was part of a system of degradation developed by British and US troops called R2I – Resistance to Interrogation – which uses sexual jibes and stripping prisoners to prolong 'the shock of capture' when detainees are at their most vulnerable (Beaumont et al., 2004). Not just the 'abuses' themselves, but their photographic documentation, may have been part of the covert policy of intelligence-gathering. Attorneys for Lynndie England, the reservist charged with 13 counts of misconduct in the case, say she was ordered by her superiors to pose with naked Iraqi prisoners so that the photos could be used to frighten and demoralize other prisoners (Washington Post, 2006). Hersh (2004c, p. 4) cites a government consultant who said: 'I was told that the purpose of the photographs was to create an army of informants, people you could insert back in the population.' The idea was that they would be blackmailed, by fear of exposure of the shameful photos to family and friends, to spy on their associates (Danner, 2004; Hersh, 2004c; Apel, 2005). According to Hersh (2004d, p. 39), Raphael Patai's book, *The Arab Mind*, (a study of Arab culture and psychology first published in 1973, which depicts sexual shame and humiliation as the greatest weakness of Arab men), was 'the bible of the neoconservatives on Arab behavior'.

Whether it was just the sharing of the photographs that was motivated by personal sousveillance, or also the capturing of the photographs, their existence and circulation generated an instance of hierarchical sousveillance. In his sworn statement to CID on 14 January 2004, Joe Darby detailed that after Graner lent him the CDs containing the 'abuse' photos, he made 2 CDs of all the photos, then reflected for a while. Darby then created another CD with the photos showing the prisoners being abused, wrote an anonymous letter and handed it in to CID on

13 January 2004 (CID Report and Statements, 2004), three weeks after initially being lent the CDs (CBC news, 2005; BBC Radio 4, 2007). This prompted CID to seize other computers and disks from members of the unit within hours, recovering hundreds of photos, CDs and videotapes (Beaumont et al., 2004). Six days later, on 19 January 2004, Lieutenant General Sanchez ordered a secret investigation into Abu Ghraib (Hersh, 2004b, 2004d), resulting in the initiation of the investigation for the Taguba Report on 31 January 2004, and various others thereafter.

PUBLICIZING 'ABUSE'

It was not until the evening of 28 April 2004 that accounts of the 'abuse' (the media's favoured term for the activities) by night shift personnel of the 372nd MP Company of the US,[21] of prisoners in Abu Ghraib came to public attention, with a report on the then US weekly, primetime television news-magazine, *60 Minutes II,* presented by Dan Rather (CBS News, 2004b). Here a small portion of the Abu Ghraib

Figure 3.1 Electrocution and soldier 11:04 p.m., Nov. 4, 2003. Placed in this position by HARMAN and FREDERICK. Both took pictures as a joke. Instructed if moved would be electrocuted. SSG FREDERICK is depicted with a Cyber Shot camera in his hands. SOLDIER(S): SSG FREDERICK (caption information taken directly from CID materials) *Source:* http://www.salon.com/news/abu_ghraib/2006/03/14/chapter_4/20.html

photographs were shown (the news programme had 12 pictures) (CBS News, 2004a). Two days later, Seymour Hersh, a renowned US Pulitzer Prize-winning investigative journalist, delivered a fuller account of the images in *The New Yorker* magazine (Hersh, 2004a),[22] having obtained, in April, the Taguba Report (which was not meant for public release) (Hersh, 2004d). An accompanying photo, one that quickly became iconic, showed a hooded Iraqi prisoner balanced on a box, wires attached to his fingers, toes and penis (Ricchiardi, 2004). In the week after the scandal broke, Hersh was given a second set of digital photographs, documenting scenes of terrified, naked prisoners and snarling dogs, which had been in possession of a member of the 320th MP Battalion. Hersh's first story was followed up by two more stories in *The New Yorker* across the following fortnight (Hersh, 2004b, 2004c).

The Washington Post also claimed to have over a 1000 digital photos comprising both touristic shots of soldiers in Iraq and the 'abuse' photos (Davenport, 2004), publishing 10 on 6 May (Washington Post, 2004), and more across the following fortnight (Guardian.co.uk, n.d.; White et al., 2004), and disclosing previously secret sworn statements by Abu Ghraib prisoners alleging that they had been ridden like animals, sexually fondled by female soldiers and forced to retrieve their food from toilets (Ricchiardi, 2004). In the US, *The Washington Post* became the lead news organization on the story as it steadily published from its large cache of photos and assigned considerable reporting resources to the story (Bennett et al., 2007). The mushrooming scandal commanded the 17 May covers of *Time*, *Newsweek* and *US News* and *World Report*. Abu Ghraib dominated the headlines for a month as top national newspapers brought to light new aspects of the debacle on their front pages (Ricchiardi, 2004).[23] These photographs were rebroadcast by global satellite news broadcasters (Hamm, 2007) and posted widely on the internet, on activist sites such as Human Rights Watch, Amnesty International, Notinourname.com and Anti-war.com (Davenport, 2004).

Interestingly, the Arab media (including *al-Jazeera* and *al-Arabiya*) did not particularly dwell on this scandal. This low profile can be explained partly by relentless American pressure on the Arab media in Iraq during this period not to incite violence, which left these stations more cautious than usual (Lynch, 2006). In June 2003, the CPA had issued a public notice prohibiting 'Iraq media organizations from broadcasting or publishing material that would seriously undermine security and civil order in Iraq' (Coalition Provisional Authority, 2003). However, the images were powerful enough not to need constant recirculation. *Al-Jazeera* and *al-Arabiya* broadcast the outraged reaction of the Islamic Middle East. Egypt's *Akhbar al-Yaum* splashed the word 'Scandal' across the front page above smiling US soldiers posing by naked, hooded prisoners piled in a human pyramid. The Kuwaiti newspaper *al-Watan* warned that the 'barbaric' treatment would rally Islamic fundamentalists (Ricchiardi, 2004).

Impact of Publication of Images

Whereas by February 2004, a national survey of Iraqis found that 48 per cent agreed that it was absolutely or somewhat right that US-led coalition forces invaded Iraq in Spring 2003 (Oxford Research International, 2004), by May 2004, 82 per cent of Iraqis in a confidential CPA public opinion survey disapproved of the American military presence (Lynch, 2006, p. 218). The torture scandal presaged a nationwide crimewave in Iraq (robberies, rapes, kidnappings and carjacking) and aided the insurgency by alienating large sections of Iraqis (Ricks, 2006). Indeed, after a comparative lull in insurgencies across the first few months of 2004, by August 2004, attacks against the Coalition, the Iraqi Security Forces and Iraqi civilians exceeded 2,500 in that month, making it the most violent since June 2003 (Wright & Reese, 2008). This disaffection did not dissipate. A poll, carried out in mid-2006 for the US Department of State and reported by *The Washington Post*, found that a strong majority of Iraqis wanted the US-led Coalition forces to withdraw immediately from Iraq, saying that their swift departure would make Iraq more secure and decrease sectarian violence, with similar results from a World Public Opinion poll in September 2006[24] (Paul & Nahory, 2007).

Even before Abu Ghraib, a 2002 Gallup survey across nine predominantly Muslim countries showed that more than 85 per cent felt that the West did not respect Muslim values or beliefs and did not treat the Muslim world fairly in its international relations (Nisbet et al., 2004). The Abu Ghraib images further infuriated Muslims around the world, and infused their popular culture, purchasable at marketplaces, adorning walls in painted murals and becoming tools of protest in the Middle East (Hesford, 2006; Hamm, 2007). The fact that the prisoners' tormentors in many of the photographs are grinning, demonstrably enjoying their work, made the images perfect symbols of the subjugation and degradation that many perceived the American occupiers had inflicted on Iraq and the Middle East, instantly demolishing the

Coalition's claims to moral superiority regarding democratic values and human rights (Cook, 2004; Danner, 2004). The photographs drew attention also to the fact that some 10,000 Iraqis languished without trial in various US-run prisons, often arrested on the basis of anonymous tip-offs, bearing an uncanny resemblance to the practices of Saddam Hussein's regime (Tripp, 2007).

The photographs rallied elements of Arab sentiment to the cause of Islamic extremism (US Senate Armed Services Committee, 2008, p. xii). Several days after the publication of the photos, on 11 May 2004, came the gruesome decapitation of Nick Berg, the 26-year-old, American freelance contractor conducting telecommunications work in Iraq, captured in April 2004. In the video of his death, entitled 'Abu Musab al-Zarqawi Slaughters an American', broadcast on *al-Ansar* website (affiliated with al-Qaeda), Berg was surrounded by five masked men reading a lengthy statement claiming that his execution was retaliation for the abuses at Abu Ghraib (al-Marashi, 2004).[25] This appears to be the first manifestation in Iraq of the phenomenon of kidnapping foreigners and releasing video recordings of their captivity and execution on the websites of Sunni insurgent groups (al-Marashi, 2004, Nakash, 2006; Hill, 2008).[26] Further hostage videos from Iraq repeatedly demanded that prisoners at Iraqi prisons be released (Hill, 2008).

Official Attempts to Control the Images

The Bush administration made concerted attempts to control the communication of the Abu Ghraib 'abuses'. By 2004, as arguments for invading Iraq that rested on finding WMD or eliminating Iraq's links to al-Qaeda were publicly discredited, the US needed to lean more heavily on its third justification for war – that of liberating the Iraqi people. Yet, this was dealt a severe blow by the publicization of the Abu Ghraib images (Ricks, 2006). Vice President Dick Cheney's concern throughout the Abu Ghraib scandal was its potential impact on the re-election of George Bush in the November 2004 US presidential elections: the revelations, if left unchecked, could provoke more public debate about the wisdom of the Iraq War and the intelligence operations used to wage Bush's ongoing War on Terror (Hersh, 2004d).

Hoping to prevent the Abu Ghraib images from being leaked to the press, the Bush administration restricted copies of, and access to, the photographs and videos. The US Army went to great pains to retrieve all copies of the images in their initial investigation in January 2004 (CID, 2004). The Taguba Report, itself, does not present the images, ostensibly because of: 'the extremely sensitive nature of these photographs and videos, the ongoing CID investigation, and the potential for the criminal prosecution of several suspects' (Taguba Report, 2004, p. 16). The question of how the photographs made it to *CBS*'s *60 Minutes II* remains unclear. Some accounts claim that it was leaked by one of the 'abusers'' family so that the individual would not be scapegoated by the US Army; others suggest that the photos came from within US military or political circles, as part of a process of deep internal disagreement over aspects of the war (Coyne, 2004; Dao & Lichtblau, 2004; Hersh, 2004d).

A second major element of control was to attempt to delay inevitable publication, once the photos were leaked. Two weeks prior to broadcasting, *60 Minutes II*'s producer, Mary Mapes, received an appeal to her patriotism from the DoD to delay the broadcast given the tension on the ground in Iraq, especially with US hostages still in Iraqi hands (Beaumont et al., 2004; Cockburn, 2007). *60 Minutes II* honoured this request for a fortnight, but as the photos began to circulate elsewhere, and on learning that Seymour Hersh would be publishing the story in *The New Yorker*, CBS ran the exposé (CBS News, 2004b; Cohen, 2004b). Yet, the Abu Ghraib pictures publicized by *CBS* and other media were only a fraction of the images collected by the CID. The full dossier of the CID's photographic evidence includes 16,000 photos (only 200 were made public) and 112 videos (Hamm, 2007). From mid-2004–2006, human-rights and civil-liberties groups were locked in a legal battle with the DoD, demanding that it release the remaining visual documents from Abu Ghraib, as it was the public's right to know. The Pentagon's argument, that release of the records might endanger soldiers in Iraq by inciting further violence, was rejected by a federal district court in September 2005, but release of the photographs in the suit was delayed as the government appealed (Benjamin, 2006). It was not until more than two years after the mainstream media's original publication of the photos, that the 6 June 2004 CID investigation report, along with 1,000 photographs, videos and supporting documents from the Army's probe, was made available to salon.com.[27]

A third, and arguably most important, element of control was damage limitation, framing the story to deflect blame from US policy (Cockburn, 2007). While *CBS* initially delayed breaking the story, Pentagon public affairs planners drafted an 11-page media response.

Their plan was to focus on Darby's role as an honest whistleblower and the army's swift – if largely secret – investigation (Beaumont et al., 2004; Cockburn, 2007). On 30 April 2004, two days after *CBS* broke the story, President Bush introduced the frame that he would consistently repeat: 'The actions of a handful of soldiers . . . should not taint the tens of thousands who serve honorably in Iraq' (Bennett et al., 2007, p. 102). The military's Taguba report, leaked to renowned, and therefore highly credible, investigative reporter, Seymour Hersh, in April, localized the 'systemic and illegal abuse' (Taguba, 2004, p. 16) problem to 'several members of the military police guard force' (Taguba, 2004, p. 16) and a failure of leadership at the prison level to provide appropriate training and oversight of personnel. The Taguba Report was swiftly followed by the Fay-Jones Report (initiated in March 2004 and released in 23 August),[28] the Schlesinger Report (chartered on 12 May 2004 and released on 24 August 2004) and the classified Church Report (initiated in May 2004, its Executive Summary released on 10 March 2005)[29] (Bennett et al., 2007; Wright & Reese, 2008).[30] None of these analyses suggest that the abuses were policy, sanctioned through the chain of command.

While the pictures clearly show abuse, whether or not this abuse constituted torture depended upon the involvement of official bodies. Torture is defined by Article 1 of the UN Convention against Torture (UNCAT) as:

> any act by which severe pain or suffering, whether physical or mental, is intentionally inflicted on a person . . . at the instigation of or with the consent or acquiescence of a public official or other person acting in an official capacity. (Office of the High Commissioner for Human Rights, 1984)

Defense Secretary, Donald Rumsfeld, claimed that he had no idea that abuses were happening in Iraqi prisons until Darby alerted the investigators in January 2004, and on 7 May in a statement to the joint Senate Armed Services Committee hearing, he accepted full responsibility, without taking any of the blame (FDCH E-Media, 2004; Bennett et al., 2007; Cockburn 2007). Indeed, as, and after the story broke, the US government avoided the use of the word 'torture' (Hochschild, 2004).

Investigative reporter, Seymour Hersh's, first two stories in *The New Yorker* largely reproduced the framing of the Taguba Report (Hersh, 2004a, 2004b). However, his first story tentatively introduced a torture frame, for instance by reporting remarks from Gary Myers, Frederick's civilian attorney, 'that culpability in the case extended far beyond his client' (Hersh, 2004a, p. 4); and his third story was wholly framed by the torture frame (Hersh, 2004c). In response, the US administration bolstered its own framing by attempting to undermine Hersh's credibility, despite his long pedigree as an investigative journalist (for instance, he reported on the My Lai massacre in Vietnam). His detailed reports on Abu Ghraib in *The New Yorker* were dismissed by Pentagon spokespeople as 'outlandish' and 'conspiratorial,' and although his reports were initially noted in US mainstream publications, they were soon beaten back by officials and did not ignite a second front in the story (Bennett et al., 2007, p. 57).

As the story broke, President Bush decided to speak directly to two Arab networks in two 10 minute interviews, to reach Arab audiences with the US administration's framing of abuse. However, Bush did not apologize to the Arab community, leaving this for his aides at a later date. Instead, by saying things such as 'it's also important for the people of Iraq to know that in a democracy, everything is not perfect, that mistakes are made', Bush infuriated and insulted most Iraqis (Jamail, 2007). Furthermore, Bush spoke on the wrong channel: despite advice from the State Department, he refrained from appearing on *al-Jazeera*, choosing the more conservative *al-Arabiya* along with the US-government-financed satellite TV station, *al-Hurra* which no one watched or found credible (Wright & Graham, 2004; Lynch, 2006; Tatham, 2006). Choosing *al-Arabiya* could be rationalized on the grounds that *al-Jazeera* had a poor reputation with Iraqis, many having regarded it as too sympathetic to Saddam Hussein's regime, while *al-Arabiya* was relatively popular inside Iraq. Yet, *al-Arabiya* did not have the wider transnational audience of *al-Jazeera* (Lynch, 2006).

The Bush administration's strategy of media control was enormously successful in the US across 2004. While foreign western news sources, including those in the UK (apart from *The Times*), were more likely to frame Abu Ghraib as a torture story, US reporters did so only in the early weeks after the photos were released, with torture also entering the news through sources such as former detainees and human rights organizations like the ICRC (Bennett et al., 2007), and Hersh's investigative journalism (Hersh, 2004a, 2004c). However, after the initial two weeks of publicization of the photos (by which time the Bush administration's news management was in full swing) until the end of summer 2004, US mainstream press[31] reported the story as the Bush administration wanted it – as a case of low-level abuse. This can be explained not only by the Bush administration's news management strategies, but an absence of powerful government champions capable of challenging the Pentagon and White House; news organizations' caution about the legal implications of their language use; and the fact that the torture-policy frame was not easy for Americans, including journalists, to entertain, as it did not fit their national self-image (Bennett et al., 2007). Correspondingly, in an *ABC/Washington Post* poll in the wake of the 2004 scandal, 60 per cent of respondents classified what happened at Abu Ghraib as mere abuse, not torture (Sharrock, 2008). It was not until late 2005 when Republican Senator John McCain had mobilized enough Senate votes, backed by military officers, to force the president to accept a legislative admonition against torture, that the US news used the term 'torture' more prominently, if still cautiously, to talk about high-level tactics in the War on Terror (Bennett et al., 2007). Yet, for several years, no independent commission was set up to investigate the policies that led to torture (Hamm, 2007). Instead, between May 2004 and September 2005, the few 'abusers' from Abu Ghraib were convicted in courts martial, sentenced to federal prison time and dishonourably discharged from service, while the commanders of the MP and MI outfits involved were demoted or reprimanded for failing to train their troops adequately (Beaumont et al., 2004; Follman & Clark-Flory, 2006; Walsh, 2006).

Meanwhile, in the wake of Abu Ghraib revelations and in the handover of power in June 2004 to the Iraqi Interim Government (discussed in Chapter 4), Coalition commanders turned over hundreds of prisoners to the Iraqi Ministries of Defense, Justice and Interior – the latter a highly militarized department with little civilian police experience and a harsh sectarian reputation. Given the continuing insurgency, Iraq's prisoner count grew from 5,000 in April 2005 to 20,000 in April 2007, with thousands of security detainees detained without charge or trial (Amnesty International, 2006; Paul & Nahory, 2007). Even while the US authorities claimed to have stopped all 'abuses' after Abu Ghraib, torture continued in secret interrogation centres, FOBs and Iraqi prisons during interrogations, where US and UK intelligence personnel could be present while preserving deniability (Amnesty International, 2006; Human Rights Watch, 2006; Paul & Nahory, 2007).[32] It was not until April 2009 that the frame of 'isolated abuse' was categorically overturned – and this after the Bush administration had served its full 2 terms. Under new US president Barack Obama, in April 2009, a newly unclassified 232-page bipartisan Senate Armed Services Committee report (itself the result of an 18-month inquiry) revealed that the 'abuses' were, indeed, government policy (Nasaw, 2009). The report shows a paper trail going from the then Defence Secretary,

Donald Rumsfeld, to Guantánamo to Afghanistan and to Iraq and Abu Ghraib regarding the use of coercive interrogation methods. The techniques – based on practices detailed in military courses on survival, evasion, resistance and escape, known as SERE – included the removal of clothing, hooding, treating detainees like animals, slapping, and the exploitation of phobias, including fear of dogs. The report emphasized that SERE techniques were used by the military to 'better prepare U.S. military personnel to resist interrogations and not as a means of obtaining reliable information' (US Senate Armed Services Committee, 2008, p. xvii), and that their use in Guantánamo (authorized by Rumsfeld, on 2 December 2002) in an attempt to extract information from inmates was counter-productive as the techniques were based, partly on Chinese Communist techniques used during the Korean War to elicit *false* confessions. The report concluded that, contrary to the US government's assertion that a 'few bad apples' were to blame for the Abu Ghraib 'abuses', responsibility ultimately lay with high-level Bush officials for policies that 'conveyed the message that physical pressures and degradation were appropriate treatment for detainees' (Miller & Barnes, 2008; US Senate Armed Services Committee, 2008). As the executive summary states:

> senior officials in the United States government solicited information on how to use aggressive techniques, redefined the law to create the appearance of their legality, and authorized their use against detainees. Those efforts damaged our ability to collect accurate intelligence that could save lives, strengthened the hand of our enemies, and compromised our moral authority. (US Senate Armed Services Committee, 2008, p. xii)[33]

REPERCUSSIONS: CLAMPING DOWN ON WEB-BASED PARTICIPATORY MEDIA

As a result of the Abu Ghraib experience, the military moved quickly to restrict future pictures of torture ever being recorded. Within weeks, if not days, of the military authorities learning of the photographic evidence of torture in Abu Ghraib, photography was banned in military compounds in Iraq. This is evidenced in the sworn statement of David Ophiton Sutton, 229th MP Company, Baghdad on 10 February 2004:

> Recently there was a memorandum put out about things you're not supposed to do. I don't know if that was a knee-jerk reaction to something that happened, but it specifically says things in there about mistreatment, photography, and contraband stuff like that. (Taguba Report, 2004, annex 74, available at Cohen, 2004a)

Similarly, following Abu Ghraib, the UK military immediately banned mobile phone and digital cameras in the UK military and, it has been observed that all operations since in the Middle East have been framed by Abu Ghraib (interview with UK military expert, June 2008).

In 2005, a Pentagon review was launched to better understand the overall implications of blogging and other internet communications in combat zones (Hockenberry, 2005). As Christopher Conway, a lieutenant colonel and DOD spokesperson observes:

> It's a new world out there. . . . Before, you would have to shake down your soldiers for matches that might light up and betray a position. Today, every soldier has a cell phone, beeper, game device, or laptop, any one of which could pop off without warning. Blogging is just one piece of the puzzle. (Hockenberry, 2005, p. 1)

By 2005, miliblogging – that is, blogging by military personnel, was still officially tolerated by the Pentagon, although it was being monitored with a view to understanding and controlling it. This is unsurprising given Christensen's (2008) findings that without much effort, clips and videos (uploaded across 2006 and 2007) can be located on *YouTube* that, among the mundane footage of daily, everyday activity also show radically different images of the war to that which the military wished to project, with most of the material shot by US or Coalition troops themselves. One example shows US soldiers taking obvious pleasure in violent fighting against Iraqis who get gruesomely eviscerated (Christensen, 2008). Thus, in the spring of 2005, Pentagon policy required all military bloggers inside Iraq to register with their units, giving unit commanders the authority to review blogs and other communications before they were sent, and directing commanders to conduct quarterly reviews, to ensure that bloggers were not violating operational security or privacy rules (this rule does not apply to soldiers outside Iraq) (Hockenberry, 2005; Andén-Papadopoulos, 2009). Continuing into 2006, while there was no specific Pentagon policy that banned troops from posting graphic material online, troops who have served in Iraq and Afghanistan were 'hearing the message that they should consider carefully what videos they upload to the web' (Greene, 2006). Meanwhile, US Central Command – responsible for troops in Iraq and Afghanistan – had a team reading blogs and responding to what they considered inaccuracies about the War on Terror. Their concern was that these videos and stills might be used by enemies to propagate the notion that US military members were barbaric warmongers (Greene, 2006). The Army also created the Army Web Risk Assessment Cell to monitor compliance.

Given that military blogging and vlogging were still allowed in 2005, this also allowed the generation of spontaneous, authentic and positive depictions of the military to emerge, as shown in the following case study.

IS THIS THE WAY TO ARMADILLO?

Is This the Way to Armadillo is a popular, spoof music video, produced by UK soldiers and circulated across the military. The original song on which it is based, *Is This the Way to Amarillo*, recorded by Tony Christie and released in the UK in 1971, tells of a man travelling to Amarillo, Texas, to find his fiancée. On 14 March 2005, it was re-released expressly with the intent of proceeds going to British charity, Comic Relief.[34] Here, the song, *(Is This the Way to) Amarillo* (2005), was performed by popular UK comedian, Peter Kay (lipsynching to Tony Christie's voice), during the evening of Comic Relief's live television extravaganza on BBC's Red Nose Day, and was later released as a single. In the accompanying video, Peter Kay cheerily mimes the song accompanied by various celebrities largely from UK pop music and light entertainment television. The video consists almost entirely of Kay perpetually walking jauntily towards the camera flanked by different pairings of the celebrities, in front of increasingly bizarre backgrounds. It was the number one single in the UK for seven weeks and became the UK's best-selling single of 2005, selling over a million copies.

Given the lip-synching nature of Kay's visual treatment of this song, it spawned many light-hearted imitators online – or 'internet memes' (faddish jokes or practices that become widely imitated, spreading through distributed networks in ways that the original producers cannot determine or control (Burgess, 2008)). Examples include BBC One's late-night political gossip show, This Week, starring presenter Andrew Neil, (used for its opening titles in the run-up to the 2005 UK election); and *Show Me the Way to Aberystwyth* sung by the producer of BBC Radio One's Chris Moyles Show, Aled Jones (about the Welsh town of Aberystwyth).[35] The spoof, *Is This the Way to Armadillo*, came from a UK Army cavalry regiment – the Royal Dragoon Guards – stationed at their al-Faw base in Iraq towards the end of their six-month peacekeeping tour. Their video featured Lucky Pierre (a joke reference to three-in-a-bed gay sex) as Peter Kay, and was directed by The Munganator.[36] In the spoof, Lucky Pierre marches through their Iraqi camp mimicking Peter Kay's jaunty walk, and summoning up pairs of fellow squaddies (instead of celebrities) along the way. At the video's end, three portable toilets come into view with the doors on two swinging open to reveal a pair of naked squaddies. Sergeant (Sgt.) Stokoe, who came up with the idea, said it had been created as a morale boost to entertain troops stationed in Basra after Kay's version of *(Is This the Way to) Amarillo* attained anthemic status among soldiers. The Dragoon Guards e-mailed their video to Army friends in London, but so many tried to download it that it crashed an MoD server, causing the MoD to alert units to delete the e-mail from their systems (BBC, 2005a, 2005b).

While not 'official' military communication, it was sanctioned by Supreme Comd. Allied Forces al-Faw. It raises a smile when you mention the spoof to anyone in the military because it reminds them of being back with the soldiers, who, when bored, 'get up to mischief, and they have a great sense of humour' (interview with UK military expert, June 2008). The editor of *The Sun*, on seeing the spoof, told the UK military that it was great public relations, and that they should not be worried (interview with UK military expert, June 2008). Subsequently, it was publicly very much approved by the military authorities:

> The MoD said the spoof was 'brilliant' and the crash did not cause problems. A spokesman said: 'The soldiers maintaining their morale on operations is always important. The fact that it proved so popular in the office and caused the system to crash is unfortunate, but this did not affect operations and the system is up and running again.' (BBC, 2005b)

The following day, UK Defence Secretary, John Reid, paid tribute to the Royal Dragoon Guards when opening the Queen's Speech debate on defence in the Commons. As of November 2009, the *YouTube* video (added 20 June 2006) has now been seen 121,970 times and generated 162 text comments. On the whole, most comments enthused about the video, such as: 'So great seeing how these guys can still have a great time in such a situation . . . . Keep it up! Freakin funny'(19phil88, 2008). While this volume of viewings and responses does not compare with the most popular *YouTube* videos such as Judson Laipply's *Evolution of Dance* (viewed 129,561,261 times with 1,492 video responses and 409,507 text comments as of November 2009), it still represents a significant audience.[37]

CONCLUSION

With the Abu Ghraib images and *Is This the Way to Armadillo*, we see the challenges that web-based participatory media can pose to careful official control of information, as well as the branding opportunities presented to different parties – al-Qaeda militants in the case of Abu Ghraib, and the UK military in the case of *Is This the Way to Armadillo*. However, such impactful instances of web-based participatory media are rare, and, certainly in 2004–2005, appeared to depend upon the amplification and credibility conferred by mainstream media's attention. There are many instances of military spoof music videos that do not make mainstream news – for instance, the Royal Navy's *YouTube* version of Queen's *Bohemian Rhapsody* called *Royal Navy's Bohemian Rhapsody*[38] and the Navy's spoof of the *Numa Numa Song*, called *Navy Numa Numa*.[39] *Is This the Way to Armadillo* gained wider national exposure beyond the military in-group to which it was e-mailed *because* it was picked up by mainstream media – notably the *BBC* – probably because the *BBC* themselves had already done several of their own spoof music videos based on *(Is This the Way to) Amarillo*. *Is This the Way to Armadillo* would therefore be firmly on the radar of *BBC* journalists.

By the same token, it is notable that Abu Ghraib, while the most publicized of military 'abuses', was not isolated, but in fact perpetrated across Iraq, Afghanistan and Guantánamo Bay (ICRC, 2004; Schlesinger, 2004; Walsh, 2006; The Aitken Report, 2008). That Abu Ghraib received so much attention is no doubt due to the mainstream news media's circulation of the 'abuse' photographs. The importance accorded to mainstream media circulation can be seen in the continuing attempts to restrain release of further pictures. In response to legal action filed by the American Civil Liberties Union (ACLU), the Pentagon was ordered to release further pictures from more than 60 criminal investigations between 2001 and 2006 of military personnel suspected of abusing detainees in Afghanistan and Iraq by 28 May 2009. While the new White House administration under Barack Obama said it would not oppose this court ruling, as that date approached Obama changed his mind. The reasons Obama gave for this U-turn were that the new pictures would serve no purpose beyond confirming what was already known; and that additional photos could inflame anti-Americanism posing additional danger to US troops in Iraq and Afghanistan (al-Jazeera, 2009; The Independent, 2009).

However, since 2006, mainstream media have become more attuned to, and co-optive of, web-based participatory media (as the following chapters will show). Across 2006, a number of US mainstream newspapers experimented with blogs, real-time traffic coverage, reporters carrying digital cameras and more. By 2007, some of the most popular bloggers were already being assimilated by establishment media (Robinson, 2006; Project for Excellence in Journalism, 2007; Bivens, 2008). Thus, rather than web-based participatory media needing mainstream media for amplification, they also attract mainstream media's attention because they are already popular. This changing media ecology warranted, in the military's view, greater attempts to control military-generated web-based participatory media still further (Hall, 2007). Given the popularity of internet communication in war zones, after a period of monitoring what its troops posted online, particularly images showing aftermaths of combat (Greene, 2006; Andén-Papadopoulos, 2009), the Pentagon launched a wide-ranging effort at control over information, using OPSEC as its rationale. On 19 April 2007, US Army Regulation 530–1 noted that whereas classified information had long been subjected to multiple procedures to protect it, unclassified information had not. It noted that traditional DoD security programmes focus on classified information and are unable to prevent unclassified 'indicators' from being revealed – indicators being 'data derived from open sources or from detectable actions that adversaries can piece together or interpret to reach personal conclusions or official estimates concerning friendly capabilities, activities, limitation, and intentions' (Army Regulation 530–1, 2007, p. 31). It cites soldiers' 'blogs' as a particularly 'significant vulnerability' (Army Regulation 530–1, 2007, p. 35–36). Indeed, as far back as 2000 it was known through discovery of al-Qaeda's *Declaration of Jihad Against the Country's Tyrants – Military Series* that al-Qaeda advised explicitly that 'openly and without resorting to illegal means, it is possible to gather at least 80% of information about the enemy' (Hoffmann, 2006a, p. 11).[40] Since then, reports such as the 9/11 Commission Report (Kean, 2004) and a British government report on the genesis and execution of the 7 July 2005 suicide bomb in London, as well as trials of al-Qaeda operatives, highlight the internet's prominent role in furnishing operatives with all the information they required to carry out the attacks (Hoffmann, 2006a).

As such, across 75 pages, US Army Regulation 530–1 details the scope and process of OPSEC to prevent indicators from revealing critical information (information important to the successful achievement of US objectives and missions or which may be useful to a US adversary) (Army Regulation 530–1, 2007, p. 1). Thus, OPSEC was now to operate throughout the entire spectrum of conflict operations and all data sources, rather than just combat operations and classified sources. Now, all Department of the Army (DA) personnel (active component, reserve component to include US Army Reserve, Army National Guard, and DA civilians) and DoD contractors must:

> g. Consult with their immediate supervisor and their OPSEC Officer for an OPSEC review prior to publishing or posting information in a public forum.
>> (1) This includes, but is not limited to letters, resumes, articles for publication, electronic mail (e-mail), Web site postings, web log (blog) postings, discussion in Internet information forums, discussion in Internet message boards or other forms of dissemination or documentation. (Army Regulation 530–1, 2007, p. 4)

In addition, this Directive stipulates that the Commander of Army Web Risk Assessment Cell (AWRAC) is responsible for reviewing the content of the Army's publicly accessible websites to ensure compliance with OPSEC procedures: 'Web sites include, but are not limited to, Family Readiness Group (FRG) pages, unofficial Army web sites, Soldiers' web logs (blogs), and personal published or unpublished works related to the Army' (Army Regulation 530–1, 2007, p. 12).[41]

Citing similar OPSEC reasons, as well as personnel's responsibility to comply with the Official Secrets Act, copyright and patent laws, the UK MoD took similar steps to control the wider media environment. In August 2007, it released an instruction that covered all members of the UK military including civil servants, cadets and volunteers, and all media or means of communicating with the public. In addition to standard news media and published material, it included web-based participatory media (Ministry of Defence, 2007, 2008). The instruction was one of control in a fragmented media environment. In terms of contact with journalists: 'The guiding principle for all contact with the news media contact is that it must be referred to the appropriate D News [Director of News] staff,' who would then delineate what could be discussed. In terms of communicating in public through non-news channels including self-publishing on the web or via mobile devices and contributing 'to any online community or shared electronic information resource available outside Government, for example a bulletin board, newsgroup, wiki, online social network, multiplayer game or other information-sharing application' communicators must consider the impact of the material carefully:

> both in terms of the effect on its intended audience but also on any unintended audience through any wider coverage by the media. All personnel must make every effort to minimise the scope for misreporting and misrepresentation and avoid straying beyond the issues that they have been approved to speak on. Individuals should ensure that they seek authorisation in sufficient time to allow proper consideration of their request.' (Ministry of Defence, 2008, p. 3)

Advance, upwardly referred security clearance is needed on *all* communication with the public (Ministry of Defence, 2007, p. 4; 2008, p. 4). The enormity of this attempt at total control over military information can be seen when comparing this with previous *war-time* censorship provisions in wars for national survival. For instance, Carruthers (2000) notes how the UK Government's Defence of the Realm Act in WWI imposed broad and vague prohibitions against the collection or publication of information about the war, or any material that might directly or indirectly be useful to the enemy, the vagueness resting on omission of any definition of how utility may be gauged, so pushing the press towards self-censorship for fear of transgressing a boundary whose precise location was unspecified. In an era of globalized, converged media, where enemies can access the same global media as traditionally media-rich western audiences, the vague requirement that all Web 2.0 postings from all military personnel must take account of effects on 'any unintended audience' (Ministry of Defence, 2007, p. 3, 2008, p. 4) or the ability of adversaries to 'piece together or interpret' open source data (Army Regulation 530–1, 2007, p. 31) suggests a draconian attempt to censor at source.

Meanwhile, the MoD maintains that:

> New and emerging internet technologies present significant opportunities for communicating with the public. Service and MoD civilian personnel are encouraged to use self-publishing on the internet or similar channels to communicate with the public directly, but should ensure that the rules on prior authorisation, conduct and behaviour, collective and personal security, use of official IT, data protection and communicating in public are followed. (Ministry of Defence, 2008, p. 2)

Such efforts at control will undoubtedly stifle creativity and spontaneity in military user-generated content. Indeed, military bloggers warned that these regulations could have a chilling effect on their writing (Sipress & Diaz, 2007); and *YouTube* removed dozens of soldiers' videos from its archives and suspended the accounts of some users who had posted them (Andén-Papadopoulos, 2009). As such, the military is unlikely to be able to capitalize in the future on user-generated content such as *Is This the Way to Armadillo*, thereby stymieing the MoD's aim that user-generated content could enhance the reputation of Defence (Ministry of Defence, 2007).

As noted in the introduction to this chapter, in 2007 the US DoD and UK MoD launched their own channels on *YouTube* in the hope of benefiting from viral marketing and spreadability (Jenkins, 2007) – the process of seeding the web with advertising or marketing content that niche users will want to pass on to their peers, often through e-mail, in return for material or reputational incentives (Jenkins, 2006a; Castells et al., 2007). The hope here is that openly distributed, official, military-generated clips be picked up not only by journalists but by aspiring lay video-makers repurposing these online resources to create their video, so allowing information management to operate behind user-generated content (McKelvey, 2007). Lieutenant Colonel (Lt. Col.) Christopher Garver, a spokesman for US forces in Iraq, stated that the content to be seeded would be 'great footage' shot by the military's combat cameramen (Smith-Spark, 2007). Indeed, one of the video clips with the most hits on MNF-I is a short clip of a sniper battle focusing on Coalition soldiers taking aim on an Iraqi rooftop scene, generating distant puffs of smoke, titled *Battle on Haifa Street, Baghdad, Iraq* (2007), posted on 10 March 2007 with 4,214,636 views by November 2009. However, given their sanitized depictions, the viewing figures of most clips are comparatively low. For instance, in August 2008 (a randomly chosen month), the most viewed videos on the UK military's official *YouTube* site included a shooting in Afghanistan (with 19,008 views), and a UK soldier set to be Miss England (with 15,210 views). Although consciously crafted viral advertising and marketing can be very successful (Castells et al., 2007), as self-conscious pieces of commercial information they are always in danger of failing as marketers misjudge their target (usually niche) audience, or fail to deliver content sufficiently desirable for users to voluntarily forward to others. Indeed, rather than content with high production values, McStay (2007, p. 43) suggests that successful viral advertising that contributes to the 'branding of the self' is often 'low-fi,' [42] (p. 42) 'edgy, controversial and subversive' (p. 42). Indeed, when such user-generated content authentically emerges and circulates of its own accord, as in *Is This the Way to Armadillo*, it can become a prime opportunity for brand enhancement, as long, of course, as the user-generated content is suitable to the brand. As Abu Ghraib showed, the difficulties of banning the creation and distribution of user-generated content in the era of web-based participatory media are immense, although given the US-led covert policy of torture in interrogations, it is obvious why the military would attempt such control. However, such control then minimizes the likelihood that spontaneous, authentic and positive depictions of the military will be circulated.

NOTES

[1] www.americasarmy.com/ [Accessed 1 November 2009].

[2] http://www.youtube.com/mnfiraq [Accessed 1 November 2009].

[3] http://www.youtube.com/user/armyweb [Accessed 1 November 2009].

[4] This state-destroying motive of insurgency is, perhaps how it differs from 'terrorism', which is defined by the US State Department as intended ' (i) to intimidate or coerce a civilian population; (ii) to influence the policy of a government by intimidation or coercion; or (iii) to affect the conduct of a government by assassination or kidnapping' (US State Department, 2009, Title 18, Part I, Chapter 44, Section 921, No.22 (c)).

[5] The ICRC is an independent agency that monitors application of, and respect for, the Third and Fourth Geneva Conventions regarding the treatment of persons deprived of their liberty (ICRC, 2004).

[6] This estimate comes from independent British-based group, Iraq Body Count, based on their evaluation of numbers reported by local hospital officials, the Health Ministry and mainstream media accounts.

[7] By November 2003, out of a total of 160,000 Coalition troops, the UK contributed 10,500 (Ministry of Defence, 2003b).

[8] In the 2003 version of FM 3–13, this aspect of IO doctrine included three related capabilities: PA, civil-military operations and defence support to public diplomacy. Furthermore, PA staff officers, organizationally, were subordinated to IO staff (Field Manual (FM) 3–13, 2003; Wright & Reese, 2008).

[9] *The Christian Science Monitor, Los Angeles Times, The New York Times, The Wall Street Journal, The Washington Post, ABC News, CBS News, CNN* and *NBC News.*

[10] http://www.dvidshub.net/ [Accessed 1 November 2009].

[11] http://www.pentagonchannel.mil/ [Accessed 1 November 2009].

[12] The IMN also included the newspaper, *al-Sabah* (Lynch, 2006).

[13] *Al-Hurra,* broadcasting since February 2004, is a US-based and US-government-sponsored 24/7 Arabic-language satellite television news channel that reports on regional and international events to 22 countries in the Arab region.

[14] http://www.microsoft.com/windowsxp/downloads/updates/moviemaker2.mspx

[15] In the UK, by 2005, the internet was in 57 per cent of households, and by 2006, 69 per cent of the US were internet users (Abdulla, 2007b).

[16] Security detainees meet the requirements based on UN Security Council Resolution 1546 and its extensions. They are classified as individuals that may be held for imperative reasons of security because they are suspected of insurgent activity (Perry et al., 2009).

[17] 'Hard site' was the nickname for part of the main prison building – Tiers 1A and 1B – where 'MI holds' were kept and where US forces operated. This was where most of the prisoner 'abuse' occurred (Cohen, 2004a).

18 This is the protected enclave in central Baghdad housing the new Iraqi Government and western military and administrative headquarters.

19 The acronym 'CID' comes from the original Criminal Investigation Division formed during WWI, which is retained today for continuity purposes.

20 *The Rush Limbaugh Show*, airs weekdays daily in the US. In 2005, its minimum weekly audience was 13.5 million listeners – the largest radio talk show audience in the US.

21 This was a unit attached to the 320th MP Battalion, part of the 800th MP Brigade.

22 These were posted online on 30 April 2004 and published in the 10 May 2004 issue.

23 For compilations of reportage around the world, see Sourcewatch (2008).

24 This was conducted by the Program on International Policy Attitudes at the University of Maryland.

25 Al-Zarqawi used this video to announce his presence in Iraq. His movement, initially called Tawhid wa Jihad (Monotheism and Jihad), launched lethal attacks on foreign contractors, oil pipelines, the Iraqi Interim Government's deputies, mosques, civilians and Shi'i religious leaders. A month before the January 2005 elections, al-Qaeda officially adopted al-Zarqawi's group, and, with this promotion, al-Zarqawi renamed his organization 'al-Qaeda in Iraq' (Engel, 2008).

26 The first such video in the world to appear showed the execution of Wall Street Journal reporter, Daniel Pearl in Karachi in February 2002 (Ayres, 2005).

27 A small portion of the photographs are archived at: http://www.salon.com/news/feature/2006/02/16/abu_ghraib/ [Accessed 1 November 2009]. A larger archive containing 279 photos and 19 videos along with the original captions created by Army investigators is at: http://www.salon.com/news/abu_ghraib/2006/03/14/introduction/index.html [Accessed 1 November 2009].

28 In March 2004, Major General George Fay was appointed to investigate the operations of the 205th MI Brigade. In June 2004 the Army folded that inquiry into an investigation headed by Lieutenant General Anthony Jones into higher-level MI policies and practices in Iraq. Their report is commonly referred to as Fay-Jones (Fay, 2004; Jones, 2004; Wright & Reese, 2008).

29 Conducted by Vice Admiral Albert T. Church, into Department of Defense interrogation policies in Afghanistan, Iraq and Guantánamo Bay, it found 'no connection between interrogation policy and abuse' (cited in Amnesty International, 2006, p. 12).

30 Other US military reports had previously been conducted into interrogations of detainees in Iraq – the Miller report (produced on 9 September 2003) and the Ryder Report (produced 5 November 2003 and released in March 2004) (Ryder, 2003).

[31] US news outlets examined were The *Washington Post* and CBS from January to August 2004; and between April 2004 and mid-January 2005, the *Atlanta Journal Constitution, Boston Globe, Chicago Sun-Times, Los Angeles Times, New York Times, Cleveland Plain Dealer, San Francisco Chronicle, Seattle Times, St. Petersburg Times,* and *USA Today* (Bennett et al., 2007, p. 91).

[32] All detainees held by US forces are scheduled to be turned over to the Iraqi authorities, or released, by 1 December 2009 (Perry et al., 2009).

[33] Reports of abuse in 2003–04 by UK troops in Iraq, some of these also coming to light via photographs and videos taken by the soldiers, some publicized by the British tabloid, *The News of the World*, were investigated by the Aitken Report, which blames the actions on a handful of soldiers and unclear policy on how to deal with civilian detainees (The Aitken Report, 2008).

[34] Comic Relief was founded in the UK in 1985 and is supported by the BBC.

[35] http://chrismoyles.net/mw/lyricsamarillo.shtml [Accessed 1 November 2009].

[36] The Peter Kay character was played by Staff Sgt. Roger Parr, from Runcorn, Cheshire. Captain Mungo Ker filmed the video (BBC 2005a, 2005b).

[37] *Evolution of Dance* can be viewed at http://www.youtube.com/watch?v= dMH0bHeiRNg [Accessed 1 November 2009].

[38] Officers and staff on HMS Campbelltown produced this video while on patrol in the Indian Ocean. It was uploaded on 10 December 2005. It can be viewed at http://www.youtube.com/watch?v=DerD7RNMbDQ [Accessed 1 November 2009].

[39] It was uploaded on 17 February 2006. It can be viewed at http://www. youtube.com/watch?v=puVmKfCwb4M&feature=related [Accessed 1 November 2009].

[40] This manual is a compendium of terrorist tradecraft assembled by al-Qaeda in the 1990s (Hoffmann, 2006a).

[41] This Directive was presaged elsewhere. For instance, arising from their experience in Afghanistan since 2002, in September 2006, Canada's Chief of Defence Staff issued a general order restricting publication of information and images to the internet by members of Canada's Armed Forces (Canadian Forces General Order 136/06, 2006).

[42] A key characteristic of viral advertising is its low-fi status (low-budget production values) these lending a degree of authenticity (McStay, 2007).

Chapter 4

CONTROLLING SADDAM HUSSEIN'S IMAGE
His Capture (2003) and Execution (2006)

. . . for seizing the reins of the global media, for founding and framing the new digital democracy, for working for nothing and beating the pros at their own game, TIME's Person of the Year for 2006 is you.

(Grossman, 2006)

INTRODUCTION

Highlighting the extremes of totally controlled surveillance and uncontrolled sousveillance, two case studies are examined in this chapter within the context of state-building activities in Iraq from 2003 to 2006. The first case study is the internationally televised inspection of Saddam Hussein, dishevelled and disempowered, on his capture (13 December 2003) seven-and-a-half months after the declared end of major combat operations. This image was captured by the US military and propagated for Coalition propagandistic ends in the hope of quelling the growing insurgency and reassuring ordinary Iraqis that Saddam Hussein could never return to reinstate his regime. The second case study examined is a footage of Saddam Hussein's execution three years later (31 December 2006). Here, two versions of reality stood in stark contrast to each other – the official Iraqi government version that the execution was dignified and Saddam Hussein cowed, and an unofficial version captured on a mobile phone video by a witness at the execution that contradicted the official narrative. It was imperative for the various authorities that Saddam Hussein's execution convey the appropriate political message, with multiple governments needing to balance a complex mesh of volatile political forces; yet, the official version of the execution was utterly compromised by the mobile phone footage. This leads to a discussion about the political intent behind sousveillance and its relationship to democratic social responsibility. Before progressing to these case studies, some explanation of the political environment and the media environment is necessary.

POLITICAL ENVIRONMENT

As outlined in Chapter 2, the Bush and Blair administrations' end-goal of OIF was a democratically elected government in Iraq that would prevent Iraqi territory from being used as a base for terrorism and regional aggression thereby helping reshape the Middle East – goals perceived as crucial to American and British security following 9/11. Given these aspirations, it is wholly ironic that a consequence of OIF was that, in the ensuing chaos, al-Qaeda supporters were provided with a base in Iraq from which they could engage their enemies by inculcating insurgency there (Azzam, 2006). Furthermore, state-building is not an activity to be undertaken lightly given its need to establish a functioning political framework and given that it causes people to rethink existing political identities, values and interests (Tripp, 2007). As such, the road to democracy in Iraq was far from smooth, and was always unlikely to be a limited exercise in terms of time and cost.

Given Iraq's demographics, inevitably religion emerged as a major political issue (Mandaville, 2007). Although the Ba'th Party had claimed to be a secular, pan-Arab, socialist organization, as far back as 1977 Saddam Hussein had been paying lip-service to Islamic values as part of a strategy of patronage to cultivate certain Shi'i *ulama* (Islamic religious scholars) with the aim of controlling them (Nakash, 2006; Tripp, 2007). For instance, across the 1990s, to direct the religious energy of the Shi'i away from the regime, the Ba'th Party tolerated the activities of Grand Ayatollah Sayyid Mohammed Sadiq al-Sadr, who, unlike the leading clerics in Najaf, argued that clerics should be politically outspoken or lose the right to lead. During the 1990s, he succeeded in reconnecting the Najaf world of Shi'i clerics and seminaries (the *hawza*) with the rural communities of southern Iraq as well as with the Shi'i urban poor in Baghdad. He adapted Shi'i law to tribal custom, opened religious courts and established a network of deputies and charities in cities and villages, filling a void left by the state during the years of sanctions and contracting government welfare services. Inevitably under Saddam Hussein's regime, as Mohammed Sadiq al-Sadr became a focus for mass loyalty among Iraqi Shi'a, he was assassinated in Najaf in 1999. However, his movement, made up mainly of Shi'a of poor background, remained intact after his assassination under his son, Muqtada al-Sadr, who went underground, re-emerging vigorously in the power vacuum that followed the 2003 collapse of the Ba'th (Nakash, 2006; Tripp, 2007). Indeed, for Iraq's majority Shi'i population, an end to minority Sunni rule with the collapse of Saddam Hussein's regime represented an unprecedented political opportunity (Mandaville, 2007), and the long-suppressed *hawza* reasserted itself. Three Shi'i clerics competed for leadership of the *hawza*: Sayyid Muqtada al-Sadr (a young, rabble-rousing radical who exploited the huge respect the Shi'a held for his late, clerical father, Mohammed Sadiq al-Sadr, and uncle);[1] Ayatollah Sayyid Mohammed Baqir al-Hakim (who, on fleeing Iraq to Iran, founded the Supreme Council for the Islamic Revolution in Iraq (SCIRI) in 1982 – a revolutionary group dedicated to overthrowing Saddam Hussein's regime – gaining him immense credibility among the Shi'a on his return to Iraq in May 2003); and the Grand Ayatollah Sayyid Ali al-Husayni al-Sistani (with the death of other leading ayatollahs in Iraq, including Mohammed Sadiq al-Sadr in 1999, al-Sistani emerged as the pre-eminent Shi'i cleric remaining in Iraq). Although the American administration was aware of the rise of Shi'i power in Iraq, it was unwilling, or potentially unable, to challenge it. After all, in 2003 the Shi'i senior clerics were tolerant of the Americans. Al-Sistani himself has been reluctant to get directly involved in worldly affairs, and he urged his followers not to take up arms against the Americans. The general strategy of the Shi'a in post-war Iraq was to allow the Americans to stabilize the country while they focused on making Iraq's *hawza* more powerful than the rival Iranian *hawza* that had filled the power vacuum in the Shi'i world created by Saddam Hussein's oppression of Iraq's Shi'a (Engel, 2004, 2008; Nakash, 2006).

However, despite his basic belief that clerics should stay out of politics, Grand Ayatollah al-Sistani was drawn into the power vacuum in Iraq (Nakash, 2006). Bremer felt that Iraq needed a constitution before creating a government, as did the Sunni Arabs and Kurds in order to guarantee their rights in the Shi'i-dominated state that would likely result from elections (Wright & Reese, 2008). Responding to fears that the US was trying to impose a secular, federal constitution on Iraq, al-Sistani issued a *fatwa* on 26 June 2003 stating that it was unacceptable for an Iraqi constitution to be generated by people who were appointed by the occupation forces rather than elected (Nakash,

2006; Tripp, 2007; Engel, 2008). This move dealt a blow to Bremer's original plan, published in September 2003, of having the US formally occupy Iraq for several years, wherein a constitution would be written and ratified by Iraqis, followed by a general election, followed by dissolving US occupation authority (Ricks, 2006). Taking into account al-Sistani's demands, on 15 November 2003 the CPA and the IGC announced an agreement for transfer of power to an appointed (unelected) Iraqi Interim Government (IIG) to take over from the CPA in June 2004, charged with organizing elections for an Iraqi parliament by January 2005 (Fawn, 2006). After these nationwide elections, the Iraqi parliament would form a transitional government, which would write the constitution. Once written, the constitution would be subject to national referendum by October 2005, and if accepted, elections would be held for a fully sovereign parliament by December 2005, which would serve a four-year term (Tripp, 2007; Engel, 2008). However, for many reasons, the legitimacy of the various interim institutions set up to guide Iraq to democracy – the CPA, the IGC, the IIG and even the fully sovereign parliament – were rejected by key sections of the Iraqi population, as explained below.

The IGC was appointed on 13 July 2003 by the CPA to help it transfer full political sovereignty to Iraq (Tripp, 2007). However, the IGC's 25 members were not elected, but chosen by Bremer in negotiation with the UN special representative for Iraq and the seven dominant, formerly exiled, parties, and so was not a democratic outcome, no matter how ethnically balanced its membership (Dodge, 2005; Jabar, 2007).[2] The IGC was dominated by nine members of the exiled opposition with long-established links to the US administration, such as Ahmed Chalabi and Ayad Allawi. The CPA, operating in an isolated manner from within the heavily fortified Green Zone in Baghdad (for security reasons), had little chance of successfully reaching out to the Iraqi people, in direct contrast to the *hawza* (Lynch, 2006; Engel, 2008). Furthermore, under, the CPA and IGC, Iraqi state assets were rapidly and illegally disposal of and corruption was rife (Barakat, 2005; Klein, 2007). Unsurprisingly, then, opinion polls showed widespread mistrust of the IGC's politicians (Oxford Research International, 2004; Dodge, 2005; Lynch, 2006).

Legitimacy did not improve with the transfer of power from the IGC to the IIG in June 2004 under UN Resolution 1546 (even though al-Sistani bestowed his conditional approval) (Nakash, 2006). The United States retained significant de facto power in Iraq and the UN's Resolution recognized the need for the continued presence of Coalition military forces. The IIG, with Ayad Allawi as prime minister, was still an unelected body, its members appointed by the IGC that had doled out positions to its own members' families, tribes, business partners and political parties with little regard for local opinion. About two-thirds of its members had foreign (mainly British or American) passports and few of these former exiles commanded any popular support inside Iraq, which gave them personal interest in delaying the creation of real democratic institutions (Fawn, 2006; Lynch, 2006).

Under the CPA and IGC, the insurgency grew – a clear sign of growing disaffection, drawn mainly from the now dismantled, Sunni-dominated Ba'th Party, foreign fundamentalist groups such as al-Qaeda and domestic Islamists. Sunni disenchantment with the US-led Coalition has already been explained in Chapter 3. Added to this, they felt threatened by moves towards democracy that would empower the majority Shi'a. Al-Qaeda's involvement in the insurgency kept its name on the international agenda in what was seen by many in the wider Muslim world as resistance to US occupation, its targets mainly UN representatives (in August 2003), and after the UN withdrew, foreign envoys, US forces, Shi'i civilians and religious leaders (Azzam, 2006; Jabar, 2007; Engel, 2008). The domestic Islamists were the by-product of the fact that Saddam Hussein had allowed the organization of Sunni Islamist groups, including fundamentalist Salafis with Wahhabi inclinations, seeking to use them to counterbalance the Shi'a. Furthermore, in the final days of his rule, Saddam Hussein sanctioned the formation of Islamic *Fedayeen* groups (a ruthless paramilitary force), turning them into part of the military wing of the Ba'th Party. Although the leading Shi'i cleric, al-Sistani, urged the Shi'i not to fight the US-led coalition, Muqtada al-Sadr urged the opposite across 2004, leading two Shi'i rebellions against the Americans, radicalized by the CPA's insistence that the Iraqi state be secular, pro-US and dominated by former US exiles, that majority rule be blocked, and that Shi'i Islamists be marginalized, leading al-Sadr to denounce the IGC as non-representative.[3] Sections of the Shi'a were further radicalized by the fact that the de-Ba'thification orders had been reversed in 2004 and that the US had signed over Fallujah to former Ba'th Republican Guard officers in April 2004 – these acts reaffirming Shi'i fears that the US intended to bring the Ba'th Party back to power. Furthermore, Americans had not prevented scores of political assassinations of Shi'i leaders across 2003–2004 at the hands of militant Sunni adversaries (Nakash, 2006). As the security situation remained unstable, many Iraqis sought refuge in sectarian formations that felt safer and more reliable than a weak central government still largely beholden to the US and its ongoing military occupation (Mandaville, 2007). For instance, there were various Shi'i militia belonging to different political parties and forces – al-Sadr's Mahdi army, SCIRI's al-Badr Brigade, and militias belonging to al-Da'wa and Hizbullah.[4] Meanwhile, the US Bush administration alleged that there was evidence that Iran was giving tactical and material support to the Iraqi Shi'i insurgency (Beehner & Bruno, 2008).

January 2005 saw one of the highest number of violent attacks in any of the months after the declared end of major combat operations in May 2003 (with close to 3,000 attacks) (Wright & Reese, 2008). Despite this unstable environment, on 30 January 2005, the first post-Saddam Hussein elections were held for the (transitional) Iraqi National Assembly to replace the IIG (Jabar, 2007). Various Sunni insurgency groups pledged a bitter war of violence to undermine the elections, dispatching suicide bombers to kill election workers (Fawn, 2006; Munson, 2006; Nakash, 2006). Nonetheless, in defiance of the Sunni insurgency, the various Shi'i parties came together (apart from Muqtada al-Sadr's supporters) to run on a single list – the official *hawza* list – in bloc 169 (called the United Iraqi Alliance (UIA), a coalition of al-Da'wa and SCIRI parties). The UIA stressed, on Shi'i-run television channels, that voting was a religious duty, in a campaign powered by Grand Ayatollah al-Sistani and the *hawza*'s network of mosques and seminaries (Engel, 2008). The Shi'i parties also withstood Sunni propaganda that they planned to establish a Shi'i theocracy in Iraq, instead stressing the importance of keeping Iraq unified and writing a constitution that guarded the Islamic character of Iraq while respecting the rights of Iraqis of all religions and sects (Nakash, 2006).

Over 14 million Iraqis were registered to vote (Wright & Reese, 2008) – no mean achievement in a country with no democratic traditions and in the middle of an insurgency. Voter turnout was approximately 8.5 million voters – 58 per cent of eligible voters (Jabar, 2007; Tripp, 2007). Although a significant achievement, the elections did not mean that Iraq was now a fully functioning democracy. At least eight candidates were assassinated before the election (Jamail, 2007), and candidates were unable to make themselves known, because the security situation had prevented public campaigning. Only the names of the party leaders were widely known (Danner, 2005c). The electorate could vote only in those parts of Iraq with effective military protection (Barakat, 2005). On election day, 34 Iraqis and 11 Coalition solders died as several polling stations were bombed (Fawn, 2006;

Wright & Reese, 2008). Significantly, a large majority of Sunni Arabs boycotted the elections, feeling disenfranchised and alienated by de-Ba'thification, and perceiving the US as treating all Sunnis as terrorists – particularly after the 2004 attacks on Fallujah (Tripp, 2007; Engel, 2008; Wright & Reese, 2008). Because of low Sunni participation in the vote, the Shi'i and Kurdish blocs ended up being over-represented in the new Iraqi National Assembly. This strengthened the rejectionist and militant Islamist groups among the Sunni Arab community, delegitimized the democratic process as one that would provide fair power-sharing and reinforced the logic of using force to respond to perceived institutional injustices (Jabar, 2007).

Despite these many shortcomings, the January 2005 elections allowed the US and UK political authorities to signal that their goal of democratizing Iraq was successful, and much attention was given to securing western coverage of this story. The day before the Iraqi elections, the number of embeds had risen from a post-war lull of 35 in December 2004 to 164 (Wright & Reese, 2008). On election day, the military ensured that insurgents' violence would not make television news, banning all vehicles, so that any explosions would be limited to the size of bomb that could be carried on foot. The military's most effective Information Operations (IO) rule was that still and video cameras were admitted only into five predetermined and highly protected polling places where one had to pass through cordons of US military, Iraqi military, Iraqi police and finally Electoral Commission security, the first three cordons performing searches and all four checking credentials and identification (Danner, 2005c). Correspondingly, in the West, the iconic television pictures of the election were of scores of Iraqis in line, waving their purple-inked fingers (the mark designed to prevent people from voting twice), smiling in powerful images of democracy (Danner, 2005c; Jamail, 2007; Engel, 2008). This was narrated on US news networks by voice-overs over-optimistically claiming that 'probably more than 80 percent' had voted and that 'The Sunnis are voting, the Sunnis are voting' (Danner, 2005c). Yet, although US mainstream media coverage of cheering, jubilant Iraqis boosted Bush's ratings in US opinion polls, such images did not signify the professed gratitude towards the Bush administration for bringing them democracy, but rather a desire for an end to US-led occupation and for genuine self-determination, as the candidates had promised they would demand (Jamail, 2007).

The resulting Iraqi Transitional Government's (May 2005–May 2006) main function was to draft a permanent constitution of Iraq.

The constitution that emerged was one of the most progressive in the Middle East. It guaranteed equal civil liberties for women, prohibited the return of a dictator, reserved a role for Islam in government but also stipulated that 'no law may be enacted that contradicts the principles of democracy' (Iraqi Constitution, 2005, Article 2) and tilted the balance of institutional powers in favour of strong regional governments at the expense of a weak central government (Iraqi Constitution, 2005; Dawoody, 2006; Engel, 2008). However, the constitution is weak regarding freedom of expression and freedom of the press. While necessarily (given Iraq's insurgency) prohibiting 'racism or terrorism or accusations of being an infidel (takfir) or ethnic cleansing' (Iraqi Constitution, 2005, Article 7), it left freedom of expression and of the press vaguely defined and created the possibility for the Iraqi authorities to restrict these freedoms on grounds of 'public order' and 'morality' (Iraqi Constitution, 2005, Article 38). The constitution was ratified in a national plebiscite on 15 October 2005, by 78 per cent to 22 per cent, with the Shi'i and Kurdish provinces voting in favour and the Sunni Arab provinces against (Tripp, 2007). Many Sunnis opposed the federalism written into the constitution and the lack of clarity in terms of oil-revenue sharing. Yet, realizing that their boycott of the January 2005 elections had only weakened their voice and power, this time most Sunnis expressed their commitment to the political process by participating in the referendum but rejecting the constitution. Nonetheless, a powerful minority, particularly the Salafi insurgents, opposed the process altogether and continued to wage sectarian war (Jabar, 2007), extending this from the normal targets of US and Iraqi troops, politicians and Shi'i religious leaders to Shi'i civilians because they had voted (Engel, 2008).

Approval of the constitution paved the way for general elections in December 2005. The official turnout for the parliamentary elections was 80 per cent, over 20 per cent more than in the elections for the transitional parliament 11 months earlier. The election returned the Shi'i bloc, the UIA (now comprised of an alliance between al-Da'wa, SCIRI and al-Sadr – who had been persuaded by al-Sistani to end his rebellion) as the largest single bloc (winning 41 per cent of the vote), but with no overall majority. The Kurds won 22 per cent and the Sunnis only 19 per cent despite a strong turnout in cities like Ramadi and Fallajuh. After a process of long negotiations, in May 2006 a coalition government was formed under the leadership of Prime Minister Nouri al-Maliki (of the UIA and al-Da'wa in particular), with Jalal Talabani as president. This was the first government to take office in Iraq on the basis of the nationally vetted constitution and fresh elections (Jabar, 2007; Tripp, 2007; Engel, 2008).

The US-led coalition had three paramount concerns in this post-war period regarding the installation of democracy in Iraq. The first was to create a government that was sympathetic to US interests (Knightley, 2003; Barakat, 2005). Yet, a truly democratic Iraq was always likely to be led not only by the Shi'a, who are the majority of Iraqis, but by those Shi'i parties that are the largest and best organized – SCIRI and al-Da'wa. These parties happened to be those blessed by the religious authorities and nurtured in Iran for over two decades, with all the ideological and financial ties this implied. As such, the overthrow of Saddam Hussein boosted Iran's regional influence – an outcome far from the intention of the Bush administration, which continued to see Iran as its major strategic adversary in the area, particularly after the election of Mahmud Ahmadinejad as Iranian president in 2005 and the growing dispute over possible Iranian development of nuclear capability (Tripp, 2007; Perry et al., 2009). The second concern of the US-led coalition was to create a government that was nationally uni-fied, preventing Iraq from splintering into its three main ethnic group-ings of Shi'a, Sunni and Kurds, and forestalling a civil war – the latter of which would show that OIF had been ill-advised (Stansfield, 2006). Such a split would also be worrying to the US in that a decentralized or divided Iraq would invite Iranian expansion into the Shi'i-dominated areas of Iraq removing the main check on Iranian influence in the Gulf area (Lynch, 2006; Nashashibi et al., 2007). The US-led coali-tion's third concern was to create a government that was deemed legit-imate. Yet, even the democratically elected al-Maliki government in 2006 suffered legitimacy problems in that large cross-sections of the Sunni community did not approve of the constitution nor of the insti-tutions and power arrangements it had brought about.

Certainly, after the removal from power of Saddam Hussein, Iraq's growing insurgency suggested that large sections of the population per-ceived the governing bodies as illegitimate, threatening the break-up of Iraq. Whereas in 2005, insurgency groups in Iraq appeared divided over practices and ideology, by 2006 there was gradual convergence around more unified practices and discourses around Sunni Arab identity, with virtually all adhering publicly to a blend of Salafism and patriotism, diluting distinctions between foreign jihadis and Iraqi combatants (International Crisis Group, 2006). These sentiments were capitalized upon by al-Qaeda in Iraq's al-Zarqawi, who was not killed by the US until 7 June 2006, while the security situation deteriorated dramatically with militias wreaking havoc in Iraq's cities. By 2006, Sunni suicide bombers and Shi'i death squads operated wherever Sunni and Shi'a lived in proximity, especially in Baghdad (Perry et al., 2009). Whereas by the end of 2003 there were 12,049 civilian (that is, non-combatant) deaths from violence (gunfire, executions, suicide attacks and vehicle bombs) in Iraq, 10,750 across 2004, and 14,841 across 2005, this yearly slaughter almost doubled to 27,684 across 2006 (iraqbodycount, 2009).[5] The government was unable to act effectively on the security front, not only because its armed forces were not yet fully ready, but because many of the militias on the ground had ministers in the government, and hence the government was not seen as neutral but rather a party to the conflict or, at best, unable to control its own factions (Jabar, 2007; Tripp, 2007). This prolonged and widespread violence lead to the flight from Iraq of the middle classes, weakening the social groups who opposed political violence and strengthening radical and militant voices within political parties, the army and police force (Jabar, 2007; Paul & Nahory, 2007) thereby jeopardizing 'the political gains the Iraqis had made' (Bush, 2007). Iraqis who could afford it escaped to Jordan and Syria and by April 2007, an estimated 1.9 million Iraqis were displaced within the country and over 2.2 million were refugees abroad (Library of Congress, 2006; Paul & Nahory, 2007; UNHCR, 2007). As Tripp (2007, p. 303) puts it, while all 'the formal trappings of constitutional and democratic government seemed to be in place,' they were 'little-connected to the life-and-death struggles that formed the texture of a much more local, violent and communal politics across the country'.

Amid such ongoing chaos, and deficits in government legitimacy, several key events needed to be carefully controlled in terms of their potency in further fuelling or quelling the insurgency. However, before discussing the key events of the capture of Saddam Hussein and his execution, the media environment must be elucidated.

MEDIA ENVIRONMENT

The period from 2003 to 2006 saw the media environment in Iraq rapidly changing, with different groups having varying success in exploiting it. As Chapter 3 detailed, after the end of major combat operations a plethora of private, and increasingly critical, media in Iraq were launched. As is normal in conflict zones and post-conflict peace-building and democratic development, the CPA engaged in information intervention to manage the transition from Saddam Hussein's state-controlled media to what they termed the 'Iraqi Free Media' (Guntzel, 2007; Wide angle, 2007). As such, in mid-May 2003, the focus of US military's Information Operations (IO) in Iraq switched from undermining Iraqi military morale (the focus during the invasion and 3 month pre-invasion timeframe) to encouraging Iraqi support for the Coalition's political objectives. This included influencing Iraqis to support Coalition efforts to build a new Iraqi Government, and neutralizing anti-Coalition elements and propaganda (Engel, 2008; Wright & Reese, 2008). Given the proliferation of media outlets in Iraq, in autumn 2003 US Embassy public affairs experts and military intelligence agents formed a sixty-person team to produce a daily brief called *The Mosquito* – a summary of the rumours and tabloid journalism circulating in Iraq's TV and press, collected so that they could be rebuffed and used to refine the information campaigns run by the Coalition authorities (Shanker, 2004; Engel, 2008). Undoubtedly, this knowledge fed into the US military's multimillion-dollar covert campaign across 2004–2005 to plant paid propaganda in the Iraqi news media. The propaganda, including optimistic accounts of Iraq's democratic future, was planted via the Lincoln Group, a Washington-based PR firm hired in 2004 after military officials concluded that the US was failing to win over Muslim public opinion (Gerth & Shane, 2005; Library of Congress, 2006).

Recognizing the importance of official media in facilitating a western-style democracy, mainstream media organizations and media management processes were simultaneously established by the CPA and the US Army across 2003 (as in the Iraqi Media Network (IMN), referred to in Chapter 3) (Wright & Reese, 2008). However, while the CPA had declared freedom of the Iraqi press and assembly on assuming power in May 2003, this was not formally enacted until almost a year later – in March 2004 in Order No. 65, *Iraqi Communications and Media Commission* and Order No. 66, *Iraq Public Service Broadcasting* (Coalition Provisional Authority, n.d.). More quickly enacted, in June 2003, was the CPA's Order No. 14, *Prohibited Media Activity*, which banned the media in Iraq from inciting violence, civil disorder, alterations to Iraq's borders by violent means or advocating the return of the Ba'th Party (The Coalition Provisional Authority, n.d.). This order came in response to *al-Jazeera* airing a tape in spring 2003 from Ayman al-Zawahiri, al-Qaeda's main ideologue, which castigated Arab countries allied to the Coalition and called on Muslims to rise up and attack western embassies and interests (Miles, 2005b). The CPA often accused Arab media of exaggerating the violence and chaos in Iraq. Yet, official Iraqi media under the CPA lost credibility by erring in the opposite direction, talking up Iraq's security and stability, and failing to bring to Iraqis the kind of information they needed to discuss, rationally, the emerging political system (Lynch, 2006). As Lynch (2006, p. 219) succinctly puts it:

> The CPA never fully resolved the inherent conflict between the concept of a free independent, critical media and a concept of the media as a vehicle for conveying a particular political narrative. Nor did it resolve the tension between the military imperative of controlling information and the political imperative of creating a free and independent press.

Following the CPA's lead, the IGC periodically attempted to enforce control over information. Arab satellite news stations, in particular, were a focus of concern. Given that the CPA early on lifted Saddam Hussein's ban on TV satellite receivers but failed to begin satellite broadcasting itself until February 2004 (when *al-Hurra* started), this left a gap in which Iraqis got their news from Arab satellite news stations. According to Charles Krohn, a veteran of Army PA: 'What this means is that for the first nine months, we essentially forfeited the contest for hearts and minds to the competition' (Ricks, 2006, p. 209). Attempting to influence these stations' output, in September 2003, the IGC ordered the closure of *al-Jazeera* and *al-Arabiya*, given their perceived contempt towards the Iraqi opposition parties that had become the Iraqi face of the US-led occupation (Lynch, 2006; Tatham, 2005). In December 2003, the IGC expelled *al-Arabiya* for two months for playing an audiotape several times from Saddam Hussein in July 2003, in which he urged Iraqis to resist the American-led occupation. Although this was not the first message from Saddam Hussein (a letter had already been published in the London-based newspaper, *al-Quds al-Arabi*, and a tape had been given to the *Sydney Morning Herald*) it was the first time Saddam Hussein's voice had been heard on a TV network since his regime's fall (Miles, 2005b; Lynch, 2006; Zayani & Ayish, 2006). In November 2003, after the IGC raided *al-Arabiya*'s offices, Rumsfeld claimed to have seen evidence that *al-Jazeera* and *al-Arabiya* were cooperating with insurgents. Yet, compelling images, particularly those taken after bombings, can be taken safely only by people from the community that has been hit, and to function as a reporter in such locations requires some understanding of the local militia – a situation that does not necessarily mean approval (Loyn, 2007). Nonetheless, *al-Jazeera* was particularly suspect because it received so many 'exclusive' videos from Ba'th Party members and other insurgent groups (Miles, 2005b; Lynch, 2006; Engel, 2008). As the insurgency advanced, *al-Jazeera*'s journalists in Iraq were often arrested, beaten, and harassed by US troops, and their Baghdad offices periodically closed, in efforts to prevent coverage of the insurgency (Miles, 2005b; McNair, 2006; Jamail & al-Fadhily, 2007). Perhaps as a result of threats of expulsion and pressure placed on its financier in Qatar, perhaps harkening back to its claims to objectivity, perhaps resulting from a desire to position the channel as the leading Arab media service with a global orientation, in July 2004, *al-Jazeera* became the first and only Arab television network to create a professional code of ethics, seeking to strengthen its ability to report diverse views in a manner consistent with liberal pluralistic norms (Roy, 2004; Miles, 2005b; Tatham, 2006).[6]

Alongside direct control over Arab satellite news stations' outputs, the process of establishing a new Iraqi media culminated with the Coalition's creation of the Combined Press Information Centre (CPIC) within Multi-National Force-Iraq (MNF-I)[7] in July 2004, shortly after the establishment of the IIG. The CPIC represented all branches of service and operated 24/7 in Baghdad. Here, Army units worked with the Iraqis to develop a media culture and organization suited to a democracy. This included training local Iraqi media personnel in western-style journalism, emphasizing the responsibility journalists have in a democracy to present accurate, objective accounts, training local media representatives in broadcasting live interviews with local civic and religious leaders, showing Iraqis how to gather, write, edit and package stories for television without governmental direction, and training on journalistic professional standards. Army PA officers also trained local leaders on the role of media spokespersons in government. Influence over broadcast news remained the most pressing need for the Coalition as surveys published in June 2005 found that 70 to 80 per cent of Iraqis received their news from satellite or ground-based television (Wright & Reese, 2008). However, as of 2006, most of Iraq's broadcast media was owned by political factions as conditions did not make the operation of commercial media outlets profitable (Library of Congress, 2006). This would allow sectarian footage to emerge at crucial moments, so undoing some of the CPIC's work, as shown in the second case study in this chapter.

While Iraqi mainstream media were being totally rebuilt across 2003–2004, and given the extensive control exercised over it by the CPA, IGC and the Iraqi government, Sunni insurgents became highly adept at using participatory media, some of this web-based where global audiences were sought. Across 2004–2005, they simultaneously developed more sophisticated combat and media management techniques to make their groups appear more capable than they really were and to discredit the Coalition and Iraqi Security Forces (ISF). Reaching the Iraqi masses, since late 2003, compilation videos of successful insurgent attacks on US forces (*mujahideen* films), often filmed from multiple camera angles with high-resolution cameras, set to inspiring religious soundtracks or chanting, sold in Baghdad markets for as little as 50 cents on video CDs (Brachman, 2006; Hoffmann, 2006a; Johnson, 2007). As Hoffmann (2006a) details, such films variously: impart practical, tactical advice to insurgents on planning and executing attacks and using weaponry; appeal for financial contributions; and solicit recruits globally to come to Iraq. Insurgents' videos also feature *khutba* – a form of oratory or rhetorical mode of speaking that predates Islam, entailing eloquence, style and cogency – which, when used in these videos, contain strong elements of religious and/or nationalist discourse (Khoury-Machool, 2007). As Hoffmann (2006a) notes, their goal is to explain and legitimize their use of violence, employing theological arguments and treatises, for example, to differentiate between 'illicit terrorism' and 'licit terrorism'. The more prominent insurgent organizations in Iraq established dedicated information offices that functioned as online press agencies – issuing communiqués, and developing and posting new content for their websites, often several times a day (Hoffmann, 2006a; Engel, 2008). Given that internet penetration in Iraq was very low, insurgents' main audience here was potential al-Qaeda recruits abroad, as well as Arab TV stations. More than a dozen insurgent groups produced their own videos which they posted on the web, allowing them to be far more responsive to events than the Coalition's slower, more centralized Information Operations systems (Hoffmann, 2006a; Johnson, 2007; Wright & Reese, 2008). Decapitation videos of captured Iraqis were also broadcast on insurgent groups' websites to serve as a warning for any Iraqis serving in the interim government's security forces or collaborating with the Coalition (al-Marashi, 2004). Better known to western audiences, were hostage videos of kidnapped westerners (Hill, 2008), described as the insurgents' version of 'shock and awe' (al-Marashi, 2004).

Western states have long attempted to curb media reporting of terrorism as a central facet of counter-terrorism strategy (Curtis, 1984; Miller, 1994; Carruthers, 2000). This recognizes that terrorism is a media management strategy adopted by groups who feel excluded from political discourse; and that terrorists' mere attraction of news coverage, let alone the specific broadcasting of their ideologies or demands, can help establish their legitimacy and credibility as well as demonstrating the state's vulnerability (Schmid & de Graaf, 1982; Paletz & Schmid, 1992). Where terrorism does receive coverage in mainstream western media, it is normally without the historical background or political context that would allow terrorists to justify their actions (McNair, 2007). However, this sort of control is impossible with the internet and globally connected media (Wright & Reese, 2008). Many insurgency groups in Iraq shrewdly exploited the glaring absence in western news coverage of graphic portrayals of violence by dispatching camera people among combatants, reinforcing the view that the western media presents at best a sanitized version of conflict, failing to admit real Muslim suffering, or at worst that it is complicit in the events (International Crisis Group, 2006). Insurgents would release their video communiqués to Arabic news channels, enabling them to reach recruitable young Muslims in the region. For instance, insurgents' video footage, such as American soldiers being killed in sniper attacks and by Improvised Explosive Devices (IED), was rebroadcast on television stations like *al-Zawra* (since November 2006), run by former Sunni parliamentarian Mishan Jibouri, and very popular among Sunnis (Johnson, 2007; MixMax, 2008). Insurgents also knew that the broadcasts would be picked up by channels such as *CNN* or the *BBC*, spreading fear across western audiences, and in the case of hostage videos, instigating rallies against the occupation of Iraq in hostages' countries, so pressurizing world leaders to meet insurgents' demands (al-Marashi, 2004; Shaw, 2007). As Curtis (2007) suggests, such videos make a mockery of the US military's fantasy of control in the information war.

When General George W. Casey Jr. assumed command of MNF-I on 1 July 2004, realizing that it had to compete with the graphic imagery of violence in Iraq, he created the concept called 'the drumbeat of steady progress,' to publicize emphatically the steady march toward Iraqi assumption of responsibility for every aspect of their political, economic and military lives (Wright & Reese, 2008). However, in comparison to insurgents' rapid and flexible use of web-based participatory media, the US military and governmental communications systems in Iraq were slow (USA Today, 2006; Wright & Reese, 2008). The US military's response is usually through traditional channels like press releases, but these can take hours to prepare, particularly given that the Coalition's CPIC had to ensure that their facts were accurate. As such, press releases were often outdated by the time they were issued. Lieutenant Colonel (Lt. Col.) Barry Johnson, director of the military's press operations in Baghdad until September 2006, complains that:

> The military wants to control the environment around it, but as we try to [do so], it only slows us down further . . . All too often, the easiest decision we made was just not to talk about [the story] at all, and then you absolutely lose your ability to frame what's going on. (Johnson, 2007, p. 2)

According to a draft report produced by the Baghdad embassy's director of strategic communications, Ginger Cruz, despite spending hundreds of millions of dollars, by the end of 2006 the US had lost the battle with insurgents for Iraqi public opinion (International Crisis Group, 2006; Johnson, 2007).

Ironically, the deteriorating security situation, while confounding US attempts to control information within Iraq and the Arab world, allowed President Bush greater control over information in the West. As the insurgency gathered momentum from the spring of 2004 and across 2005 and 2006, foreign journalists' ability to move around and report was heavily constrained due to the deteriorating security as hotels were mortared, cars bombed and journalists kidnapped. Consequently, most foreign journalists only left the hotels when embedded with the US military (Ricks, 2006; Jamail & al-Fadhily, 2007). The harder it became for reporters to collect information as a result of the security deterioration, the easier it was for the Bush administration to assert that steady progress was being made in Iraq but that cowed western reporters simply were not seeing it (Lynch, 2006; Ricks, 2006; Engel, 2008). As such, whereas Reporters Without Borders' 2002 press freedom index (which ranks countries by how they treat their media, looking at the number of journalists who were murdered, threatened, had to flee or were jailed by the state) ranked Iraq a dismal 130th, the 2006 index pushed Iraq even further down to 154th position in a total of 168 listed countries (Jamail & al-Fadhily, 2007).

By the end of 2006, therefore, the execution footage of Saddam Hussein was disseminated in a media environment more firmly entrenched in the capabilities of Web 2.0 – an environment which saw, among other things, the phenomenon of mobile phone blogging (moblogging) using camera phones becoming more culturally established, allowing many more people to aspire to the status of the photojournalist (Rheingold, 2003; Goggin, 2006) – whether citizen journalist or insurgent terrorist. Alongside mobile phone developments, the global media environment was more firmly entrenched in the phenomenon of convergence. For instance, by 2006 a variety of media convergence features were observable in the UK, including: *Sky* and the UK's independent mobile phone retailer, Carphone Warehouse, entering the broadband market; and *Sky* and *Google* becoming partners. These were made possible by broadband entry speed of 2 Megabits, with up to 8 Megabits per second becoming commonplace as thousands more homes in the UK become part of the audio- and video-capable broadband platform. These developments generated audience/user demand for greater control over choice of content, mobility of media and participation (Richards, 2007). For instance, by 2006, millions of users became familiar with online video as video-sharing website, *YouTube*, reached a critical mass of short video clips (Lovink, 2008), and was acquired by *Google*.[8]

The sousveillant medium of capture in the second case study examined in this chapter was the mobile phone. By 2005 an estimated 2 to 10 per cent of Iraq's population had mobile phones, with people in Iraq using satellite phones, US-area code mobile phones, or new (in 2003) oversubscribed Iraqi mobile phones (albeit all three suffering from heavy static and frequent disconnection), as landlines in Iraq were rare, having been severely disrupted by the 2003 Iraq War and subsequent sabotage (Banbury, 2004; Library of Congress, 2006; United Nations Development Program, 2009). Indeed, countries with inadequate fixed line infrastructures make the use of mobile telephony more attractive to telecom operators seeking to enter these markets; and citizens, faced with long waiting periods and unreliable service from fixed-line operators, are more likely to turn to wireless telephony when it becomes available (Castells et al., 2007). Internet access in Iraq expanded much more slowly after the 2003 Iraq War, following the end of full state control under Saddam Hussein. Whereas in 2000 there were an estimated 12,500 internet users in Iraq (Abdulla, 2007b), by 2005 an estimated 36,000 people (still only about 0.1 per cent of Iraq's population) were using the internet. The main access points were hotels and internet cafés in Baghdad, Basra, and Kurdistan (domestic internet landlines remained unreliable) (Library of Congress, 2006). Thus, although Iraqi use of these technologies expanded since the end of major combat operations in May 2003, their overall levels were still low. Iraq's low level of mobile phone and internet penetration may help explain why the US military and Iraqi authorities were taken by surprise by the transmission of the unofficial mobile phone footage of Saddam Hussein's execution.

CONTROLLED IMAGE: THE CAPTURE OF SADDAM HUSSEIN

On 14 December 2003, Lieutenant General Rick Sanchez and Ambassador Paul Bremer announced that US special operations forces troops and soldiers from the 4th Infantry Division had captured Saddam Hussein on the previous day (Fontenot et al., 2004). Coming seven-and-a-half months after the declared end of major combat operations, this was a significant political moment. As part of the strategic aim to destroy Iraq's Ba'thist regime, Coalition forces had assumed the task of hunting down regime officials – often referred to as high-value targets – to prevent their escape or going underground to lead an armed resistance. Across 2003, a number of key members of Saddam Hussein's regime either turned themselves in on hearing that they were on the most-wanted list, or were captured (Wright & Reese, 2008). According to the US military, Saddam Hussein was captured by Major General Raymond Odierno's 4th Infantry Division, facilitated by hostile interrogation-derived information of several of Saddam Hussein's relatives and bodyguards (MSNBC, 2003; Schlesinger, 2004; Engel, 2008).[9] In an operation called Red Dawn, the division's 1st Brigade Combat Team and Task Force 120, a special operations team that had been hunting high-value targets in Iraq, surrounded the village of ad-Dawr near Tikrit (the Sunni heartland) not far from Saddam Hussein's birthplace of Auja, and after a careful search, found him hiding in a hole in the ground on a farm (Ricks, 2006; Wright & Reese, 2008).

The Bush administration and the CPA believed that Saddam Hussein's capture would be a significant turning point in the Coalition's campaign in Iraq, as indicated by the excitement in Bremer's voice when he announced on television to Iraqis and Coalition leaders in Baghdad, 'Ladies and Gentlemen, we got him!' Saddam Hussein's capture was important in quelling any thoughts among his supporters that he could return to reinstate his regime, thereby also reassuring ordinary Iraqis. Up until Saddam Hussein's capture, his 'presence' weighed heavily on the occupying powers, with Arab satellite channels proving his continued existence through audio and video-taped broadcasts, where he declared the continuation of fighting and called for 'jihad' – a call subsequently taken up by preachers during their Friday sermons (De Quetteville, 2003; Tumber and Palmer, 2004; Zayani and Ayish, 2006). Indeed, documents seized by the US military when it took Saddam Hussein into custody indicated that he had been in regular contact with those organizing the resistance (Dodge, 2006). Notably, Saddam Hussein's moment of capture predated the official hand-over of sovereignty to the IIG in June 2004 by 6 months during a period in which insurgencies were rife, rising steadily from around 600 violent attacks per month in July to around 1,300 by November 2003 (Wright & Reese, 2008). Perhaps in an attempt to quell such insurgencies, the media were told that Saddam Hussein had not resisted capture, despite carrying a pistol – a detail widely cited in UK and US mainstream media on 14 and 15 December.[10]

Repeatedly shown on *BBC News* on 14 December 2003 was, as the presenter put it, the 'extraordinary' news conference given by Paul Bremer at Coalition headquarters in Baghdad. The 'dramatic pictures of the day' behind the caption, 'Saddam Captured: Saddam Hussein arrested in Tikrit', were as follows. We see a close up of the face of a dishevelled, white-bearded Saddam Hussein. He is standing against a white, tiled wall, while a white man in uniform and surgically gloved hands inspects Saddam Hussein's long, unkempt, hair for lice, then puts a spatula in his mouth, and pokes around his gums to get a saliva swab to verify that this was the real Saddam Hussein, and not a body double. The ambient sound is of men cheering, whistling and loudly shouting and jeering in Arabic, 'down with Saddam', 'death to Saddam'. The camera pulls out to reveal that the images of Saddam Hussein are on two flat-screen TVs in a conference room, with four men at a podium, one of them Paul Bremer (BBC, 2003a).[11] On *BBC News 24*, another American at the podium presenting this clip to the press conference goes on to say that Saddam Hussein is being examined here in order to ensure his medical well-being. However, the Americans would realize that they were contravening the Geneva Convention relative to the Treatment of Prisoners of War (Geneva Convention, 1950b) and Geneva Convention relative to the Protection of Civilian Persons in *Time* of War (Geneva Convention, 1950a), where Article 3, 1c of both Conventions prohibits 'Outrages upon personal dignity, in particular, humiliating and degrading treatment' for 'Persons taking no active part in the hostilities, including members of armed forces who have laid down their arms'. Furthermore, Article 13 of the Geneva Convention relative to the Treatment of Prisoners of War (Geneva Convention, 1950b) states that 'prisoners of war must at all times be protected . . . against insults and public curiosity'. Yet, the US believed that to quell the insurgency in Iraq, the capture of Saddam Hussein was not enough. He needed to be presented as defeated rather than defiant, willingly giving himself up to the Coalition authorities. This would generate maximal shock value particularly when contrasted with his predominant historical image.

Certainly, western discursive constructions of Saddam Hussein had long vilified Saddam Hussein as a threat, enemy and tyrant – constructions dating back to his invasion of Kuwait in 1990 and re-energized by the 11 September 2001 terrorist attacks, after which Iraq was publicly suspected of harbouring terrorists and developing WMD, as detailed in Chapter 2. For instance, a common strategy was to liken Saddam Hussein to a madman (Post & Panis, 2005) (a discursive process of de-legitimization, as Foucault (1965) notes), or Hitler (Kellner, 1992, 1995; Dorman & Livingston, 1994; Berman, 2004). Berman (2004) observes how the Hitler analogy changed over time. During the 1991 Gulf War, the analogy, repeated endlessly by Israel (Simpson, 2003) pointed out the unprovoked annexation of foreign territory (Kuwait), but quickly came to signify the brutality of the Iraqi regime in its occupation of Kuwait. During the 2003 Iraq War, the use of the metaphor not only pointed out the Iraqi regime's brutality to its own population, but the global threat it posed as carrier of WMD, echoing the classical totalitarian aspiration to world domination.

Meanwhile, Iraq's own official projections of Saddam Hussein, such as in speeches, statues and murals, were of a strong man, a war hero (Barakat, 2005), a great nationalistic leader unifying the wider pan-Arab nation against western aggression (Post & Panis, 2005; Nakash, 2006) or the spread of Iranian Islamic fundamentalism (Kellner, 1992; Tripp, 2007). For instance, Syria's invasion of Lebanon in 1976 and its military action against Palestinian forces there allowed Saddam Hussein to cast doubt on Syrian leader, al-Asad's, pan-Arab credentials and to pose as champion of the Palestinian resistance movements. Even Iraq's invasion of Kuwait in 1990 was accompanied by Arab nationalist unification rhetoric, the annexation presented as a rectification of injustice committed by UK imperialism in separating Kuwait from Iraq when originally defining the boundaries of the Iraqi state (Simpson, 2003; Nakash, 2006; Tripp, 2007). Feeding the cult of the personality, he likened his rule to that of militant kings of the ancient Assyrian and Neo-Babylonian empires, verging at times on self-deification (Bakir, 2009). For instance, Saddam Hussein designed the Victory Arch – a monument, opened in Baghdad in August 1989 to celebrate Iraq's (unconvincing) victory over Iran in 1988. Here, two steel forearms rise out of the ground, each fist holding a sixty-six-foot-long sword, the two swords crossing to form the apex of the arch about 130 feet above the ground. As the invitation card sent to guests on the opening day describes it:

> The ground bursts open and from it springs the arm that represents power and determination, carrying the sword of Qadisiyya.[12] It is the arm of the Leader-President, Saddam Husain himself (God preserve and watch over him) enlarged forty times. It springs out to announce the good news of victory to all Iraqis, and it pulls in its wake a net that has been filled with the helmets of the enemy soldiers, some of them scattering into the wasteland. (Makiya, 1991, p. 2)

This steel was made by melting down the actual weapons of Iraqi 'martyrs' killed in the war, and 5,000 real Iranian helmets, taken from the battlefield are gathered up in two bronze nets. The two forearms are not sculpted objects that might have idealized the body parts, but castings taken from plaster casts of Saddam Hussein's own arms and then enlarged, showing veins and hair follicles (Makiya, 1991). This projection of the leader's irreducible uniqueness (through the casts) into the artistic edifice displays the absolute priority of personal power, such displays necessary to help cow the Shi'a and Kurds (Makiya, 1991; Berman, 2004). Politically, the discourse of hero-worship was reinforced by Iraqi government policy which throughout the 1990s had steadfastly rejected the demands of the US and the international community, despite persistent violation of Iraqi sovereignty through US and UK patrolling of no-fly zones in the north and south, periodic bombing and 13 years of harsh sanctions (Dodge, 2005; Tripp, 2007). Saddam Hussein also wanted to project his people's 'love' for him, and giant photographs of him adorned government buildings – carrying bowls of rice (Saddam the Provider), brandishing rocket-propelled grenades (Saddam the Protector), eating bread with poor villagers (Saddam the Man of the People) and surrounded by adoring schoolchildren (Saddam the Father) (Engel, 2008).

According to Major Brian Reed, the operations officer of the 1st Brigade Combat Team who helped lead Red Dawn, on his capture Saddam Hussein raised both hands and declared in English, 'I am Saddam Hussein. I am the president of Iraq, and I am willing to negotiate' (McCarthy, 2003c). No official photographs of Saddam Hussein's moment of capture were released, although a month later, an unofficial one of a US soldier posing for the camera as he pinned Saddam Hussein's body and face to the ground shortly after having pulled him from his 'spider hole,' was published on the US website Military.com.[13] The photograph was e-mailed to the person who posted it online (former journalist and contributor to Military.com, John Weisman), by a friend in special forces who was proud of what his former colleagues in Iraq had accomplished. Although the military requested that the photograph be removed from the site on the grounds that it was a security risk, Weisman denied the request, writing on his website: 'I'd like to see this photograph posted in every public building in the US so Americans can be reminded to thank the American soldiers who put their lives on the line every day to keep this nation safe and free' (Clifton, 2004). Nonetheless, the first footage broadcast in the West of the captured Saddam Hussein was on 14 December 2003, the day following his capture, where for the first time, we were presented with Saddam Hussein not only as de-deified, ragged and with six months of beard (much of it white) but as captured beast, disempowered, controlled and intruded upon (BBC, 2003a; Bakir, 2009). In the 14 December 2003 *BBC News 24* broadcast of the US press conference given by Paul Bremer, clips from a military video of the 'spider hole' where Saddam Hussein was captured are also shown. Here his bestiality differs in tone to the predatory bestiality previously conferred upon him by the West – for instance in US presidential speeches (Lazar & Lazar, 2004) and US mainstream media, where he was regularly referred to as a monster and the Butcher of Baghdad (Kellner, 1992). Rather, US and UK mainstream reportage made much use of prey-oriented bestial analogies, with widespread citation of the phrase 'caught like a rat' – a phrase uttered by Major General Raymond Odierno (Bakir, 2009).[14]

Capturing Saddam Hussein without a fight, denied him the opportunity to honour his claim that he would be a martyr, but never a captive (Fontenot et al., 2004). Indeed, his capture appeared to temporarily disrupt the Sunni insurgency as the number of insurgent attacks in the winter of 2004 dropped to about 800 per month – significantly below that of the preceding autumn. The televised parading of Saddam Hussein on his capture may well have been to pre-empt what turned out to be the most common reaction in Iraq – disbelief – with Iraqis insisting that the capture was a fake, a put-on by Saddam Hussein and the Americans to confuse them (Engel, 2008). However, his undignified parading was very unpopular in al-Anbar province; and the display was seen as disgraceful in other parts of the Arab world (Ricks, 2006). From the later rise in insurgency, it appeared that Sunni insurgents (drawn from Saddam Hussein's *fedayeen*, the *mukhabarat*, former Ba'th Party members, aggrieved tribes and the newly unemployed and disenfranchised) had used the time merely to regroup and consolidate in the Sunni heartland, while other insurgent groups added to the fray (Wright & Reese, 2008). Removing Saddam Hussein may have made it easier for Iraqis who hated him but also disliked the Americans to support the insurgency in their fight for their country, honour and Islam (Ricks, 2006). Thus, April–July of 2004 saw around 2000 violent attacks per month, rising to a monthly average of around 2,800 across August 2004 to January 2005 (Wright & Reese, 2008). According to an IGC report, Saddam Hussein's incarceration following his capture:

> gave the insurgency renewed momentum, dissociating it from the Baathist regime and shoring up its patriotic, nationalist and religious/jihadist credentials. By the same token it facilitated a rapprochement between the insurgency and trans-national jihadi networks, which had been hostile to a partnership with remnants of a secular, heretical regime. (Cited in Wright & Reese, 2008, p. 102)

While the post-war insurgency in Iraq was volatile and difficult to control, at least the Coalition was able to control the release and framing of this disempowering image of Saddam Hussein, thereby signalling the might of the Coalition forces as well as the end of Saddam Hussein's regime. The selectivity of this controlled image of the moment of bestialization is noteworthy when we consider that, as he was captured, he confidently identified himself as the President of Iraq, ready to negotiate, and within hours of his capture, he had regained his composure, in characteristic defiant, grandiose mode (Post & Panis, 2005) – a stance he maintained throughout his televised trial and, as the following section will show, his execution.

LOSING CONTROL: THE EXECUTION OF SADDAM HUSSEIN

The IIG assigned an Iraq Special Tribunal for Crimes Against Humanity to try the top members of Saddam Hussein's regime for war crimes as defined by the International Criminal Court. Saddam Hussein's televised trial began on 19 October 2005 and continued intermittently through the summer of 2006 (Library of Congress, 2006). While standing accused of seven crimes, including the killing of tens of thousands of Kurds in the late 1980s, assassinating political opponents and religious leaders, invading Kuwait in 1990 and murdering thousands of Shi'a after the 1991 Gulf War, Saddam Hussein was charged first with a relatively minor crime – the unlawful killing in 1982 of 148 villagers in the mainly Shi'i village of Dujail following a failed assassination attempt. While this trial was proceeding, a second trial began in the summer of 2006 in which Saddam Hussein and another group of associates faced charges for al-Anfal (the killing of over 100,000 Iraqi Kurds in 1988) (Engel, 2008). Throughout, Saddam Hussein sought to use the televised trial as a platform to indict the Iraqi government as a US puppet, and to mobilize Iraqis against the occupation. The Iraqi government (and the US and UK) sought to use the trial to remind Iraqis and the world of the regime's crimes, to allow relatives of Saddam Hussein's victims to get satisfaction of seeing him brought to account, and through the proceedings to demonstrate that a new rule of law now applied in Iraq (Tripp, 2007). Saddam Hussein was sentenced to death two days before the US congressional mid-term elections in November 2006, where polls predicted the Republicans would lose both houses of Congress. A diplomat at the US embassy in Baghdad said to *NBC* journalist, Richard Engel: 'We're doing everything we can to make sure they're done by the midterm elections. But don't report that. This is an entirely Iraqi process' (Engel, 2008, p. 306). Indeed, Amnesty International condemned the trial, and the subsequent appeal, as rushed and flawed in process (Cox, 2006).

It was imperative that Saddam Hussein's execution convey proof of death to Iraqis – a detail initially overlooked by the US-led Coalition on killing Saddam Hussein's two, widely hated, sons, Uday and Qusay on 22 July 2003. As Salam Pax ranted several days later:

> It is so unbelievable how they have wasted a chance to show Iraqis they really are doing something. It was the most useless of press conferences, first off this Sanchez speaks only in Militar-ese, meaningless words come out of his mouth while we are all hanging on the edge of our seats waiting for one single picture, definitive proof. It is so easy, all it takes is to show us the friggin' corpses. They do have them. Someone did see them and when asked why it wasn't sown to the public they came up with the moral issues stuff. Habibi it didn't bother you that all those Iraqis, Americans and British are being killed for dubious reasons, so why suddenly become so squeamish? Give the Images to Jazeera, moral issues have never stopped them from showing gruesome images, let them do your dirty work. All I care about is knowing, seeing, being 100% doubt free and that press conference proved nothing. (Pax, 2003f)

Proof of death had long been used in Iraq, to signal regime change. In February 1963, when the Ba'thists succeeded in killing President Qassem (himself installed in 1958 in a coup to remove the royal family), in a gangland execution, the grisly pictures of the bodies of the President and his entourage were shown repeatedly on national TV to prove he was really dead. The pictures always ended with the same sequence: the camera followed a soldier as he walked over to Qassem's body, pulled the head up by the hair, and spat in the dead face (Simpson, 2003). However, showing death and executions on national television is not something that the media in the US or UK normally does. In the UK, it infringes Ofcom-regulated notions of decency and taste. Yet, there has been a recent history of execution footage freely available online (as explained earlier in this chapter). The delay in proof of death of Uday and Qusay was corrected quickly, with the CPA releasing photographs of them on 24 July 2003, two days after their killing. US Defense Secretary Donald Rumsfeld said providing proof of the brothers' deaths could demoralize the remnants of Saddam Hussein's regime that were battling US troops, convince Iraqis that the regime was not coming back, and encourage Iraqis to come forward with information, and that the chance of saving US lives outweighed ethical sensibilities (CNN, 2003).

As well as providing proof of death, Saddam Hussein's execution needed to signal 'Iraqi ownership' of the state-building process, as his trial had been designed to do (Post & Panis, 2005; Tripp, 2007). However, Engel (2008) observes that while appearing Iraqi, the trial was an American proceeding. The US government had trained the judges, flown in legal advisors, built the courtroom, ran the simultaneous translations booth and the media company that coordinated the satellite uplink, as well as holding Saddam Hussein in custody. While, by the time of his execution in December 2006, a constitutionally elected Iraqi government had been in place for seven months, throughout his trial, Saddam Hussein continued to demand that he be referred to as the President of Iraq, denying the court's authority to strip him of his title (Post & Panis, 2005). Saddam Hussein's execution was intended to dash any illusion that he could ever lead his supporters back to power, so minimizing the risk of fuelling the ongoing insurgency. As noted earlier, despite three major elections in Iraq across 2005, by the year's end the insurgency had intensified. Since the bombing by al-Qaeda of one of the most sacred Shi'i holy shrines in Iraq – the al-Askariyya shrine in the Sunni Arab town of Samarra in February 2006 – and the cycle of retributory violence this generated as Sunni mosques were attacked by al-Sadr's Mahdi army, Iraq had effectively descended into a medium-level sectarian civil war between Shi'i and Sunni militias, centred mainly on Baghdad (Library of Congress, 2006; Jabar, 2007; Tripp, 2007).[15]

Beyond Iraqi considerations, the Coalition authorities also needed to consider the impact of Saddam Hussein's execution on the wider Arab and Muslim world. Indeed, on announcing his execution, people took to the streets in protests and mourning across the globe (Owen, 2006; McElroy, 2007). Iraq, sitting on the critical sectarian fault line of the Middle East – the Sunni-Shi'i spilt – risks any conflict there gaining momentum from the involvement of neighbouring states, with Iran strongly supporting the Shi'a and with Saudi Arabia, Kuwait, Jordan and Syria sympathetic to the Sunni (Danner, 2005a; Perry et al., 2009). Given the complexity and fragility of the political and security situation in a climate of mounting insurgency, maximum control over the presentation of Saddam Hussein's execution was needed – including who should execute and be executed with him, and where and when the execution should occur.

In terms of who should execute Saddam Hussein, in order to signal Iraqi ownership of the state-building process, this had to be the Iraqi state. After Saddam Hussein's execution, one of the witnesses, Iraqi National Security Adviser, Mowaffak al-Rubaie, stressed Iraq's autonomous control in this procedure and that no Americans were present during the hour of execution. In terms of who should be executed with him, two other co-defendants – Barzan Hassan, Saddam Hussein's half-brother, and Awad Bandar, the former chief judge of the Revolutionary Court – had been expected to face execution with Saddam Hussein, but al-Rubaie said their executions were postponed 'because we wanted to have this day to have an historic distinction' (Raaman et al., 2006). In terms of where the execution should take place, it had to be outside the heavily fortified US Green Zone, in Baghdad. Iraqi officials contemplated holding a public hanging at a sports arena in Baghdad, allowing tens of thousands of Iraqis to attend and satisfying public demand for revenge as well as certainty that Saddam Hussein's demise was final. However, such an event would have been vulnerable to attack by Sunni insurgents; and American officials believed it would inflame the Muslim world and prompt unfavourable comparisons with Afghanistan's Taliban regime (Harnden, 2006). Instead, Saddam Hussein was executed in a secret location – which turned out to be the Kazimiya military intelligence headquarters under his regime, famous for executing al-Da'wa party members (Engel, 2008). Precisely when the execution should happen was the subject of debate between Iraqi officials, the final decision indicating the hand of sectarianism. Saddam Hussein's appeal against his death sentence failed on 26 December, the court instructing that he should be hanged within 30 days (Tweedie, 2007). In fact, he was hanged within five – his route to the gallows expedited for various reasons including Iraqi government fears of conspiratorial rescue efforts (Parker & Colvine, 2006); and the desire to avoid mounting international pressure against the death penalty from human rights groups, and surrounding Arab and European countries (Parker & Hamdani, 2007). Under Iraqi law, no execution can be carried out during religious holidays. The three-day Muslim holiday of Eid al-Adha began on Saturday 31 December 2006 for the Sunni and Sunday 1 January 2007 for the Shi'a, who now controlled the government (Santora et al., 2006).[16] Given that there were 30 days to choose from for the execution, the decision to execute Saddam Hussein on the Saturday could well have been interpreted by the Sunnis – comprising more than 85 per cent of the world's Muslims – as a major sectarian slight (Senanayake, 2007), indicating that the Shi'i-dominated government wanted revenge against Saddam Hussein. Whether or not the timing was wise is another matter, but what is clear is that such decisions were carefully deliberated, with the aim of exercising political control over a volatile situation battling with the desire for sectarian revenge.

Official Media Representations

Saddam Hussein's arrival at the gallows was captured on film by Ali al-Massedy, Iraqi Prime Minister Nouri al-Maliki's official videographer (Owen, 2006; Blogs of war, n.d.). The Shi'i-run TV stations were the first to break the news that Saddam Hussein was dead, obviously having received calls from someone in the execution chamber – perhaps the chosen judge who presided over the execution (Munir Haddad – a man whose brother and over 24 other relatives had been killed by Saddam Hussein) (Engel, 2008). Al-Massedy's footage was played repeatedly on *al-Iraqiya* several hours later (CNN, 2006; Harnden, 2006). It shows Saddam Hussein being led up the gallows' steps by masked guards, the rope placed over his head as the executioner reads rituals from the Koran. Broadcasters cut the footage shortly before the trapdoor opened (Owen, 2006). *Al-Iraqiya* television repeatedly ran the visual footage juxtaposed with images of national monuments, replacing the original audio with patriotic music as an announcer declared that 'the criminal Saddam was hanged to death' (CNN, 2006; Owen, 2006), these words taken from al-Maliki's written statement: 'Justice, in the name of the people, has carried out the death sentence against the criminal Saddam, who faced his fate like all tyrants, frightened and terrified' (Owen, 2006).[17] This official version of the execution was packaged to convey that justice had been served in a respectable, dignified manner and that Saddam Hussein had been treated humanely (Bakir, 2009). Meanwhile, a Shi'i TV station aired nothing but clips of Saddam-era abuses and mass graves. One station created a graphic of Saddam Hussein with a noose by his neck, and another broadcast pictures of his face in the crosshairs of a gun (Engel, 2008). The privately owned Iraqi Shi'i channel, *al-Biladi*, also showed a separate, grainier video, of what it said was Saddam Hussein's body after the execution. The footage showed the man identified as Saddam Hussein lying on a stretcher, covered in a white shroud, with only his head exposed and eyes closed (Raaman, et al., 2006), his neck twisted at a sharp angle and apparent bloodstains on his neck and part of the shroud (Bunrs & Santora, 2006; Parker & Colvine, 2006).[18] Iraqi governmental control was exercised over some channels' treatment of the execution. For instance, on 1 January 2007, the Baghdad office of *al-Sharqiya* satellite channel which broadcasts from Dubai was ordered closed by the Iraqi government on grounds of inciting sectarianism as, following the execution, a news reader had appeared wearing black mourning clothes (Jamail & al-Fadhily, 2007).

The carefully selected sequences of the execution shown on *al-Iraqiya* were immediately broadcast to a global television audience of more than one billion (Owen, 2006). Generally, across the UK national newspaper websites (tabloids and broadsheets) the front-page 'execution' image used was a still image from the official Iraqi pre-execution film, depicting Saddam Hussein with the noose around his neck.[19] British television broadcast what the Iraqi government wanted shown – the official, silent, cut-before-the-drop film (Helmore, 2007). No mainstream broadcaster in the UK used the moment when the trap door opened (Bakir, 2009). Further television footage showed the corpse in the white death shroud (Owen, 2006). Thus, the official Iraqi version of the execution prevailed in the British mainstream press and television news. Given that it was past 10 p.m. on the American East Coast, at the heart of the New Year's weekend when Saddam Hussein was executed, US mainstream news had little coverage of the hanging, having poured their resources into a week's worth of coverage following the death of former US President, Gerald Ford whose funeral had been earlier that day. America's 24/7 news networks – in particular *CNN*, *Fox News* and *MSNBC* – offered live coverage before and after the hanging, confirming that the former Iraqi dictator had been hung, but offering no video upon confirming the news (Salama, 2007).

Unofficial Media Representations

The authorities' ability to control this event was shattered by a two-minute, 36-second act of user-generated content, filmed covertly by Saddam Hussein's Shi'i executioners on a mobile phone camera through the railings of the gallows' scaffold, and uploaded to the web 12 hours later, that same day (Bakir, 2009).

The grainy, handheld, shaky footage showed that rather than being frightened and terrified as the Iraqi Prime Minister proclaimed, (Owen, 2006), in the moment before his death Saddam Hussein was heard repeatedly to denounce 'the Persians' and 'the Americans,' and to call for all Iraqis to resist them, stating that he was unafraid of death and shouting 'Allah is great', 'the Muslim Ummah will be victorious', and 'Palestine is Arab' (Keesing's Record of World Events, 2006). After the rope was secured around his neck, some of the witnesses present taunted him, shouting 'You destroyed Iraq' (Engel, 2008, p. 309) and chanting loudly 'Muqtada, Muqtada, Muqtada,' a chant used by supporters of Muqtada al-Sadr, leader of the Mahdi Army (the main Shi'i militia). Another voice could be heard on the video praising the late Grand Ayatollah Sayyid Mohammed Baqir al-Sadr (Engel, 2008). Saddam Hussein repeated the name ironically and asked 'Do you consider this bravery?' A Shi'i version of an Islamic prayer was recited by some of those present as an apparent sectarian insult. As Saddam stood on the gallows, one observer was heard to tell him to 'go to Hell'. Saddam Hussein retorted, 'The hell that is Iraq?' Amid these exchanges, a man appealed for propriety, pleading. 'Please, stop. The man is facing an execution.' Saddam Hussein began to recite the *Shahadah*, an act of faith performed by Muslims prior to death, but before he had completed the second recitation, the trapdoor was opened and he fell to his death (Keesing's Record of World Events, n.d.; Engel, 2008; Bakir, 2009). At this point, the crowd in the execution room erupted in celebration, taking pictures, with the camera flashes giving the room the eerie, slow-motion effect of a strobe light. 'The tyrant has fallen,' one of the onlookers shouted. 'Let him swing for three minutes,' another voice called out as the mobile phone video showed a close-up of Saddam Hussein's face as he swung (Bennett, 2007; Engel, 2008, p. 311).[20] For about 15 seconds after the trap door had opened, the camera phone lingers on Saddam Hussein's forcedly upturned face, lit from above, swinging from the rope. This personal and intimate intrusion is particularly disturbing given Sontag's (2002) observation that within the West, there is a powerful impulse against showing the naked face of the dead.

This illegally captured footage was quickly posted on the internet – this despite the fact that a national state of emergency, ongoing in 2006, authorized the Iraqi government to monitor communications (Library of Congress, 2006), a task made easier by the fact that at the time of the execution, few Iraqis had access to mobile phones, and even fewer were using the internet. Undoubtedly, its upload and rapid spread was facilitated by the smallness of the video file, taking up just over one megabyte (Johnson, 2007). It appeared first on the Finnish-registered Arabic website, Anwarweb.net, and sped across the world via the file-sharing websites *YouTube*, *Google Video* and *Revver*, uncoordinated and uncontrolled, accessed by people directly without the intermediary control of politicians or media organizations (Bennett, 2007; Bakir, 2009). The internet offered all possible variations of the execution, for example pre-hanging without sound; hanging with sound; hanging without the drop and convulsions; or the full, two-minute 36-seconds unedited cut (Helmore, 2007).[21] In less than 24 hours, it had more than a million hits on *YouTube* (Engel, 2008).

After it spread across the internet, the camera-phone images with their accompanying soundtrack of savage and noisy taunting by the execution's witnesses became ubiquitous across many mainstream media outlets. The new video footage was broadcast first by *al-Jazeera* early on the day after the execution (MSNBC, 2007). As Iskandar & el-Nawawy (2004) observe, a plethora of wars in the Arab world's contemporary history and the ongoing Palestinian-Israeli conflict have provided Arab audiences with years of gruesome imagery of war casualties. Furthermore, in Iraq under Saddam Hussein, executions were a common method of punishment, and by these standards the mobile phone footage of the execution was comparatively dignified as Saddam Hussein was not given over the crowds to be dragged through the streets, and neither was his body hung up for days for public display. As such, in this context, images of his execution would not appear so shocking. In the US, most mainstream news outlets, including *CNN* and *ABC*, did not broadcast the images directly, although some still directed viewers to the web footage. *CNN*'s and *ABC*'s websites aired brief parts of the video obliquely while reporting on the viral spread of the video via mobile phones in Iraq, looking over users' shoulders as they watched the video. However, these clips did not include the moment of death. Among mainstream US news outlets, the websites of *The New York Times* and *Fox News* linked to the full version of mobile phone footage, the former linking to streaming video on LiveLeak. com, while the latter linked to *Google Video* (with *Fox News* also posting a version of the video that showed almost everything except the moment of execution itself) (Sass, 2007). In the UK, according to Peter Horrocks, head of *BBC* television news, decisions on what to show were, as ever, influenced by editors' perceptions of public taste and 'appetite' for 'images of violence' as well as knowledge that millions of licence payers were already watching them online (Luckhurst, 2007). For instance, it is instructive to look at *Sky News*' response to complaints to Ofcom about their broadcast of part of the mobile phone footage on 2 January 2007 at 17:00 (where, *Sky* reported the Deputy Prime Minister, John Prescott's, reaction to the mobile phone footage, with this footage 'floated' over the audio of Prescott's comments, taken from an earlier interview). Part of *Sky News*' defence of this broadcast (which did not show the actual moment of hanging) was that the material had already been seen widely and therefore would have been unlikely to generate new exposure, even for children; and that as it is a 24-hour news channel, those watching it chose to do so, thereby reducing the chances of people coming across the coverage 'unawares', as defined by the Broadcasting Code (Ofcom, 2007).[22]

Official sources attempted to re-contain the scandal by mildly criticizing the method of execution while taking care not to suggest that this was symptomatic of concerns about the trial and sentencing (Bakir, 2009). Predictably, the mobile phone footage bolstered Iraqi Prime Minister al-Maliki's status among the Shi'a, but drew the ire of many Sunni (Jabar, 2007). It reinforced the perception of the execution itself as being highly sectarian. Salim al-Jaburi, a member of the Sunni-led Iraqi Accordance Front, said on 3 January that the video would push some Sunnis further away from the political process and make national reconciliation more difficult. The voices in the video of several guards invoking the name of Muqtada al-Sadr moments before the execution strengthened the belief among Sunni Arabs that members of the al-Mahdi Army and other Shi'i militias had infiltrated the ISF at the highest levels: Sunni Arabs as well as US officials had long accused al-Maliki of being unable or unwilling to rein in the Shi'i militias (Senanayake, 2007). Indeed, al-Maliki told *The Times* in October 2008 that he regretted the way in which the sentence was carried out and that: 'Those who chanted were punished. There was no major violation apart from the chanting.' However according to the head guard at Saddam Hussein's tomb, who was one of the people that helped bury his corpse, Saddam Hussein's body was stabbed six times after he was executed – an allegation denied by the Iraqi government (Haynes, 2008). Within hours of Saddam Hussein's death, up to 80 people died in 5 bomb attacks across Iraq as his Sunni Muslim followers fought their Shi'i rivals (FoxNews, 2006; Owen, 2006). The release of the mobile phone footage prompted thousands of Sunnis to protest in al-Anbar province, while residents of Fallujah – the target of a multimillion-dollar hearts-and-minds campaign – renamed the city's main thoroughfare the Street of the Martyr Saddam Hussein (Johnson, 2007). The Iraqi blogger, Riverbend (2006), described the execution as a 'lynching'. Other bloggers saw both the trial and execution as entirely sectarian – 'showing Saddam's execution like a Shiite revenge' (Sooni, 2006). El Delilâh, a female Iraqi blogger, protested that:

> Saddam Hussein was executed only for the Dujail charges of crimes against humanity, putting in brackets that they were crimes against Shiites. I do not take differences in religions and ethnics seriously, yet I cannot see anything other than Shiite vengeance . . . and absolute disregard to the thousands and thousands of Iraqi Kurds who have suffered genocide. He did deserve to die, yet he did not die for his crimes against Iraqis. The government made sure he only died for his

crimes against Shiites, cancelling all other entities and therefore enforcing the differences upon Iraqis, deepening the gap of sectarianism within. (Él Delilâh, 2007)

Politically, therefore, the execution – both the official version, and then intensified by the mobile phone footage – exacerbated perceptions of sectarianism going to the very heart of the democratically elected government, and further destablizing Iraq.

CONCLUSION

The case studies show that as web-based participatory media became more entrenched within convergence cultures, carefully staged political events could now be more readily subverted. Web-based user-generated content of Saddam Hussein's capture in 2003 came to light, but only a month later, and it did not contradict the official narrative – in fact reinforcing the Coalition's desired projection of Saddam Hussein as captured, disempowered beast, an image designed to quell the growing insurgency. By contrast, the mobile phone footage from 2006 emerged much more quickly – within hours of the depicted event, and massively contradicted the official Iraqi government and US and UK government-sanctioned versions, undoing their projection of a non-sectarian, stately execution and a fearful Saddam Hussein. Furthermore, it was picked up immediately by Arab satellite news broadcasters with no ethical qualms about showing gory footage, thereby conferring on it the authoritative stamp of journalistic credibility, then making its way quickly to western broadcasters (Bakir, 2009). The ability of governmental strategic political communicators to control information in a global media landscape where the media's standards of taste and decency differ according to country and specific media environments (mainstream media versus internet) is, now, demonstrably lacking.

So, can we determine the political intent behind sousveillance and its relationship to democratic social responsibility in these case studies? We should remember that for Mann, the concept and practice of sousveillance was initially situated in the larger context of democratic social responsibility, aiming to disrupt the power relationship of Panopticon surveillance, and aiming for social engagement and dialogue (Mann et al., 2003). As Chapter 1 summarized, there are two main theories of public sphere involvement in democratic dialogue – Habermas' public sphere that offers an idealized, consensus-oriented model of democracy and participation focusing on the ideal of achieving rational consensus on the common good; and more conflict/compromise-oriented approaches as espoused by Mouffe, (2000, 2005), more based on argument, rhetoric and persuasion to reach compromise among passionately held different interpretations of the common good. Despite their differences and associated stances on strategic political communication, both consensus- and conflict/compromise-oriented models stress the need for citizens' adherence to the shared democratic rules of the game, and to participate in processes of dialogue and deliberation (Dahlgren, 2007).

The official footage of Saddam Hussein's capture and execution were pieces of strategic political communication, that, in their surveillance of Saddam Hussein himself, attempted to articulate the Panoptic power of the US-led coalition and then al-Maliki's government – in a push to make Iraqis believe that there would be no return to the old regime and that the newly democratic Iraqi state was robust and would withstand the ongoing insurgency. The question examined here is whether the user-generated photos of Saddam Hussein's capture and mobile phone footage of his execution aimed to disrupt the power relationship of Panoptic surveillance, while aiming for social engagement through dialogue (be it rational, or passionate/strategic).

The user-generated photos of Saddam Hussein's capture appear to be a form of personal sousveillance – the recording of a highly significant moment from a US military member's everyday life in Iraq. However, that it was forwarded to a military personnel and veteran's website to show pride in the achievements of the special forces, and that the person who posted it refused to take the photo down despite DoD requests, suggests that the sousveillers (both the person who took the photograph and the person who posted it online) wished to challenge official narratives and their discourses of power – not concerning Saddam Hussein's capture itself, but concerning the US media's portrayal of soldiers, believing that the soldiers themselves needed greater public recognition. In their intention to challenge what they perceived to be the dominant media narrative about soldiers, and in their desire to generate greater public appreciation of soldier's achievements, this can therefore be seen as a form of hierarchical sousveillance – provocative and socially engaged, oriented towards dialogue and deliberation.

Whether Saddam Hussein's execution sousveiller intended personal sousveillance or hierarchical sousveillance is unclear. Where mobile phone cameras have become more ubiquitous, sets of social conventions and regulations have emerged around what is appropriate and inappropriate use (Castells et al., 2007). Depending on the culture, some examples of personal sousveillance are disturbing – for instance, the 'happy slapping' craze originated by teenagers in South London in 2004. Here, someone attacks an unsuspecting victim while an accomplice records the assault (normally on a camera phone) and often circulates the content immediately to peers via other mobile phones and the internet. Happy slapping is usually characterized by an effort by the attacker to make the assault seem like a comical surprise at the victim's expense, although several incidents have been violent, including rape (Sulaiman, 2005). Happy slapping is seen, perhaps, as a shortcut to fame and notoriety among the people who see the circulated images (Akwagyiram, 2005). It can also be seen as a user-generated take on popular culture, such as Music Television's (*MTV*) popular show, *Jackass* (the first series of which aired in 2000), where people perform various dangerous, crude, ridiculous and self-injuring stunts and pranks.[23] In Iraq, the popular cultural context was much darker. Horrific scenes of live killings and their aftermaths – such as Iraqis kicking and stomping on eviscerated body parts of suicide bombers and their victims – started to circulate in 2004, to become very common, captured on ordinary Iraqis' mobile phone video-clips. *NBC* Middle East correspondent, Richard Engel, describes their impact on himself over the years:

> When they first started to circulate in 2004, I felt that I had to watch them to understand. Now I thought they were an affront to what little humanity I was trying to hang on to. Watching the videos can be like breathing in a smelling salt or a bottle of ammonia. If you do it once, you remember the experience for the rest of your life. If you do it every day, you'll cause brain damage and lose your sense of taste and smell forever. (Engel, 2008, p. 361)

It is in this context that the mobile phone footage of Saddam Hussein's execution could be seen – another, disquieting, side to personal sousveillance. However, there is evidence that suggests that the mobile phone footage is more akin to hierarchical sousveillance, providing evidence to deliberately counter the Iraqi government's official narrative of the execution process. For instance, the security guard who it is believed posted the mobile phone execution footage to the internet was an employee of Iraq's prison directorate under the Justice Ministry, this ministry led by a Sunni, Hashim al-Shibli, a member of the Iraqi National Accord (INA).[24] According to Interior Ministry spokesman Brigadier General Abdul Karim Khalaf, this fact raised suspicions that the video was meant to inflame sectarian tensions (CNN, 2007). Furthermore, the rapid emergence of two more mobile phone clips also suggests political-sectarian, and possibly insurgent agendas behind the execution mobile phone footage, rather than just the human-centred capture fundamental to personal sousveillance. A second, 27-second video clip showing Saddam Hussein's condition after he was hanged – including a close-up of a bloody neck wound – appeared on the internet, according to an *Associated Press* (AP) report on *CBS News*. It was posted on an Iraqi news website that was known to support Saddam Hussein's outlawed Ba'th Party (Abdul-Zahra), suggesting that this footage had been shot and shared for sectarian reasons to further destabilize Iraq by enraging the Sunnis. A third mobile phone video emerged of the dead Saddam Hussein in an ambulance as his body was being transported for burial. The grainy video shows people gawking at, and discussing, the dead dictator's body, ending with Saddam Hussein's face being covered by the body bag, the doors closing, and the ambulance driving away. This video first appeared on a Sunni website, which frames it as more evidence that the Shi'i-led Iraqi government 'did not take into account the preservation of the dignity of the Iraqi president or guard his body after his execution' (The Jawa Report, 2007).

Thus, in a deviation from Mann's intentions for sousveillant technologies to provoke social engagement, dialogue and deliberation, while the capturing and sharing of the mobile phone footage represents a form of political engagement, and appears to be a form of hierarchical sousveillance, the insurgents' intention is an active bid to further destabilize a democratically elected government perceived as illegitimate by a minority, by provoking violence. Using sousveillant videos on the internet to provoke sectarian violence in Iraq was, by this point in time, not uncommon, as explained earlier. For instance, an October 2004 video appeared on the Jaysh Ansar al-Sunna's (Army of the Supporters of the Sunna)[25] website depicting the execution of a Shi'i Muslim, Ala' al-Maliki, who is depicted as reading a statement, similar to a forced confession, whereupon he is beheaded amid screams of 'God is Great' from the kidnappers (al-Marashi, 2004). Thus, hierarchical sousveillance, while challenging official narratives, may do so in ways designed to promote antagonism and death, rather than the deliberation towards rational consensus of Habermas' deliberative democracy (Habermas, 1995 [1981], 1996 [1962]), or towards compromise between passionately held conceptions of the common good of Mouffe's radical democracy of agonistic pluralism (Mouffe, 2000, 2005). Such examples of hierarchical sousveillance are themselves strategic political communications designed to indicate an absence of shared ethico-political democratic principles, threatening the democratic experiment being played out in Iraq.

NOTES

1 Muqtada al-Sadr's uncle and al-Da'wa party leader, Ayatollah Sayyid Mohammed Baqir al-Sadr, one of the most important Shi'a in Iraq in the 1970s, was assassinated by Saddam Hussein in 1980, because al-Da'wa had begun to organize attacks on public symbols of Iraq's regime, alerting it to Shi'i dissent (Tripp, 2007).

2 The politicians were partly chosen to reflect Iraq's ethnic divisions (13 Shi'a, five Sunni Arabs, five Kurds, a Turkoman and an Assyrian Christian); and partly due to long-established links with the US administration (Tripp, 2007).

3 The US killed up to 300 of al-Sadr's followers by August 2004, this ending only when a ceasefire was brokered by al-Sistani (Fawn, 2006).

4 In the early post-Saddam Hussein years, the two major formal Shi'i parties were SCIRI (formed in 1982 under the auspices of the Iranian government) and Islamic Da'wa (known as al-Da'wa, formed in 1958 as an Islamic revolutionary party and existing in exile during Saddam Hussein's regime) (Library of Congress, 2006).

5 Iraq body count's documentary evidence is drawn from crosschecked media reports of violent events leading to civilian death or discovery of bodies, supplemented by hospital, morgue, NGO and official figures (icasualties. org, 2009).

6 The code of ethics can be viewed at http://english.aljazeera.net/aboutus/ 2006/11/2008525185733692771.html (Accessed 23 August 2009).

7 In preparation for the handover of sovereignty on 30 June 2004, the DoD redesignated the Coalition Forces (CJTF-7) as Multi-National Force-Iraq (MNF-I) on 15 May 2004. MNF-I's main function was to provide theatre-strategic and operational-level planning and command for Coalition military forces in Iraq while working closely with the US Embassy and the IIG (Wright & Reese, 2008).

8 While *YouTube* was founded in early 2005, it was the uploading to the site on 16 January 2006 of Jon Stewart's October 2004 appearance on *CNN*'s debate show, Crossfire, that expanded *YouTube*'s audience (Mitchem, 2008).

9 Jamail (2007) offers a different account.

10 BBC.co.uk, *The Telegraph; The Guardian, Times Online, The Sun*, CNN.com, ABCnews.com, Foxnews.com and *NBC News' Meet The Press*.

11 *BBC News 24* footage can be seen at http://www.youtube.com/ watch?v=4ZYF3w_8Tgk&feature=related and BBC.co.uk footage is at http://news.bbc.co.uk/1/hi/3317429.stm (Accessed 14 October 2009).

12 The swords that Saddam Hussein is holding up are meant to represent the defeat of the Persian Sassanian empire by the invading Arab-Muslim army in the battle of Qadisiyya in AD 637, a defeat which paved the way for Iran's Islamicization (Makiya, 1991).

13 This website was started in 1999 to revolutionize the way the 30 million Americans with military affinity stay connected and informed. By 2009 it

'claims to be the largest military and veteran membership organization with 10 million members.

14 For instance, on 14 and 15 December 2003, this phrase was cited in *The Guardian*, Telegraph.co.uk, *The Independent*, *The New York Times*, CBS News. com, CNN.com; Fox News.com, *MSNBC*, and *Voice of America*.

15 This was al-Qaeda in Iraq's attempt to 'wipe away' the Shi'i heresy. The al-Askariyya mosque is associated with the Shi'i saviour, Mohammed al-Mahdi, the Hidden Imam. The Shi'a believe the Mahdi disappeared in the late ninth century, hidden by God, and will eventually return to usher in a new era of justice and salvation. Thus, Samarra was the Shi'i gateway to the divine (Engel, 2008).

16 Eid al-Adha (Feast of the Sacrifice) is celebrated by Muslims around the world at the climax of the Hajj pilgrimage to Mecca.

17 For footage, see BBC (2006).

18 http://www.youtube.com/watch?v=CWlIejw4Z7M [Accessed 1 November 2009].

19 This image was used on 30 December 2006 by *The Sun*, Telegraph, *Daily Mail*, *The Guardian* and *The Times* Online. One tabloid newspaper (*The Sun*) includes a link to the video. One shows him being led to the gallows by his masked executioners (Daily Mail). Only one (*Mirror*) has no visual representation to accompany the article.

20 For further details, see: MacFarquhar and Burns, (n.d.); Tweedie (2007).

21 For instance, see Live leak (n.d.) and Militant Islam Monitor.org (n.d.).

22 The Broadcasting Code recognizes broadcasters and audiences' right to freedom of expression, including the right to receive and impart information and ideas (Ofcom, 2007).

23 *Jackass* has spawned many imitators, such as *MTV*'s Welsh *Dirty Sanchez* (known as *Team Sanchez* in the US) (available at: http://dirtysanchez. yomego.com/ [Accessed 1 November 2009]).

24 The INA started as an Iraqi opposition group in 1990, led by secular Ba'thist, Ayad Allawi, in exile under Saddam Hussein's regime. It attracted dissident Ba'thists and defectors from those social groups favoured in Iraq, mainly Sunni Arabs who predominated in the security services and officer corps.

25 Before late 2003, it was previously known as Ansar al-Islam (The Supporters of Islam), and before that, Jund al-Islam (The Soldiers of Islam). Jund al-Islam emerged in September 2001, made up of Kurdish Islamists with ties to al-Qaeda. Its main base was destroyed by US Special Forces and Kurdish militias during the 2003 Iraq War, scattering its members across Iraq (al-Marashi, 2004).

Chapter 5

SOUSVEILLANCE AND STRATEGIC POLITICAL COMMUNICATION
Developments and Implications

INTRODUCTION

This book has examined a number of instances throughout the first decade of the twenty-first century, some demonstrating supreme control over strategic political communication whereas others show how emergent, sousveillant, web-based participatory media took the political and military authorities by surprise. Exploring how the mainstream adapts to these emergences/emergencies lays the ground for this final chapter. I present my understanding of the extent and limits of control over strategic political communication in the era of web-based participatory media, particularly with regards to our own co-optation as compliantly sousveillant individuals. Here I summarize the key features of sousveillance cultures, then draw out the implications for strategic political communication now and in the future. However, before delving into these aspects, given that the detail of the political and media contexts around the chosen case studies from 2002 to 2006, has been integral to understanding the operation, and import of sousveillance in Web 2.0, this chapter offers updates on key developments since 2007 in both the strategic political and media environments concerning the three main protagonists studied in this book – the US, UK and Iraq.

POLITICAL ENVIRONMENT 2007–2009

People continue to be killed in Iraq regularly, albeit now less frequently. Out of Coalition forces, it is US military deaths that are by far

147

the highest. Coalition military deaths in Iraq totalled 580 in 2003, this almost doubling to 906 in 2004 where it remained roughly constant year on year until a sharp drop in 2008 (322 casualties) and 2009 (137 casualties as of November 2009) (icasualties.org, 2009). Iraqi deaths are too numerous to be counted properly, and the following figures are under-reported. As the previous chapter detailed, insurgents' yearly slaughter of Iraqi civilians reached its highest figure of 27,684 across 2006, this falling slightly to 24,529 across 2007, and more sharply to 9,222 across 2008 and to 3,362 by September 2009 (iraqbodycount, 2009). Since March 2003, nearly 200 journalists and other media workers have been killed in Iraq, which ranks as the most dangerous country in the world for reporters (Callamard, 2009; Ryan & al-Ansary, 2009). The mission of democratizing Iraq has, therefore, generated a heavy price in blood and hardship.

As detailed in Chapter 4, the prolonged and widespread violence and displacement across 2006 highlighted the extent to which the Iraqi state was fictional rather than real (Library of Congress, 2006; Kalyvas & Kocher, 2007). It was within this context that Bush announced 'the Surge' on 10 January 2007, deploying more than 20,000 soldiers and marines into Iraq and extending the tour of 4,000 marines already in the province of al-Anbar (Jabar, 2007; Wright & Reese, 2008).[1] The aim was to work alongside the Iraqi armed forces to break the insurgency's momentum and establish security in Baghdad. The plan aimed to regain public confidence in the central authorities and the US, and to encourage local communities to participate with the authorities in establishing security, thereby helping the Iraqi government to resuscitate national reconciliation (Jabar, 2007; Engel, 2008). For Bush, the overall objective was to establish a, 'unified, democratic federal Iraq that can govern itself, defend itself, and sustain itself, and is an ally in the War on Terror' (Bush, 2007).

Yet, the Surge was not actually implemented on the ground until mid-2007. Preceding the Surge, and arguably more important, was the al-Anbar Awakening, followed by others. As noted in Chapter 3, by September 2006, al-Anbar was under total insurgent control as local Sunni insurgents strategically allied themselves with foreign Sunni al-Qaeda fighters against what was perceived as US occupation. Iraqi Sunnis provided local knowledge, logistics, and up to 95 per cent of personnel, while experienced foreign al-Qaeda fighters provided training, expertise and financing. Yet, as early as 2005, some Sunni tribes in al-Anbar became disenchanted with al-Qaeda's control of traditionally tribal money-making activities, al-Qaeda's violent activities against tribal leaders that had forced them to cede control, and al-Qaeda's declaration on 15 October 2006 that al-Anbar now comprised the Islamic State of Iraq (McCary, 2009). Consequently, the 'Awakening' started as coalitions between tribal *sheikhs* uniting to maintain security, and paid directly by the US military, becoming an ad-hoc armed force numbering nearly 100,000 by 2008, now called the Sons of Iraq (SOI) (Rubin & Cave, 2007; McCary, 2009). Indeed, exploiting tribal hierarchies and rivalries in Iraq had been used as a means of maintaining control as far back as the nineteenth century Ottoman state, and utilized under Saddam Hussein's regime which recognized tribal *sheikhs'* authority to regulate their tribes' affairs, granting patronage to those who cooperated, withholding it from those who did not, and withdrawing it from those who appeared too powerful (Makiya, 1998; Nakash, 2006; Tripp, 2007). The Ba'th regime thus set the stage for the emergence of tribalism as a potent force following the regime's collapse (Nakash, 2006). Indeed, SOI became instrumental in reversing the spiral of violence in Sunni areas as they were able to provide that most vital and difficult aspect of counterinsurgency – identifying insurgents (McCary, 2009; Perry et al., 2009). This change in US strategy – a combination of the Surge and courting and financing tribal *sheikhs* – eventually halted Iraq's descent into civil war (Department of Defense, 2007; McCary, 2009; Perry et al., 2009).

The UN's mandate for an American military presence in Iraq expired at the end of 2008. Although, by 2008, the Iraqi Security Forces (ISF) were still not fully capable (Wright & Reese, 2008), on 17 November 2008, an Agreement was signed between the US and Iraq on the *Withdrawal of United States Forces from Iraq and the Organization of Their Activities During Their Temporary Presence in Iraq*, stipulating that all US military forces will be withdrawn from Iraq by the end of December 2011. During this time, the US mission in Iraq would change from combat operations to advising and assisting the ISF (Perry et al., 2009). Similarly, in December 2008, in a joint statement with Iraqi Prime Minister, Nouri al-Maliki, UK Prime Minister, Gordon Brown (who had taken over leadership of the Labour Party from Tony Blair on June 2007), announced that the 4,100 UK troops serving in Basra would leave Iraq by the end of July 2009, as, indeed, they did (BBC, 2008a). Despite this deliverance of ultimate sovereignty back to Iraq, national unity remains threatened by the fact that the constituent elements of Iraq's federal state have different visions. The Kurdistan Regional Government (KRG) aspires for greater autonomy and territory. The Shi'a want to consolidate majority power over Iraq's national government, security forces and oil revenues.

The Sunnis want to dilute Shi'i national power and govern in predominantly Sunni provinces. Meanwhile, violent extremists like al-Qaeda in Iraq have an undiminished appetite for violence there, but lack the physical means, popular support and (for the moment) foreign backing to reignite large-scale violence. Furthermore, one of its principal causes, source of recruitment and fund-raising – the US occupation – is ending; and its 'parent' al-Qaeda has now stressed jihad in Afghanistan, Pakistan and Yemen rather than in Iraq (Acharya & Quiggen, 2009; Perry et al., 2009). Nonetheless, as troops withdrew, across summer and autumn 2009 Iraq was subjected regularly to suicide bombs from foreign jihadists from its still porous borders with Syria (BBC, 2009a; Perry et al., 2009; Reuters, 2009a).

Yet, 2009 seemed to offer new hope. Ending the Bush era, in November 2008 Barack Obama was elected US President on the slogans 'Yes we can' (McCormick, 2008) and 'Change we can believe in' (Obama, 2008) – a reference to his promise to change things for the better for ordinary people suffering from poverty and lack of opportunity. Acutely aware of the centrality of the Middle East and the importance of key symbolic acts, Obama's first television interview as US President was granted to *al-Arabiya* on 26 January 2009 – seen in the US as a prominent voice of moderation in the Middle East (MacLeod, 2009).[2] This was an unprecedented reach-out to the Muslim world as Obama stressed that the US was 'ready to initiate a new partnership based on mutual respect and mutual interest', and wanted 'to listen, set aside some of the preconceptions that have existed and have built up over the last several years' (The Huffington Post, 2009). With this, the Bush administration's vision – that the removal of Saddam Hussein might, domino-theory style, transform Iraq into a democratic example for other Arab nations to follow – finally dissipated.

Also offering hope, along with a change in US president, Iraq's provincial elections on 31 January 2009 were peaceful and largely perceived to be fair, with strong turnout among Sunni Muslims (who had boycotted the 2005 election) (BBC, 2009c; Brooks, 2009). This first nationwide vote in four years was seen as a test of stability before a general election due in March 2010 (BBC, 2010). Furthermore, a February 2009 survey for the *BBC, ABC News* and Japanese broadcaster *NHK* suggests that the political system favoured by most Iraqis across all major ethnicities is a democracy (64 per cent in February 2009 compared to 49 per cent in 2004) as opposed to a government headed by one person for life (14 per cent supported this in February 2009, down from 28 per cent support in 2004) or an Islamic state

(19 per cent supported this in February 2009, down slightly from 21 per cent support in 2004). It also suggests that Iraqis are more hopeful about the future. Compared to a poll taken in March 2008, 65 per cent say their lives are going very or quite well (up 11 per cent), and there is a 16 per cent increase – to 30 per cent – of those who think things will be much better in Iraq in a year's time. (However, this is a decrease from 70 per cent in 2004 who said their lives were going well or quite well, and 41 per cent in 2005 who thought things would be better in Iraq in a year's time.) The poll indicates that sectarian and terrorist violence and insecurity are no longer the main concerns of most Iraqis (although they remain worried about civil war, ethnic or religious tensions and weak government with bad leaders) and that they are increasingly pre-occupied with more conventional worries such as the economy, inflation, corruption and unemployment. Indeed, standards of living are still lower than they were before the 2003 invasion and pre-war oil production peak levels were higher than in 2007 (United Nations Development Program, 2009). The *BBC/ABC/*NHK poll further notes that Iraqis remain unhappy about the role foreign powers play in their country, particularly Iran, the US and UK. There were mixed views about whether the 2003 invasion was right, with 42 per cent feeling it was right but 56 per cent feeling that it was wrong. This compares relatively poorly to 49 per cent feeling it was right but 39 per cent that it was wrong in 2004 (BBC, 2009b). These results suggest that, with time, although more Iraqis became in favour of democracy, more also felt that the price paid for democracy was too high.

Media Environment 2007–2009

The media's function in facilitating the democratic process is well-documented (see Chapter 1). In transitional states, if the media begins to function effectively, it consolidates statehood and a broader sense of national identity (Anderson 1983) and socializes mass and elite audiences to democracy's rules (Gunther & Mughan 2000). The opinion poll results detailed in the previous section suggest that these socialization processes were at work in Iraq. However, as this book has detailed, the installation of democracy in Iraq was a long, structural process, with the establishment of a media system that pertains to be free a part of the process, but not the determining factor. Prime Minister Nouri al-Maliki is seen as generally supportive of a free media, as enshrined in Iraq's Constitution – that, as Chapter 4 notes, only vaguely defines freedom of expression and freedom of the press and allows these to be restricted on grounds of public order and morality. As of 2009, Iraqis had a choice of between some 200 print outlets, 60 radio stations and 30 TV channels in Arabic, Turkmen, Syriac and two Kurdish dialects. Although investigative reporting is still in its infancy, journalists are able to write articles against key state institutions – an unusual state of affairs in the Middle East. However, journalists complain that more progressive media laws are needed, and, reflecting the traits of Iraq's new democratic environment, most media outlets remain dominated by powerful sectarian and party patrons who set the editorial tone and decide what to cover. Journalistic harassment, bribery and self-censorship are rife, particularly in semi-autonomous Kurdistan, where libel is a criminal offence. As the March 2010 Iraqi elections loomed, and given critical coverage by non-state media outlets of the devastating bomb attacks on government ministries across summer and autumn 2009 which seriously eroded the government's security credentials (and therefore its chances of re-election), Iraq's communications minister, Faruq Abd al-Qadir, tightened control over Iraq's media. Measures included the introduction of a £3,000 licence fee for all broadcast media outlets; ordering staff of the 58 media and television stations operating in Iraq to apply for work permits; ordering all government ministers and departments to deny governmental access to anti-administration channels such as *al-Sharqiya* satellite channel; warning ISPs and internet cafes they would block access to offensive websites; and appearing to authorize the ISF to beat up journalists covering routine security stories. In the mean time, embracing advertising as an alternative to party funding has been hindered by the poor state of Iraq's economy outside the oil sector. As such, the media have yet to become commercially sustainable enterprises let alone watchdogs keeping government under scrutiny (BBC, 2009b; Callamard, 2009; Chulov, 2009; Ryan & al-Ansary, 2009).

Strategic political communication about, and in, Iraq continues unabated. For instance, Saudi-based *al-Arabiya* was used by the Saudi government to provide a platform for Saudi clerics, often to Iraq's dismay, who accused it of inflaming sectarianism. Yet, more recently, Saudi TV has given airtime to salafi clerics to issue *fatwas* banning jihad in Iraq to dampen sectarianism (Perry et al., 2009). That Saudi trans-national media can be both instruments of violent escalation and venues for reconciliation represents a loss of control over Iraq's media environment by Iraqi, US and UK governments. As such, the US continues to devote resources to manipulating the media environment and content in Iraq to engage various audiences globally, and support Iraq's government (Pincus, 2009). Meanwhile, in the US, mainstream media's portrayal of the success of the Surge, together with the economic crisis that engulfed the US in 2008, meant that Iraq dropped off mainstream news' and the public's agenda (Project for Excellence in Journalism, 2008; Castells, 2009). In the UK, across 2007–2009, representing a failure of the government's strategic political communication efforts, the public remained critical of the Iraq enterprise. An Ipsos-Mori poll (11–13 May 2007) showed that the vast majority disapproved of the way Bush and Blair were handling the current situation in Iraq, with 85 per cent and 77 per cent disapproval respectively (Ipsos MORI, 2007). An ICM poll for the *Sunday Telegraph* (12–13 March 2008) found that 65 per cent of respondents felt that five years on, invading Iraq was the wrong thing to have done, with 67 per cent believing that it was unlikely that democracy would be fully established in Iraq in the foreseeable future (ICM, 2008). As Chapter 2 noted, a survey, conducted by ComRes in March 2009, found 72 per cent of those questioned believed there should be an official inquiry into the UK's role in the invasion of Iraq (BBC Radio 5 Live, 2009).

Resistance to strategic political communication also continues in staged media events that play to the aesthetics and flow of information within converged media. An example is the shoe-throwing incident on 14 December 2008 by Iraqi journalist, Muntadar al-Zaidi, working for private, Iraqi-owned TV station, *al-Baghdadiya*. At a press conference in Baghdad held by the outgoing President Bush,[3] al-Zaidi shouted insults in Arabic at Bush ('This is a farewell kiss, you dog;' 'This is from the widows, the orphans and those who were killed in Iraq') and threw each of his shoes at Bush's head in quick succession, causing Bush to duck to avoid them. Al-Zaidi deliberately bought Iraqi-made shoes, which were dark brown with laces, suggesting that he had pre-planned his symbolic act: hitting someone with your shoe soles is deeply insulting in the Middle East. Moments after al-Zaidi was roughly arrested,[4] *al-Baghdadiya* TV suspended normal programming to play messages of support, saying that al-Zaidi should be freed because he had been exercising freedom of expression – something that the Americans had promised to Iraqis on ousting Saddam Hussein. Arabic TV stations repeatedly showed footage of the incident, which was also front-page news in many newspapers, generating days of rallies in support of al-Zaidi across the Middle East (Abdul-Zahra, 2008; AFP, 2008a, 2008b; BBC 2008b, 2008c). This symbolic shoe-throwing designed to attract global attention was quickly available globally, online, on US and UK mainstream media's websites. Within two days of the incident, there were over 5,000 versions on *YouTube*, totalling over 8 million views, acquiring 11 of the top 20 most-watched videos spot, with people uploading videos of the incident to *YouTube* at an average rate of 209 per hour (The Economic Times, 2008).

This example illustrates that convergence continues, unabated, as indicated in Chapter 1. Notably, as audiences continued to move online, as of 2007, major broadcasting organizations such as the *BBC*, *CNN* and Australia's *ABC* re-organized to allow user-generated content greater prominence in their news gathering, as did Middle Eastern media organizations (al-Harthi, 2008; Horrocks, 2008; Knight, 2008; Mitchem, 2008). In the US online news sector, much activity in 2007 was about partnerships: for instance, ABCNews.com partnered with *Facebook*, and CBSNews.com teamed up with *Digg*,[5] training multimedia reporters and adopting new technologies like 'crowd sourcing' to get audiences involved in designing coverage before the fact and reacting to it afterward (Project for Excellence in Journalism, 2008). Web 2.0, and its ease of producing, commenting upon and sharing content enabled media organizations with internet presence to track what stories, and presentational styles work with audiences (Whitwell, 2008), allowing media producers to improve editorial quality and restructure editorial policy according to audience feedback. This increases income for the media organization, for instance, through SMS, mobile channels and web advertising, capitalizing on the fact that by 2009, over a quarter of the world's population (or 1.9 billion people) had access to a computer at home (International Telecommunication Union, 2009). Once-new Web 2.0 media forms, like blogging, now run alongside mainstream media, sometimes in competition, and sometimes as co-opted form, with journalists perceiving blogging as a reporters' tool (Singer, 2005; Lowrey & Mackay, 2008; Marshall & Project for Excellence in Journalism, 2008). Newer forms of web-based participatory media appear to be gaining acceptance as part of mainstream media – as in micro-blogging that emerged in 2006 through social networking sites such as *Twitter*, enabling people to publish short messages ('tweets') through the internet and mobile phones. Hashtags – a human convention that facilitates real-time search on shared events – encourages real-time response, allowing retweeted 'information cascades' to spread breaking news rapidly across *Twitter* (O'Reilly & Battelle, 2009, p. 9). For instance, during the Mumbai terrorist attacks of November 2008, an interplay emerged between *Twitter* and mainstream media in India, where, for the first time, both were listening to each other, and mainstream media was quoting *Twitter* as a source (Townend, 2008).

Feeding convergence, in terms of media flows, the use of sousveillant technologies continues to proliferate exponentially in the hands of the masses. In early 2007, 2.2 billion people had mobile phones, and by September 2009, this stood at over four billion (International Telecommunication Union, 2009). By 2007, most countries in Western Europe had 3G mobile phone telephony networks in operation (3G being digital devices with high-speed broadband capacity) and North America was in the early stages of introducing 3G (Castells et al., 2007, p. 11).[6] In the middle of 2007, *Flickr* contained about 600 million images – a figure that had doubled by 2008 (Manovich, 2008). In February 2007 more than 250 sites offered online video (Holahan, 2007; Richard, 2008), although *YouTube* remains the major source (Mitchem, 2008). Globally, Web 2.0 sites – especially social networking sites – remain popular. As of September 2009, the global top 20 websites included 6 social networking sites (*Facebook, YouTube, Myspace, Twitter, RapidShare* and *QQ.com* (a Chinese instant messenger portal)) and two weblog publishers (*Blogger, Word Press*) (alexa.com, 2009).[7] Since 2005 there has been a clear trajectory towards constant capture and broadcasting of one's everyday life as evidenced by the likes of *YouTube* (2005–) and *Yahoo!Live* personal broadcasting service (2008–) (Manovich, 2008).

In the Middle East, the biggest expression of convergence is the combination of satellite television (which continues to proliferate) and information flows from mobile phones. By 2006 there were 263 free-to-air satellite television channels targeting the Arab world, with pay-per-view providers bringing the total close to 400, including 23 satellite channels devoted to news and 19 that broadcast only religious programmes (Maluf, 2007). Many Arab television channels comprise six-hour slots – this allowing all sorts of media content – including actualité produced by students with shaky hand-held cameras, and some channels totally dedicated to viewers' SMS messages (Kraidy, 2006). The Middle East saw mobile phone usage growing rapidly across the first few years of the twenty-first century. Mobile phone penetration was estimated at 4 per cent in 2000, 12 per cent in 2003, and 28 per cent by 2005, although with huge regional variations (United Nations Development Program, 2005, 2009). By 2007, the Middle East was transitioning from 2G (digital mobile phones) to 3G (Castells et al., 2007), and by 2008, the mobile markets of Israel, Bahrain, Qatar and the United Arab Emirates (UAE) appeared to be saturated (Lewis et al., 2008). As Chapter 1 indicated, across 2000–2008, the growth in internet users globally has been greatest in the Middle East, albeit from low levels. Whereas in 2000 there were only 3, 284,800 internet users in the Middle East (representing about 3 per cent of the Arab population), by 2008 there were 45, 861,346 – a penetration rate of 23 per cent, again with big regional variations (Internet World Stats, 2009).

Iraq largely remains outside of this push towards sousveillant technologies, remaining 'an analog society' by 2009 (Levy, 2009, p. 1). While many Iraqis have mobile phones – 62 per cent in 2009, up from almost zero in 2003 – coverage is patchy (Levy, 2009). Iraq lacks a coherent high-speed fibre-optic cable network with few homes having broadband or personal computers. In 2008 there were only 275,000 internet users in Iraq, representing a 1 per cent penetration rate (Internet World Stats, 2009). Yet, the will to engage is there, if the infrastructure can be provided. Out of the minority who are digitally active online, Iraqis have embraced blogging as a way of sharing their life in a post-Saddam Hussein world. The website *al-bab* ('the door') – dedicated to linking to the most interesting of websites written in English about the Middle East – links to 21 from Iraq (al-bab, 2009). While banned under Saddam Hussein's regime, mobile phones became so entrenched in Iraqis' daily lives by 2006 that, according to study by Zawya (an online information service) over 80 per cent of respondents said their phones had become a necessity, while 43 per cent described them as a best friend: note that their prime use in this period was to check, daily, on the safety of loved ones in the ongoing insurgency (Economist Intelligence Unit, 2006). It is possible that sousveillant mobile technologies, combined with global convergence cultures, may provide the much-needed push to further expand freedom of opinion and expression, as well as freedom of information, and that these will be used by the majority of Iraqis in the furthering of democracy, rather than being utilized mainly by insurgents for antagonistic ends (as detailed in Chapter 4).

TOWARDS SOUSVEILLANCE CULTURES

Undoubtedly, the urge and practice of dissent has always been with us, and people exploit the participatory media technologies at hand to mark and spread their dissent. However, the rise of web-based participatory media and sousveillance cultures have made it easier for many more to record and spread this dissent globally, unimpeded by traditional media's commercial distribution restrictions such as pre-defined circulation runs or paid-for airtime, or the need for expert knowledge in media production. Mann has long maintained that the 'informal nature of sousveillance, with its tendency to distribute record-ings widely, will often expose inappropriate use to scrutiny, whereas the secret nature of surveillance will tend to prevent misuse from com-ing to light [Mann, 1995]' (Mann, 2005, p. 641). Indeed, by the end of 2006, the internet was awash with sousveillant civilian footage – for instance of police abuse in Malaysia, union-busting in Zimbabwe, and women posting photos of men who had harassed them (Hoffman, 2006b).[8] By 2009, G20 protesters in London openly collected sousveil-lant footage of the police presence to deter police officers from exces-sive use of force and to provide evidence for legal action against the police where excessive force was used. Meanwhile, pilot tests by police in 2006–2007 of 'body worn video devices' – typically small cameras attached to the head – were pronounced a success by the Home Office in that they led to a drop in complaints against the police, vindicating the police's own versions of events (Rohrer, 2009). Just as the Panopti-con operates through potential or implied surveillance, so sousveil-lance might also operate through the credible threat of its existence. As the ubiquity and awareness of sousveillance widens, it is this that may most empower citizens – by making the state and indeed, all stra-tegic political communicators, realize that their actions may, them-selves, be monitored and exposed at any time. The permanent potential for sousveillance from so many (as opposed to more formalized exposés at the hands of investigative reporters, a small media elite) raises the likelihood that power abuses will be captured on record which can then be used to hold power-abusers and manipulators to account, pro-viding of course, that there is a functioning legal system and/or public sphere (with mechanisms in place to translate popular demands and moral outrage into real-world change).

Some of the key features of sousveillant cultures as realized in web-based.participatory media and revealed in the case studies examined in this book are issues of anonymity; the blurring of boundaries between personal and hierarchical sousveillance and its implications for resistance and social change; and the interplay between semi-permanence and instantaneity. These are discussed below.

Anonymity

Given their ease of circulation and recirculation, web-based participa-tory media are much more *noticeable* than other forms of participatory media, foregrounding a range of cultural and political activity that would otherwise remain hidden from the masses and their governmental institutions (Jenkins, 2006a). This *lack of secrecy* is, perhaps, a key difference to previous resistance-based participatory media forms and social practices (Scott, 1990). As Fandy (1999, p. 127) observes at the birth of Web 2.0, with reference to Saudi resistance-based new media forms:

> sites of resistance are no longer the secret nooks and crannies within Saudi society but internet nodes, specific Web sites, and offices outside the country that transmit information to sympathizers inside. Neither the hidden transcripts nor the social sites of resistance conform to earlier formulations concerning resistance literature. The transcript of resistance, especially on the World Wide Web, is hidden only to those who choose not to read it or who have no access to the language.

Given this lack of secrecy, the anonymity of the sousveillers is of prime importance if hierarchical (politically or legally motivated) sousveillance is to proliferate. In the case of Salam Pax, the Baghdad Blogger, there was much debate about his identity, linked to authenticity claims, as discussed in Chapter 2. Yet anonymity was important because Salam Pax's sousveillant online activities during Saddam Hussein's regime were risky. As he later noted, when *Reuters* first mentioned his blog and URL, he e-mailed a fellow blogger, the *Legendary Monkey*, to arrange to give her his password if his site got blocked, so that she could erase all his archives:

> Things got worse when the Reuters article got picked up by other news outlets. My brother saw my agitation and I had to tell him. He thought I was a fool to endanger the family, which was true. I was kicking myself in the butt for the next couple of days. Then Blogger did get blocked. This was the end. My brother and I kept checking on Blogger.com every couple of hours. But the 'access denied' page still did not come up. I signed in, deleted the archives and stopped blogging for a couple of days. (Pax, 2003b)

More than 200,000 people went missing under Saddam Hussein's regime, many for far lesser crimes than openly criticizing the regime as Salam Pax did (McCarthy, 2003b). However, he put faith in his anonymity and the Iraqi authorities' ignorance of how to control blogging given its relative recency as a social practice (Zalewski, 2003).

In the case of Abu Ghraib, the whistle-blower, Joe Darby, was promised anonymity on handing in the CD of the photographs to CID. This was paramount as his whistle-blowing involved turning on his colleagues, some of whom he had known since high school, while the Army's credo is that soldiers protect each other. It took about five weeks before the accused were removed from Darby's base, and even then he feared retribution from other soldiers as he remained in his unit thereafter (CID Report and Statements, 2004; Bryan, 2007). Also problematic was retribution against his family in the US from those who would view his actions as putting American soldiers in prison over Iraqis. Yet, Darby's anonymity was blown spectacularly four months after handing in the CDs. He was sitting in a crowded canteen in Camp Anaconda in Iraq with hundreds of soldiers, when Secretary of Defence, Donald Rumsfeld, came on American television in a press conference that was the live feed from the Congressional hearings on Abu Ghraib, to thank Joe Darby by name for handing in the photographs (Bryan, 2007; Cockburn, 2007; Sharrock, 2008). Hersh had already named Darby in his investigative reports (Hersh, 2004c), but as Darby noted in an interview in 2008, 'Who reads the damn New Yorker?' (Sharrock, 2008, p. 7). Darby's interpretation of this naming is that Rumsfeld deliberately targeted him, and we must not forget that the Abu Ghraib 'abuse' was eventually revealed to be part of a systematic policy of torture sanctioned by Rumsfeld. Darby points out that while he subsequently received a letter from Rumsfeld:

> which said he had no malicious intent, he was only doing it to praise me and he had no idea about my anonymity . . . I really find it hard to believe that the secretary of defence of the United States has no idea about the star witness for a criminal case being anonymous. (Bryan, 2007)

After Rumsfeld blew Darby's cover, Darby was bundled out of Iraq quickly, living under armed protection for the first six months, subsequently leaving the army and testifying at the trials of some of those accused of abuse (Bryan, 2007).

If hierarchical sousveillance in circumstances like Abu Ghraib is to be encouraged, anonymity must be ensured. As Lowenthal (2008) observes, repressive governments such as Thailand, Burma and Nepal have a tendency to block internet communications, particularly video, during times of social unrest, making activists heavily reliant on commercial spaces. Yet, there are many examples of the large commercial players such as *Google* and *Yahoo* cooperating directly with repressive governmental authorities to reveal the identity of dissidents. This means that there is a real need for spaces online that are willing to protect users' anonymity and keep their subversive content online despite political or corporate pressure (Lowenthal, 2008). With this sort of situation in mind, whistle-blowing websites have been set up that guarantee anonymity, such as *Wiki-leaks*, launched in December 2006, comprising a wiki mechanism

that allows sharing of information with an internationally dispersed investigative journalism team in safety.[9] More such sites are needed.

Of course, anonymity is only necessary for hierarchical sousveillance, and tends not to be a necessary feature of personal sousveillance, the ramifications of which are explored in the final section of
this chapter.

Blurred Boundaries, Resistance and Social Change

In Mann's original conception, sousveillance had an emancipatory
political thrust, with hierarchical sousveillance a conscious act of resistance to surveillance. Yet, most of the sousveillant acts examined in this
book do not appear to have been motivated primarily by hierarchical
sousveillance, only mutating into this later. While Salam Pax's blog
drifted towards hierarchical sousveillance as he perceived the need to
educate the world regarding what was really happening in Baghdad, it
was primarily and originally motivated as personal sousveillance – the
desire to keep up communication with his friend, Raed, living in
another country. The user-generated photos of Saddam Hussein's capture were initially a form of personal sousveillance – the recording of a
highly significant moment from a US military member's everyday life –
which mutated into hierarchical sousveillance as it was posted to the
military users' website in the hope of generating greater public recognition of soldiers' deeds. The Abu Ghraib photos appear to be personal
sousveillance – at least in their sharing, and perhaps also in their
capture – mutating into hierarchical sousveillance as Darby's conscience got the better of him. The military's spoof music video was pure
personal sousveillance. It would appear, therefore, that in Web 2.0,
most people's goal is not just, or not even, to resist or come to terms
with the power yielded by traditional surveillance, but rather to participate in the capture and sharing of details – mundane and special – of
one's daily life. Indeed, out of all the acts of sousveillance examined
here, it is the various mobile phone video clips of Saddam Hussein's
execution that appear to be closest to intending hierarchical sousveillance from their inception (although again, personal sousveillance
motives cannot be ruled out). The mobile phone footage provided
evidence to deliberately counter the Iraqi government's, and US and
UK government-endorsed, official surveillance and framing of the
execution process. However, rather than having the emancipatory political thrust envisaged by Mann's conceptualization of hierarchical

sousveillance, its political thrust was one of antagonism, destabilizing the Iraqi government by further provoking sectarian violence.

At first glance, then, the optimism for progressive social change that Mann foresaw in the development of his sousveillance technologies appears to be in trouble. However, that most of these examples of personal sousveillance (except the spoof music video) mutated into acts of hierarchical sousveillance shows that sousveillant content made readily available in Web 2.0 has a potent after-life, and the potential to fuel social change. Again, the nature of the social change generated is unpredictable, and dependent on the nature of the sousveillant content, the context of its subsequent sharing, and, of course, the strength of the traditions of deliberation for democratic purposes. At the negative end of the scale, the mobile phone footage of Saddam Hussein's execution spread virally and rapidly across the web to enter mainstream Arab, UK and US television news, where it outraged Sunni public opinion across the Middle East, fuelling further the insurgency within Iraq, as the sousveillers intended. More ambivalently, the sousveillant Abu Ghraib photos were taken up by Arab, UK and US mainstream news, sparking a wide range of responses – from further insurgency in Iraq

Figure 5.1. Lynndie England 2:14 a.m., Nov. 8, 2003. SPC ENGLAND points to the penis of one of the detainees. SOLDIER(S): SPC ENGLAND (caption information taken directly from CID materials). This pose spawned the craze 'doing a Lynndie'. *Source:* http://www.salon.com/news/abu_ghraib/2006/03/14/chapter_6/27.html

through to eventual, prolonged political introspection within the US on the practice and morality of torture. Of course, these were not the only responses. In such cases, where the sousveillant images are extreme and shocking, and where they reside online as part of a 'rewind and replay' culture (McStay, 2007, p. 40), indulging a 'voyeuristic fascination with the grotesque' (p. 45), they could just as easily cultivate sublime aestheticization (Chouliaraki, 2006b); compassion fatigue – similar to that of journalists experiencing secondary traumatic stress from repeated exposure to their reported trauma victims (Dworznik, 2006); or, indeed, cultural reappropriation – as in 'doing a Lynndie' (Bad Gas, n.d.; Andén-Papadopoulos, 2009, p. 22). 'Doing a Lynndie' is the internet craze spawned by the Abu Ghraib photograph of Lynndie England pointing with her left hand (in the shape of a gun) to the genitalia of a blind-folded Iraqi prisoner in a line-up of naked Iraqi prisoners, her right hand in the thumbs-up position, a cigarette dangling from her smiling mouth. 'Doing a Lynddie' is to mimic this gesture of empowerment and emasculation, putting the person being 'Lynddied' into a humiliating position without knowing it, and secretly capturing it on camera (Andén-Papadopoulos, 2008). At the more positive end of the scale of social change, Salam Pax's personal sousveillance brought better understanding to civilians outside Iraq of the human suffering delivered by war, as strangers came to care about Salam Pax's fate while realizing that their own country's news broadcasts generated no such understanding and seemed detached from reality. In this instance, due to Salam Pax's mobilization of shared cultural frames of reference (generating identification) and authenticity (generating trust), isolated, disparate individuals were converted into a global macro-public, engaged in often-passionate dialogue with each other, imbued with a sense of social responsibility and sensitized to political abuses of power and others' geographically distant suffering.

Semi-Permanence and Instantaneity

Websites do not last forever. They may be taken down, links may become out-dated, or they may be blocked. Despite this, Web 2.0 provides what could be described as a semi-permanent, and easily accessible, database of multiple discourses. As Manovich (2008, p. 38) says: 'What before was ephemeral, transient, unmappable, and invisible become permanent, mappable, and viewable. Social media platforms give users unlimited space for storage and plenty of tools to organize, promote, and broadcast their thoughts, opinions, behaviour, and media to others.' Writing as early as 1994, Castells described the timeless time of the database, contrasting it with the temporality of TV. Timeless time is: 'a mixing of tenses to create a forever universe' (Castells, 1996, p. 433). Although these authors, in their rhetorical flourishes, ignore real constraints to ubiquitous social archiving (for instance, video file sizes are big and users must pay for large file storage, therefore acting as a disincentive to ubiquitous sousveillance online), they nonetheless capture some broad features of web-based participatory media. Given that the web can be used and searched in the manner of a database to find examples of sousveillance, the *longevity* of sousveillant footage is perhaps what gives sousveillance its agenda-building power, allowing journalists, citizens, activists, insurgents, researchers and strategic communicators the opportunity to discover and partially relive the discourse surrounding points of past significance, as well as reflecting on, and marshalling, their significance. The *recirculation* of sousveillant footage – particularly by mainstream media, ever-hungry for new content in a media environment of convergence and expanding capacity (multiple TV channels, newspapers with extensive print-based and web-based supplements, and news that runs 24/7) are also important features. Such agenda-building powers are seen as so important that some websites – for instance, thememoryhole.org[10] (2002–) and thesmoking-gun.com[11] (1997–) – dedicate themselves to providing permanent pegs in the ephemeral news ether so that important documents and statements (such as the exact wording of a political leader's remarks) will not be lost from our useful memory (Graves, 2007). More such sites are needed.

This semi-permanent archive allows information to be collected from a vast range of sources, with many Web 2.0 offerings allowing users to capture the sense of human agency, struggle, intensity and emotion that surround significant moments from the past. Web 2.0 therefore generates a sense of co-presence with the past. As Garcia (2008, p. 294) suggests:

> once archived on the net (YouTube) the temporalities of database and video converge to create a new set of temporal conditions and possibilities. Unlike film, even archived video looks 'live.' Whatever the content, the appearance of video, its core aesthetic, is never nostalgic. Try running the camcorder footage from nearly two decades ago, of the Police attacks on Rodney King.

Although mobile phone footage tends to be of low quality resolution and therefore may well, as a media form, take on historical qualities in the future (like black and white or sepia footage today), for the moment the visceral immediacy of the mobile phone footage of Saddam Hussein's execution, and image after demeaning image from Abu Ghraib, retain their 'live' look. So, while sousveillance may (or may not) instantly make mainstream news in spectacular displays – such as Abu Ghraib and Saddam Hussein's execution – the fact that it exists on the web, is searchable in the future, and transports us back to lived past moments – is just as important.

As well as its longevity, another important feature of sousveillance in Web 2.0 is its capacity for *instantaneity* and the importance this achieves in convergence cultures – as evidenced by the mobile phone footage of Saddam Hussein's execution. This capacity and appetite for instanta-neity feeds off an age-old journalistic drive to be first with the news – a push that has been intensified by the widespread arrival of 24/7 news in the 1990s (Virilio, 2002 [1991]; Lewis et al., 2004), and the converged newsroom of the 2000s (Bivens, 2008).

The characteristics of instantaneity and semi-permanence, married with the easy drift of personal sousveillance into hierarchical sousveil-lance, are the features of sousveillance cultures that are most feared by some strategic political communicators, and most exploited by others.

IMPLICATIONS FOR STRATEGIC POLITICAL COMMUNICATION
Long-Term Agenda-building

Just as the discourse of fear activated by 9/11 helped turn US and UK citizens into compliantly surveilled, risk-averse subjects (as noted in Chapter 1), so there were power effects from the discourses set up by the various acts of strategic political communication examined in this book. Both the discourse of *humanized patriotism* generated by embeds' coverage of Iraq's invasion, and the discourse of *isolated abuse* generated by the US administration's framing of Abu Ghraib, served to divert US citizens (in particular) from deliberating the horrors, morality and pol-icy driving the War in Iraq and the use of torture in the War on Terror for several years. The discourse of *disempowerment of Saddam Hussein's regime* propagated by the official footage of his capture and execution was designed to divert US, UK and Iraqi citizens from the deadly power of Iraq's insurgency and the fragility of Iraq's nascent democratic insti-tutions and nation-building project. That within all of these discourses, attention was focused on individuals (brave soldiers, abusive soldiers and Saddam Hussein) arguably activated powerful frames of identifica-tion and revulsion, while distracting from wider power structures and questions of policy. Indeed, it is the successful governmental control over US mainstream media that prompted Scott McClellan, PR advisor for George Bush from 2003 to 2006, to describe journalists as 'complicit enablers' (McClellan, 2008, p. 70). However, competing with these discourses offered by mainstream journalism was a range of alternative discourses generated by sousveillance.

In the era of web-based participatory media and convergence cultures, non-governmental and non-state actors, with their own virtual communities and networks that cut across national borders, use what I shall term the *sousveillant assemblage* to wield soft power. The *sousveillant assemblage* comprises the surveillant assemblage, but data-fattened by the proliferation of web-based participatory media and personal sousveillance that we willingly provide online. For instance, with reference to the ongoing terrorist threat, Major General Tony Cucolo, Chief of US Army Public Affairs (2008–), expressed concerns that:

> In the perpetually profit-driven and increasingly user-generated competitive 24-hour news cycle, where the attitude of some journalists may be 'I'd rather be first than right', the chances are that extremist propaganda will advance from print to web or from web to print, only to be repeated in thousands of blogs and other venues, thus giving falsehood a sense of widespread veracity and thereby influencing whole populations. (Cucolo, 2008, pp. 85–86)

Of course, it is not just journalistic inaccuracies that fuel the circulation of extremist propaganda and insurgency, but authentic, truthful, sousveillant web-based participatory media content like the Abu Ghraib photographs. Former Navy General Counsel Alberto Mora testified to the Senate Armed Services Committee in June 2008 that:

> there are serving U.S. flag-rank officers who maintain that the first and second identifiable causes of U.S. combat deaths in Iraq – as judged by their effectiveness in recruiting insurgent fighters into combat – are, respectively the symbols of Abu Ghraib and Guantanamo. (US Senate Armed Services Committee, 2008, p. xii)

As Chapter 3 noted, even with a change of administration in the US, Obama's administration was reluctant to make available further photographic evidence of the Abu Ghraib torture, indicating their perceived ongoing discursive power. It is this sort of cumulative, long-term agenda-building impact of sousveillance in Web 2.0 that may well be its most important attribute. Its power to inform or merely inflame or entertain, of course, depends upon the contexts in which the sousveillant content is presented and then used by others.

Knowing When to Relinquish Control

The case studies examined in this book show that the US and UK militaries and governments understand, and exploit, the specificity and constraints of mainstream news, particularly 24/7 television news, very well to show highly restricted truths with specific framings (as in embeds' coverage of the invasion of Iraq, Saddam Hussein's capture, the framing of Abu Ghraib as 'abuse' photos and the official version of Saddam Hussein's execution). However, as previous chapters have demonstrated, strategic political communicators did not fully understand the implications and practices of Web 2.0 and its relationship to convergence and sousveillance cultures.

The embeds' war reportage of the invasion of Iraq and the capture of Saddam Hussein, both in 2003, were exercises in supreme military control of information geared up to the demands of live, 24/7 news. In themselves, they were highly successful examples of strategic political communication. The embeds represent a thorough understanding of the communicative potential of 24/7 news during war-time. Allowing journalists such close access to the troops – in effect, a *carefully managed loosening of controls* – allowed these professional communicators to do what they do best, and as academic analysis has shown, diverted mainstream media and public attention in accordance with the US' and UK's strategic political communication aims during the crucial period of major combat operations. Indeed, across late March and early April 2003, 78 per cent of the US public said the press was doing an excellent or good job covering the Iraq War (Pew Research Centre, 2007). As major combat operations ended in May 2003 and the embeds largely went home, the military were careful to supply their own footage of their success stories. While the military supplied no visual footage of their initial capture of Saddam Hussein, they were quick to provide visual footage of their captive, and his utter submission to the military machine. Television news is obviously a medium well-understood by the military and the governments of the UK and the US. Although Iraq was persistently in US mainstream news from the end of the war to 2007, interestingly, by November 2007, poll data showed that the US public believed that the challenges and experiences of US soldiers in Iraq were receiving too little news coverage: 61 per cent said that reports about soldiers' personal experiences had been under-covered; 52 per cent said that efforts to improve conditions in Iraq were under-covered, as were ground troops in action (47 per cent) (Pew Research Centre, 2007). This perception may well have been due to the fact that the embedding programme was scaled back at the end of May 2003, being reinstituted only for major events. Perhaps having received blanket exposure to embeds who personalized the military's story during the invasion, and led audiences to care about the troops, expectations were then set among the US public that this sort of coverage was desirable and would continue.

The importance of controlling television news for domestic audiences remains a high priority for strategic political communicators. In 2007, 60 per cent of Americans said television news was their main source for information about Iraq (Pew Research Centre, 2007). However, although television is a highly important medium of mass communication, given that this is where most Americans and British get their political information and knowledge of foreign affairs from (Crawford, 2004; Pew Research Centre for the People and the Press, 2004; Ofcom, 2006a), the other case studies show that control over this medium is no longer enough where convergence cultures operate. Given that 16 per cent of Americans said in 2007 that they mostly rely on the internet for news about the ongoing Iraq War, and that this percentage increases with youth (10 per cent of 50–64 year olds, 18 per cent of 30–49 year olds, and 28 per cent of 18–29 years olds) (Pew Research Centre, 2007), the impact of information in Web 2.0 cannot be ignored by those seeking to control overall strategic political communications. However, how to influence the proliferating information online that users tap into still appears to be eluding those authorities operating within a control paradigm.

Even the most mundane personal sousveillance is potentially impactful, as evidenced by Salam Pax's blogs and the troops' spoof music video. Salam Pax offered alternative and authentic points of identification during war-time, acting as a corrective to the embedded journalistic reportage. Although his audience was relatively small compared to that of mainstream news, the blog was taken up by *The Guardian* after the end of OIF's invasion phase, and thereby garnered a larger audience. From the perspective of governments, the identification with Salam Pax cultivated by his blog is problematic for the success of the central frame that aims to divert domestic concern for the plight of 'enemy' civilians by leading US and UK audiences to identify with their own troops. Although Salam Pax's personal sousveillance was problematic for strategic political communicators, the personal sousveillance of the UK troops' spoof music video, widely circulated online and amplified further by *BBC* reportage, reminded audiences of the humanity of the occupying forces, following hot on the heels of a period where the military's humanity had been heavily tainted by the US administration's framing of torture at Abu Ghraib as mere 'abuses' perpetrated by criminally minded US Military Police. *Is This the Way to Armadillo* allowed the public to humorously and positively connect with the military personnel and from the perspective of the military's public relations, such user-generated content is gold dust. Thus, user-generated content can work unpredictably – in favour of, or against, the organization's or nation's intended strategic political communication.

It is this unpredictability that perhaps most concerns strategic political communicators. While Abu Ghraib was a spectacular example of personal sousveillance that damaged the military's image, perhaps exercising the military and political authorities the most was the military troops' blogs and their other everyday web-based participatory media communications posted on shock sites like Ogrish.com, designed to show, 'reality, it's part of our life, whether we like it or not' (Ogrish.com, 2006).[12] As Christensen (2008) observes, troops often posted graphic, brutal content of their real experiences and thoughts, documenting and revelling in the repulsiveness and viscerality of their daily task of killing, and avoiding being killed by, insurgents. By 2007, both the US and UK military had issued detailed and comprehensive instructions to all military employees regarding the need to refer upwards all public communications – including any using Web 2.0 technologies. The aim was undoubtedly to reinforce an institutional culture of control and secrecy, while making the reference upwards system an obstacle that would deter all casual, spontaneous, fun-based life-sharing impulses. Yet, this poses a PR dilemma for the military. As the UK military itself recognizes, 'the best, most direct and most compelling account of what the Armed Forces do is often given by ordinary soldiers, sailors and airmen, rather than by senior officers, civil servants or politicians' (Hall, 2007, p. 4). The media environment of Web 2.0 demands courage in relinquishing control over communication if organizations are to benefit from the gift economy in the creative commons that can arise unpredictably through user-generated content. The trepidation shown by military organizations towards their troops' personal sousveillance is mirrored by traditional advertisers more generally regarding involving consumers as a creative strategy, that, as McStay (2009) observes, requires relinquishing some control over a brand. Yet, the reward is that users may feel more empathy towards a brand than one-way advertising could ever hope to deliver.

Of course, a major problem with attempting to predict or control this permanent flow of networked user-generated content is that such endeavours appear to be impossible. The disruptive potential of web-based participatory media was no doubt feared by the US administration ever since Abu Ghraib surfaced in 2004; and the disruptive potential of camera phones has been recognized by Arab states who tightly control their media – for instance, Saudi Arabia banned the import and sale of camera phones, with religious authorities denounc-ing them for spreading obscenity (The Economist, 2004; Kraidy, 2006). Yet mobile phones were also banned from Saddam Hussein's execution chamber, to no avail. While military personnel of western governments and inhabitants of repressive states may be increasingly acculturated towards secrecy, there are no such guarantees for other producers of web-based participatory media. If control of information is problematic, attention can be paid in two directions. The first is working out how control can be further tightened – for instance, through increased censorship and spreading the ethos of self-censorship, as in the case of the military. The second direction is to explore whether attempts at control of information in a leaky world are desirable, given the impossibility of total control and the negative messages that such attempts generate.

In considering how control can be further tightened, it is worth remembering that various researchers find that even in the era of Web 2.0, the long-standing empirical finding that mass media over-rely on official sources still largely holds (Bennett et al., 2007; Bivens, 2008). Therefore, strategic political communication still works, on the whole. Focussing attention on areas that are still controllable, influential, and garner mass audiences (television news) would therefore seem more opportune than attempting to hold back the flood gates of all participatory media, particularly since it is mainstream media that largely confer credibility on, and amplification of, user-generated content. Indeed, the credibility problems that many journalists see the blogosphere and other user-generated content as beset with will ensure that user-generated content remains an avenue for exploring and gathering alternative views, to help balance official reports rather than replace them. Notably, this does depend on the nature of the user-generated content, and we must be careful not to lump them all together. For instance, blogs can be inaccurate and full of disinformation, with bloggers frequently arguing that accuracy, for them, is reached over time by relying on corrections by sheer numbers through the blogging network (Lowrey, 2006; Kalb & Saivetz, 2007). Such departures from accuracy perhaps help explain why most Americans are not turning to blogs for news (Project for Excellence in Journalism, 2008). Photographs posted online also have credibility problems as they can be doctored easily, a problem that mainstream journalism itself has to deal with (Farhi, 2006; Kalb & Saivetz, 2007).[13] By contrast, videos tend to be accepted by mainstream news, whatever their source. Even without mainstream news attention, very large audiences can be attracted when certain videos are uploaded to websites like *YouTube*, through its 'featured videos' and popular lists, or to individual blogs through an explosion of hyperlinks from other bloggers (Bivens, 2008). The Pew Internet & American Life Project's first major report on online video shows that, as of March 2007, 57 per cent of online adults had used the internet to watch or download video, and 19 per cent did so on a typical day (Project for Excellence in Journalism, 2008). It is therefore perhaps in *this* area of user-generated content that those seeking to control strategic political communications should invest their energy, as should, simultaneously, those seeking to sousveillantly challenge power structures. The UK and US military's recent attempts at seeding the internet with what looks like user-generated video content, but is in fact centrally produced, or restricting the ability of ordinary soldiers, for instance, to generate their own video imagery, may make sense in attempting to strategically control information. The restrictions on all military user-generated content makes no sense, however, and acts only to damage the ideals of the democracies that these militaries ostensibly protect.

However, rather than attempting still greater control, the more radical direction is to question the desirability of attempting information control in an inherently leaky, sousveillant world. Relinquishing control over strategic political communication would expose the military and government to greater scrutiny from all – perhaps endangering operational security, as they state, but also perhaps rebuilding trust through transparency, and building mutual understanding through allowing us closer to their cultures and modes of operations. After all, if the mission of the troops, for instance, is as necessary (for Iraq's stability, to prevent terrorism at home, and so on) as is politically claimed, then surely the public can be persuaded of this through the facts of the situation. Surely, if so persuaded of the necessity of war, we will even tolerate morally reprehensible acts such as troops enjoying their killing of potential civilians/insurgents, if we understand that in order to kill, an element of humanity must be switched off, to be replaced by an element of training. The intensification of sousveillance cultures brings with it the necessity of confronting these uncomfortable thoughts. Now it is time to open our eyes and deal with what we witness, deliberating over its acceptability according to our values, rather than succumbing to spin.

Indeed, if the US wishes to exercise soft power, it must stand by the values it publicly claims to hold dear. As President Bush himself said, 9 days after 9/11, referring to terrorists' leaders: 'They hate our freedoms – our freedom of religion, our freedom of speech, our freedom to vote and assemble and disagree with each other' (Bush, 2001). Yet, in Bush's War on Terror, civil liberties have been attacked continuously by government, as indicated in Chapter 1. If freedom of speech, expression and movement is curtailed through legislation on surveillance, and controls over information, then the principles that the West upholds will diminish in value, eroding soft power. Rather than behaving in an unprincipled manner, and then attempting to control and spin information about this bad behaviour – both actions that damage public trust in political and media institutions (Bakir & Barlow, 2007a, 2007b) – a more honest rendition of political and military aims and actions, self-regulated through perpetual potential sousveillance, may make governments more accountable and prevent the worst abuses, thereby rebuilding trust in the body politic.

Cycles of Emergence, Resistance, Reincorporation

The political expectation that media are controllable does not appear to have dissipated, despite the rise of web-based participatory media. The outgoing speech of Tony Blair – whose governance (1997–2007) spanned both Web 1.0 and 2.0 time periods – is instructive. Here, despite the Blair Labour government's push towards greater transparency, Blair viewed the 'new forms of communication' (Blair, 2007) not as a means of increasing inter-citizen dialogue, but to 'provide new outlets to by-pass the increasingly shrill tenor of the traditional media' (Blair, 2007). While recognizing that 'the new forms can be even more pernicious, less balanced, more intent on the latest conspiracy theory multiplied by five' (Blair, 2007), Blair certainly sees old media in negative terms, as obsessed with capturing the attention of the elusive audience through dwelling on scandal and controversy, and offering interpretation and commentary rather than balanced, factual coverage (Blair, 2007; Purvis, 2007). Meanwhile, the Bush administration viewed the US media as just another interest group that needed to be placated and could be manipulated (McClellan, 2008).

From the case studies examined in this book, it is the *emergent* nature of Web 2.0 that seems to be an important factor in subverting strategic political communication. Indeed, wider research on the interplay of politics and participatory culture confirms that political authorities were bad at engaging with web-based participatory media – particularly when they first emerged – as they were unhappy at relinquishing discursive control to the masses. For instance, a study of UK parliamentarians' political blogs concludes that by the end of 2005, bloggers had congregated around entrenched, static views, rarely stepping into a deliberative environment where their views could be exposed to ideas that differed from those they generated themselves (Ferguson & Griffiths, 2006). Politicians are, however, getting better at engaging Web 2.0. For instance, Obama's 2008 presidential campaign used various social media to build more meaningful relationships with voters and campaigners, keeping supporters engaged by delivering targeted, timed messages through e-mail and mobile text messaging, in addition to traditional in-person and phone canvassing (Webtrends, 2009). The targeting of messages was honed by creating precise voter profiles through using the services of political data-mining companies like Strategic Telemetry,[14] integrating traditional voter and party data with publicly available consumer information such as Census reports and voter registration files, along with e-mail, mobile and other voter contact information. Aggregating such data into a single, continuously up-dated database allowed the Obama campaign to more intimately understand its audience, allowing it to improve the accuracy of its targeted messages in terms of mobilizing campaigners and voters (Madden, 2008; Castells, 2009; Webtrends, 2009). The effectiveness of such strategic political communication techniques is evidenced in that *YouTube* users alone spent 14.5 million hours watching official Obama campaign videos – a figure that excludes user-generated videos – saving the strategic political communicators millions of dollars in TV commercials, and, unlike TV commercials, probably paying attention to the *You Tube* videos given that they were requested (Heaney, 2008). In addition to seeding the web with desirable content, the Obama campaign simultaneously, and very publicly, relinquished control over this medium. This is perhaps most tellingly evidenced by the *I Got a Crush on Obama* viral video – constituting the first real internet success of Obama's 2008 presidential campaign – this partially measured by number of spoofs it spawned.[15] In this video by satirists, *Barely Political*, a scantily dressed, attractive, Hispanic-looking US girl gushes over Obama footage to a light R&B backing track, suggestively singing, 'You can Barack me tonight.' It quickly notched up in excess of six million hits, becoming one of *YouTube*'s most popular clips of 2007. By February 2009, it had received 13,162,886 views. Although it was not created by the Obama campaign, the then Senator's mild reaction to something that might have been deemed disrespectful and off-message suggests that he understood its potential benefit to his campaign – or even more cleverly, the benefit of appearing unfazed by its existence. Obama noted that, 'It's just one more example of the fertile imagination of the internet . . . More stuff like this will be popping up all the time' (McCormick, 2008). Thus, as the Obama campaign shows, the options for strategic political communicators are not to either relinquish all control or totally retain control, but to do a bit of both at the same time, across different media, playing to each medium's strengths, while simultaneously learning more about the audience.

Yet, emergent Web 2.0 technologies like *Twitter* have also been used as a mode of resistance to confound strategic political communicators in the West and repressive Middle Eastern governments, alike, both of whom understand how to prevent information from ever reaching the public sphere. As an example of the former, in October 2009, in a landmark case, *Twitter* users, after a spontaneous online campaign to spread banned information, helped overturn an attempt by British oil trading firm, Trafigura, to prevent UK citizens from knowing what was said in Parliament. Trafigura had obtained an injunction against *The Guardian*, preventing it from reporting a question tabled by a Labour MP. The MP's question was about the implications for press freedom of an order that had been obtained by Trafigura preventing the media from publishing the contents of a report related to Trafigura's 2006 dumping of toxic waste in the Ivory Coast. The MP's question revealed that Trafigura had obtained a hitherto secret injunction, known as a 'super-injunction,' under which commercial corporations claim the right to keep secret the fact that they have been to court and where the fact of the injunction is itself kept secret. *Twitter* users posted details of the MP's question overnight, and by the following morning the full text had been published on two prominent blogs as well as in the UK satirical magazine, *Private Eye*. As a result, Trafigura withdrew its gagging attempt (Leigh, 2009).

Also in 2009, *Twitter* caught out Iran's administration, playing a significant role in fuelling and globally publicizing the largest public demonstration in Iran since the Islamic Revolution in 1979 ushered in its theocracy. The 2009 demonstrations involved hundreds of thousands of Iranians, demonstrating against the outcome of the 12 June 2009 Iranian presidential elections where the incumbent (since 2005) conservative president, Mahmoud Ahmadinejad, was declared the winner with 63 per cent of the votes. Demonstrators claimed that the vote was rigged (Worth, 2009). Although the state's national broadcaster, *Islamic Republic of Iran Broadcasting (IRIB),*[16] continued its campaign to prove that elections were fair and that the demonstrators were an illegal minority, gritty, uncensored images of the demonstrations' size and the state's violent crack-down, some taken by mobile phone cameras, were beamed around the world via various websites (Fathi, 2009), some in response to solicitation from mainstream global media such as the *BBC.* Bearing in mind that Iran has long had the highest internet penetration in the Middle East, such sousveillant activity caused the Iranian authorities to cut off phone and text-messaging services repeatedly since the election (Worth, 2009) and bloggers were ordered to remove all material that could 'create tension' from the internet or face legal action (Telegraph, 2009). As well as overt censorship, the Iranian government appeared to be engaging in a practice called deep packet inspection, which enables authorities to monitor information flows online to gather information about individuals. Deep packet inspection involves inserting equipment into the flow of all online data (e-mails, internet phone calls, images and messages on social networking sites), with each digitized packet of online data deconstructed, examined for keywords and reconstructed within milliseconds. In Iran's case, this is done for the entire country at a single choke point, and its suspected use in the 2009 demonstrations would explain both why the government allowed the internet to continue to function, and also why it has been running at a tenth of normal speed since the demonstrations (Cellan-Jones, 2009; Rhoads & Chao, 2009). Yet, the web became even more important after the Iranian government on 16 June 2009 barred foreign media from leaving their offices to report on the demonstrations. Even the US government intervened on 16 June, calling on *Twitter* to postpone a scheduled shutdown for maintenance in order to allow Iranians to continue to use the site to post images and reports of demonstrations (Telegraph, 2009). Web-based participatory media also appeared to force mainstream media to change their news agenda. For instance, after thousands of *Twitter* users adopted the hashtag, '#CNNfail' to highlight *CNN*'s lack of coverage of the Tehran protests, *CNN* stepped up its TV coverage (Cashmore, 2009). Meanwhile, news of the protests was fed back into Iran through mainstream media. The Farsi-language broadcasts of the *BBC*'s Persian channel on *YouTube,*[17] *Voice of America*'s *Persian News Network*[18] and the US-government sponsored *Radio Farda,*[19] – as well as the internet – deprived Iran of any monopoly over the means of communication (Ansari, 2009). Significantly, Iran's most powerful oversight council, the Guardian Council, announced on 22 June 2009 that although the overall vote was valid because the margin of victory was so great (11 million votes), the number of votes recorded in 50 cities exceeded the number of eligible voters there by three million, further tarnishing the presidential election (Slackman, 2009). Yet, although the demonstrators were publicly vindicated, as Howard Rheingold notes, in interview with Shel Israel with reference to these demonstrations:

> access to digital media and networks guarantees that it will be impossible to keep the world from witnessing massive oppression, but does not guarantee the victory of forces of counterpower who seek liberty from oppression. Power always wakes up and mobilizes when counterpower threatens it. (Israel, 2009)

This is a timely reminder that the ability of sousveillant activity in Web 2.0 to change entrenched power structures should not be overstated. However, as Chapter 4 has also demonstrated, the popular legitimacy of political institutions is not to be played with lightly, and where sousveillant activity undermines this sufficiently, then social mobilization leading to social change may occur – although not necessarily in a libertarian direction.

Despite uncertain social gain, the capacity to be surprised by new and unexpected social uses of new or existing media technologies is likely to remain with us. There is no possibility for perfecting control over strategic political communication in Web 2.0. Yet, as this book has highlighted, the rise of Web 2.0 is but one part of the story, the other main development being that of convergence. As convergence progresses, governments across the world appear to realize that trusted amplifiers are needed that can provide appropriate, official context and framing of content – including content from the web. Although the importance of English language broadcasting has long been realized by *Saudi Channel 2*, which has been broadcasting in English for two decades (Sakr, 2001; Ridley, 2008),[20] English language satellite TV channels with strong global footprints have proliferated across the first decade of the twenty-first century. For example, *al-Jazeera English* launched in November 2006 to provide a regional voice and a global perspective to a potential world audience of over one billion English speakers but without an Anglo-American worldview.[21] In 2007, the Iranian Government launched *Press TV*, a channel that offers expansive news coverage specifically looking at Middle Eastern and Asian affairs, broadcasting in English aimed at the West.[22] Similarly, various governments attempt to reach the Muslim public directly through the creation of satellite media channels, exploiting this medium's large potential audience. Examples include Iran's Arabic-language television news channel, *al-Alam News Network*, launched in 2003;[23] US-backed 24/7 Arabic language satellite television news channel, *al-Hurra*, launched in 2004 to counter *al-Jazeera* and *al-Arabiya*;[24] *France-24*, an international news and current affairs television channel launched in 2006, broadcasting in French, English and Arabic;[25] *Rusiya al-Yaum*, the first Russian TV news channel broadcasting in Arabic launched in 2007; and Arab language television channel, *BBC Arabic*, launched in 2008 – constituting the *BBC*'s first publicly funded international TV service.[26] Proliferating the amount of government-sponsored satellite TV channels aimed at other countries appears to be the main recourse of governments wishing to geo-politically control strategic political communication in a world of permanent and often instantaneous potential sousveillance. As long as television news remains the most important information source for the masses, governments continue to seek influence over this medium that they understand well.

THE FUTURE?

Mann's conceptualization of sousveillance, while rich, can be criticized in terms of its vulnerability towards reappropriation by Panoptic state apparatuses – a point that has been noted, not least by Mann himself (Mann, 2001; Mann et al., 2003). The problem of reappropriation suggests a certain naivety in Mann's propagation of personal sousveillance on the one hand while simultaneously espousing hierarchical sousveillance as a means of countering surveillance on the other hand:

> I feel okay with everyone picture-taking (and even everyday WebCam taking), but am uncomfortable with the video surveillance cameras that seem, these days, to be everywhere, rising over our city streets on high poles, looming over our neighbourhood stores, banks, schools and parks (Mann, 2001, p. 140)

While Mann, writing at the start of the era of Web 2.0, notes that he feels no sense of threat from being photographed, for instance, on a passer-by's cameraphone, given that his sousveillant technologies are inspired by the need to resist the Panopticon he would undoubtedly be unhappy if his personal sousveillance was then reappropriated through the surveillant assemblage by the surveillant Panoptic apparatus. Yet, the increasing drive to personal sousveillance facilitated by Web 2.0 provides ever-more data for the surveillant assemblage – itself intensified since 9/11. As Chapter 1 observed, the data-mining for political purposes of the wealth of information about ourselves that we willingly place online, as well as unwittingly reveal through other online activities (such as e-commerce), is *already* used to better target us as individual recipients of carefully crafted strategic communication, certainly in the West and developed countries (Bennett & Manheim, 2006; McStay & Bakir, 2006; Castells, 2009; McStay, 2009). Although internet penetration in the Middle East is still comparatively low, it is increasing, and given Middle Eastern countries' strict control over their media, it is likely that data-mining will come to feature in this region in time. Iran's suspected use of deep packet inspection to monitor the 2009 demonstrators may well be a taste of things to come.

At the time of writing (the end of 2009), innovatory change within Web 2.0 continues apace, with ever more users and sensors feeding more applications and platforms generating an ever-growing 'information shadow' – or aura of data capable of being captured and processed (O'Reilly & Battelle, 2009, p. 2). For instance, just as a book has information shadows on *Amazon, GoogleBooks, Shelfari, eBay, Twitter* and thousands of blogs, so a person has information shadows in their e-mails, instant messages, phone calls, tweets, blog postings, photographs, videos and government documents (O'Reilly & Battelle, 2009). While currently, information shadows are thin, they are likely to become much thicker. The stream of personal sousveillance that we willingly produce is unlikely to diminish, given its pleasureability, usefulness and increasing social embeddedness.

The implications of such continuing technological developments and their associated social practices for sousveillance and strategic political communicators are profound. Although there are regulatory safeguards on data-aggregation and data-mining online, particularly in nations with high degrees of e-commerce (McStay & Bakir, 2006; McStay, 2009), as Chapter 1 indicated, a major perceived crisis (like 9/11) may jolt nations into passing legislation that allows them such data access to protect us from [insert current bogeyman]. Meanwhile, through our personal sousveillance, we will continue to unwittingly contribute to the surveillant assemblage – forming the vastly data-engorged *sous*veillant assemblage. As our information shadows within the sousveillant assemblage become more substantial, the strategic political communication entrenched in western democracies can be honed, refined and targeted even more finely through data-mining. (Remember, Manheim (1991) sees strategic political communication as based on how professional communicators use *sophisticated knowledge about human behaviour* to mould information to accomplish specific objectives.) The data-mining of the Obama 2008 presidential campaign, informing its use of social networking sites for individual-ized communication with potential voters and campaigners, and its willing acceptance of brand-relevant user-generated content on *You-Tube*, is no doubt a sign of things to come in democracies. Concomi-tantly, authoritarian Middle Eastern regimes already engaging in strong surveillance measures may willingly embrace these surveillance technologies – from data-mining to deep packet inspection – without legal safeguards, as indicated by the 2009 Iranian demonstrations.

The still uncertain future scenario of universal surveillance/ sousveillance – or 'coveillance' – requires us all to be alert to the down-side of sousveillance as expressed in Web 2.0. Let us remember the caveats that Mann et al. (2003) place on their ideal of coveillance (Mann et al., 2003; Mann, 2004b)[27] – noting that such a scenario may, in the final analysis, only serve the ends of the existing dominant power structures by fostering broad accessibility of monitoring and ubiqui-tous data collection. Mindful of this, we should soberly weigh up the risks (for instance, in suffering, in the West, ever more targeted strate-gic political communication designed to manipulate and persuade rather than elicit deliberation; and in Middle Eastern countries, expos-ing sousveillers to identification by repressive surveillance states) with the benefits (ranging from the pleasures of sharing one's life to elicit-ing protection from abuses of power). Such risk-benefit analysis needs to be done in a climate of rationality (and therefore outside the discourse, of, for instance, War on Terror),[28] that allows us to clearly assess our values. What value judgements do we accord to the risks and benefits of ubiquitous sousveillance, surveillance and highly targeted strategic political communication? Do we want to feed the sousveillant assemblage or do we want to resist?

NOTES

[1] In mid-2006, 127,000 US troops and 19,000 non-US coalition troops from 20 countries (mostly from the UK, South Korea, and Italy) were in Iraq (Library of Congress, 2006).
[2] The interview's full text can be found at *The Huffington Post* (2009).
[3] Bush's visit to Iraq was 37 days before handing power to Obama.
[4] He was not released until 15 September 2009, and claims to have been tortured in prison (BBC, 2008c).
[5] *Digg* gets more visitors than *The New York Times*. It comprises lists of head-lines, these lists generated entirely by user recommendations. As such, the relative prominence given to stories will always be in tune with readers' interests (Whitwell, 2008).

6 Analog phones were the first generation of mobile phone technology – 1G; digital mobile phones were the second generation – 2G (Castells et al., 2007).

7 This was measured by average number of unique pages viewed by users per day and number of unique page visitors (3 month average).

8 See HollaBackNYC.com

9 See http://wikileaks.org/. A wiki is a piece of server software that allows users to freely create and edit web page content using any web browser. *Wiki-leaks*, like all participatory media, suffers from people putting inaccurate material online. It also suffered from its own success as, by 2008 it contained too much unorganized information (Global Operations Panel, 2008). By 2009 its operations were jeopardized by lack of funding.

10 http://www.thememoryhole.org/

11 http://www.thesmokinggun.com/

12 The domain now redirects to Liveleak.com, a site registered in October 2006.

13 Sometimes it is the blogosphere that draws attention to authenticity failings in mainstream journalism, as in the doctoring of a *Reuters* photo taken by a freelancer, Adnan Hajj during the 2006 Israel-Lebanon conflict (Farhi, 2006; Kalb & Saivetz, 2007).

14 http://www.strategictelemetry.com/

15 *I Got a Crush on Obama* can be viewed at http://uk.youtube.com/watch?v=wKsoXHYICqU. Spoofs included *I got a crush . . . on Hillary (take that Obama girl)* (http://uk.youtube.com/watch?v=jLSWudoqtWE&NR=1) with 2,201,401 views by January 2009.

16 http://www.irib.ir/English/

17 youtube.com/bbcpersian

18 http://www1.voanews.com/persian/news/

19 http://www.radiofarda.com/section/About_us_en/543.html

20 http://www.sauditv2.tv [Accessed 1 November 2009].

21 http://english.aljazeera.net/watch_now/ [Accessed 1 November 2009].

22 http://www.presstv.ir/ [Accessed 1 November 2009].

23 http://www.alalam.ir/English/ [Accessed 1 November 2009].

24 http://www.alhurra.com/ [Accessed 1 November 2009].

25 http://www.france24.com/en/ [Accessed 1 November 2009].

26 http://www.bbc.co.uk/arabic/ [Accessed 1 November 2009].

27 Coveillance is the situation where peers can see both the recording and the presentation of the images and where power relations are equal – such as when one citizen watches another, or where organizational surveiller and sousveiller observe each other on behalf of symmetrically distant organizations.

28 In March 2009, US Secretary of State, Hillary Clinton, said that the Obama administration had dropped 'war on terror' from its lexicon (Reuters, 2009b).

REFERENCES

19phil88. (2008). *Comment on 'Is this the way to armadillo?'* [Online]. Sent June 2008. Available at: http://www.youtube.com/watch? v= tN1mIerM1BQ [Accessed 16 October 2008].

Abdel-Latif, O. (2004). *Cyber-Struggle: Islamist websites versus the Egyptian state.* [Online] Arab Reform Bulletin. Available at: http://www.mafhoum.com/press7/220T44.htm [Accessed 14 April 2009].

Abdul-Zahra, Q. (2008). *Official: Shoe-thrower in Iraqi military custody.* [Online] *Associated Press,* 16 December. Available at: http://www.google.com/hostednews/ap/article/ALeqM5hwK_CSpBxs NuVUEaDuOwmSSCiqGwD953NQI03 [Accessed 14 October 2009].

Abdulla, R.A. (2007a). Islam, jihad, and terrorism in post 9/11 Arabic discussion boards. *Journal of Computer-Mediated Communication,* [Online]. 12(3). Available at: http://jcmc.indiana.edu/vol12/issue3/abdulla.html [Accessed 14 April 2009].

—(2007b). *The Internet in the Arab World: Egypt and Beyond.* New York: Peter Lang Publishing.

—(2006). An overview of media developments in Egypt: Does the internet make a difference? *Global Media Journal–Mediterranean Edition,* 1(1), 88–100.

Acharya, A. & Quiggen, T. (2009). *'What is "Al Qaeda" today?'* [Online] Globalbrief. (Updated 22 June 2009) Available at: http://globalbrief.ca/blog/2009/06/22/what-is-the-al-qaeda-network-today/ [Accessed 26 October 2009].

Aday, S., Livingston, S. & Herbert, M. (2005). Embedding the truth: a cross-cultural analysis of objectivity and television coverage of the Iraq War. *The Harvard International Journal of Press and Politics,* 10(1), 3–21.

Adorno, T. (1982 [1938]). On the fetish character in music and the regression of listening. In A. Arato & E. Gebhart, eds *The Essential Frankfurt School Reader.* New York: Continuum, pp. 270–299.

AFP. (2008a). *Iraqi justice to probe case of Bush shoe assailant.* [Online] AFP. 16 December. Available at: http://www.google.com/hostednews/

afp/article/ALeqM5hYS5PeLbqqmrfep6Hvo1mi7IGAtg [Accessed 16 December 2008].

—(2008b). *Arabs hail shoe attack as Bush's farewell gift.* [Online] AFP, 15 December. Available at: http://www.google.com/hostednews/afp/article/ALeqM5hg7W0HiJU6UHFKZ4Lc68A1ENatDA [Accessed 16 December 2008].

Akwagyiram, A. (2005). *Does 'happy slapping' exist?* [Online] BBC News, 12 May. Available at: http://news.bbc.co.uk/1/hi/uk/4539913.stm [Accessed 1 July 2008].

Al-bab (2009). *Best of the Arab blogs.* [Online]. (Updated 9 November 2009). Available at: http://www.al-bab.com/arab/blogs.htm [Accessed 26 October 2009].

alexa.com (2009). *Top sites. Alexa: the web information company.* [Online]. Available at: http://alexa.com/siteinfo/google.com [Accessed 2 September 2009].

Alexander, A. (2004). Disruptive technology: Iraq and the internet. In D. Miller, ed. *Tell Me Lies: Propaganda and Media Distortion on the Attack on Iraq.* London: Pluto, pp. 277–285.

Alexander, C.J. & Pal, L.A. (1998). *Digital Democracy: Policy and Politics in the Wired World.* Toronto, New York: Oxford University Press.

Al-Harthi, M. (2008). Introductory Panel. In CAMMRO, (Centre for Arab and Muslim Media Research) *4th international conference on new media and social change in the Arab and Muslim world.* London, UK. 16 June 2008. King's College, University of London.

Al-Jazeera. (2009). *US defends abuse photos reversal.* [Online] AlJazeera.net, 15 May. Available at: http://english.aljazeera.net/news/americas/2009/05/2009514175017637319.html [Accessed 1 November 2009].

Allan, S. (2004). The culture of distance: online reporting of the Iraq war. In S.Allan & B.Zelizer, eds *Reporting War: Journalism in Wartime.* London: Routledge, pp. 347–365.

Al-Marashi, A. (2004). *Iraq's hostage crisis: kidnappings, mass media and the Iraqi insurgency. Middle East Review of International Affairs,* [Online]. 8(4) Article 1. Available at: http://meria.idc.ac.il/journal/2004/issue4/jv8no4a1.html [Accessed 18 July 2008].

Alterman, J.B. (2004). The information revolution and the Middle East. In N. Bensahel and D.L. Byman, eds *The Future Security Environment in the Middle East.* [e-book] Santa Monica, CA: RAND. Available at: http://www.csis.org/media/csis/pubs/the_information_revolution_and_the_me.pdf [Accessed 6 April 2009].

—(2000). The Middle East's information revolution. *Current History,* January, 21–26.

—(1998). *New Media New Politics? From Satellite Television to the Internet in the Arab World.* Washington: The Washington Institute for Near East Policy.

Altheide, D.L. (2006). Terrorism and the politics of fear. *Cultural Studies <=> Critical Methodologies,* 6(4), 415–439.

Altheide, D.L. & Grimes, J.N. (2005). War programming: the propaganda project and the Iraq war. *The Sociological Quarterly,* 46, 617–643.

Amnesty International. (2006). *Beyond Abu Ghraib: detention and torture in Iraq.* [Online] March. Available at: www.amnesty.org/en/library/info/MDE14/001/2006 [Accessed 15 April 2009].

Andén-Papadopoulos, K. (2009). US soldiers imaging the Iraq War on *YouTube. Popular Communication: the International Journal of Media and Culture,* 7(1), 17–27.

Andersen, R. (2003). From Saving Private Lynch to the 'Top Gun' president: the made-for-TV 'reality war on Iraq'. In P. Phillips & Project Censored, eds *Censored 2004: The Top 25 Censored Stories.* New York: Seven Stories Press, pp. 219–223.

Anderson, A. (1991). Source strategies and the communication of environmental affairs. *Media, Culture and Society,* 13, 459–476.

Anderson, B. (1983). *Imagined Communities: Reflections on the Origin and Spread of Nationalism.* London: Verso.

Anderson, J.W. (2003). New media, new publics: reconfiguring the public sphere of Islam. *Social Research,* 70(3), 887–906.

—(2001). *Muslim networks, Muslim selves in cyberspace: Islam in the postmodern public sphere.* [Online]. NMIT Working Papers, Available at: http://www.mafhoum.com/press3/102S22.htm [Accessed 6 April 2009].

Andrews, R. (2006). *9/11: Birth of the Blog.* [Online] Wired, 11 November. Available at: http://www.wired.com/techbiz/media/news/2006/09/71753 [Accessed 4 July 2008].

Ansari, N. (2009). *Iran's election: people and power. Six factors, four questions.* [Online] OpenDemocracy, (Published 22 June 2009). Available at: http://www.opendemocracy.net/article/iran-s-election-democracy-or-coup [Accessed 21 October 2009].

Apel, D. (2005). Torture culture: lynching photographs and the images of Abu Ghraib. *Art Journal,* 64(2), 88–100.

Army Regulation 530–1. (2007). *Operations security (OPSEC).* [Online] Washington D.C. Headquarters, Department of the Army. Available at: http://www.ibls.com/internet_law_news_portal_view.aspx?s=latestnews&id= 1774 [Accessed 7 August 2008].

Associated Press. (2009). *Pentagon lifts media ban on coffin photos.* [Online] *Msnbc,* 26 February. Available at: http://www.msnbc.msn.com/ id/29410258/ [Accessed 17 March 2008].

Ayish, M.I. (2002). Political communication on Arab world television: evolving patterns. *Political Communication,* 19, 137–154.

Ayres, C. (2005). *War Reporting for Cowards: Between Iraq and a Hard Place.* London: John Murray.

Azzam, M. (2006). *Al-Qaeda five years on the threat and the challenges.* [Online] Chatham House, Middle East Programme. Available at: http://www. chathamhouse.org.uk/publications/papers/view/-/id/419/ [Accessed 21 September 2008].

Bad Gas. (n.d.) *Doing a Lynndie.* [blog] Avaible at: http://badgas.co. uk/lynndie/ [Accessed 15 November 2009].

Bahador, B. (2007). *The CNN Effect in Action.* New York: Palgrave MacMillan.

Bakir, V. (2009). Tele-technologies, control and sousveillance: Saddam Hussein – de-deification and the beast. *Popular Communication: The International Journal of Media and Culture,* 7(1), 7–16.

—(2007). Risk communication, television news and the generation of trust: the utility of ethos. In V. Bakir & D. Barlow, eds *Communication in the Age of Suspicion: Trust and the Media.* Basingstoke: Palgrave-Macmillan, pp. 211–237.

—(2006). Policy agenda-setting and risk communication: Greenpeace, Shell and issues of trust. *The Harvard International Journal of Press/ Politics,* 11(3), 67–88.

—(2005). Greenpeace v. Shell: media exploitation and the social amplification of risk framework (SARF). *Journal of Risk Research,* 8(7–8), 679–691.

Bakir,V. & Barlow, D. (2007a). The age of suspicion. In V. Bakir. & D. Barlow, eds *Communication in the Age of Suspicion: Trust and the Media.* Basingstoke: Palgrave-Macmillan, pp. 1–8.

—(2007b). The end of trust? In V. Bakir & D. Barlow, eds *Communication in the Age of Suspicion: Trust and the Media.* Basingstoke: Palgrave-Macmillan, pp. 205–213.

Bakir, V. & McStay, A. (2008). When the Script runs out . . . what happens to the polarised war body? Deconstructing western 24/7 news coverage of Operation Iraqi Freedom 2003. In K. Randell & S. Redmond, eds *The War Body on Screen.* New York: Continuum, pp. 165–181.

Ball, K. & Webster, F. (2003). The intensification of surveillance. In K. Ball & F. Webster, eds *The Intensification of Surveillance: Crime, Terrorism and Warfare in the Information Age.* Pluto, London, pp. 1–15.

Balnaves, M., Donald, J. & Donald, S.H. (2001). *The Global Media Atlas.* London: BFI.

Banbury, J. (2004). *Guantanamo on steroids.* [Online] Salon.com, 3 March. Available at: http://archive.salon.com/news/feature/2004/03/03/prison/index.html [Accessed 14 August 2008].

Barakat, S. (2005). Post-Saddam Iraq: deconstructing a regime, reconstructing a nation. *Third World Quarterly*, 26(4–5), 571–591.

Battle on Haifa Street, Baghdad, Iraq (2007) [Online video]. Multi-National Force-Iraq. Available at: http://www.youtube.com/watch?v=nlNORX006-c [Accessed 15 November 2009].

BBC. (2010). *Iraq election: Views from Baghdad.* [Online] BBC News Online, 3 March. Available at: http://news.bbc.co.uk/1/hi/world/middle_east/8545403.stm [Accessed 3 March 2010].

— (2009a). *Twin Baghdad blasts kill scores.* [Online] BBC News Online, 25 October. Available at: http://news.bbc.co.uk/1/hi/world/middle_east/8324546.stm [Accessed 26 October 2009].

—(2009b). *Iraqis 'more upbeat about future'.* [Online] BBC News Online, 16 March. Available at: http://news.bbc.co.uk/1/hi/world/middle_east/7942974.stm [Accessed 16 October 2009].

—(2009c). *UN hails Iraq election results.* [Online] BBC News Online, 6 February. Available at: http://news.bbc.co.uk/1/hi/world/middle_east/7874180.stm [Accessed 30 June 2009].

—(2008a). *UK troops to leave Iraq 'by July'.* [Online] BBC News Online, 17 December. Available at: *http://news.bbc.co.uk/1/hi/uk_politics/7787103.stm* [Accessed 17 December 2008].

—(2008b). *Shoe Thrower 'Beaten in Custody'.* [Online] BBC News Online, 16 December. Available at: http://news.bbc.co.uk/1/hi/world/middle_east/7785338.stm [Accessed 16 December 2008].

—(2008c). *Iraq Rally for Bush Shoe Attacker.* [Online] BBC News Online, 15 December. Available at: http://news.bbc.co.uk/1/hi/world/middle_east/7783608.stm [Accessed 16 December 2008].

—(2006). *Saddam Hussein Executed in Iraq.* [Online] BBC News Online, 30 December. Available at: http://news.bbc.co.uk/1/hi/world/middle_east/6218485.stm [Accessed 12 December 2007].

—(2005a). *'Amarillo' soldiers hail response.* [Online] BBC News Online, 18 May. Available at: http://news.bbc.co.uk/1/hi/uk/4559345.stm [Accessed 8 October 2009].

—(2005b). *'Amarillo' Video Crashes MoD PCs.* [Online] BBC News Online, 17 May. Available at: http://news.bbc.co.uk/2/hi/uk_news/4554083.stm [Accessed 14 February 2008].

—(2003a). *Saddam Hussein Captured. BBC on this day.* [Online] BBC News Online, 14 December. Available at: http://news.bbc.co.uk/onthisday/hi/dates/stories/december/14/newsid_3985000/3985287.stm [Accessed 12 December 2007].

—(2003b). *'Million' march against Iraq war*. [Online] BBC News Online, 16 February. Available at: http://news.bbc.co.uk/1/hi/uk/2765041. stm [Accessed 26 January 2009].

BBC editorial guidelines. (2009). *War, terror and emergencies*. [Online]. BBC, Available at: http://www.bbc.co.uk/guidelines/editorialguidelines/ edguide/war/editorialprinci.shtml [Accessed 2 June 2009].

BBC Radio 4. (2007). *Abu Ghraib whistleblower fears for safety of his family*. [Online] The Choice, BBC Radio 4, 7 August. BBC Press Office. Available at:http://www.bbc.co.uk/pressoffice/pressreleases/stories/2007/ 08_august/06/choice.shtml [Accessed 21 February 2008].

BBC Radio 5 Live. (2009). *BBC Radio 5 Live Poll.* [Online] ComRes. March 2009. Available at:http://www.comres.co.uk/page190751146. aspx [Accessed 21 October 2009].

BBC/*Reuters*/Media Center Poll (2006). *Trust in the Media*, [Online] *Globescan*, 3 May. Available at: http://www.globescan.com/news_ archives/bbcreut.html [Accessed 2 July 2006].

Beaumont, P., Harris, P. & Burke, J. (2004). *Catastrophe*. [Online] *The Observer*, 9 May. Available at: http://www.guardian.co.uk/world/2004/ may/09/iraq [Accessed 3 August 2008].

Bebow, J. (2003). *War diary – embedded in Iraq: riding the humvee with Col. Cowboy*. [Online] *The Detroit News*, 26 April. Available at: http:// courier-journal.gannettonline.com/gns/iraq/20030426–21793. shtml [Accessed 30 October 2009].

Beehner, L. & Bruno, G. (2008). *Iran's Involvement in Iraq. Council on Foreign Relations* [Online]. (Updated 3 March 2008). Available at: http:// www.cfr.org/publication/12521/ [Accessed 14 October 2009].

Beier, J.M. (2007). Grave misgivings: allegory, catharsis, composition. *Security Dialogue*, 38(2), 251–269.

Benjamin, M. (2006). *Salon exclusive: The Abu Ghraib files.* [Online] Salon.com, 16 February. Available at: http://www.salon.com/news/ feature/2006/02/16/abu_ghraib/ [Accessed 8 August 2008].

Bennett, J. (2007). Counterblast: a short film about killing Saddam. *The Howard Journal*, 46(2), 194–196.

Bennett, W.L., Lawrence, R.G. & Livingston, S. (2007). *When the Press Fails: Political Power and the News Media from Iraq to Katrina.* Chicago: University of Chicago Press.

Bennett, W.L. & Manheim, J.B. (2006). The one-step flow of communication. *The Annals of the American Academy of Political and Social Science*, 608, 213–232.

Berman, R. (2004). *Anti-Americanism in Europe: A Cultural Problem*, [e-book] Silicon Valley: Hoover Press. Available at: http://media.

hoover.org/documents/0817945121_83.pdf [Accessed 1 November 2009].

Bivens, R.K. (2008). The internet, mobile phones and blogging: how new media are transforming traditional journalism. *Journalism Practice*, 2(1), 113–129.

Blair, T. (2007). *Full text: Blair on the media.* [Online] BBC.co.uk, 12 June. Available at: http://news.bbc.co.uk/1/hi/uk_politics/6744581.stm [Accessed 10 November 2008].

—(2004). *Statement on Butler report (14 July 2004)* [Online]. Number10. gov.uk. Available at: http://www.number10.gov.uk/Page6109 [Accessed 29 October 2009].

Blinderman, E. (2002). International law and information intervention. In M. Price & M. Thompson, eds *Forging Peace: Intervention, Human Rights and the Management of Media Space.* Edinburgh: Edinburgh University Press, pp. 104–138.

Blix, H. (2004). *Disarming Iraq.* New York: Pantheon.

Bloch-Elkon, Y. (2007). Studying the media, public opinion, and foreign policy in international crises: the United States and the Bosnian Crisis, 1992–1995. *The Harvard International Journal of Press/Politics*, 12(4), 20–51.

Blogs of war. (n.d.). *The man who filmed Saddam Hussein's execution: 'I Saw Fear.'* [blog] Available at: http://www.blogsofwar.com/ 2006/ 12/30/video-saddam-husseins-execution-hanging-shown/ [Accessed 16 December 2007].

Blood, R. (2002). Weblogs, a history and perspective. In J. Rodzvilla, ed. *We've Got Blog: How Weblogs are Changing Our Culture.* Cambridge, MA: Perseus, pp. 7–16.

Bodi, F. (2004). Al Jazeera's war. In D. Miller, ed. *Tell Me Lies: Propaganda and Media Distortion in the Attack on Iraq.* London: Pluto Press, pp. 243–250.

Boulos, M.N.K. & Wheeler, S. (2007). The emerging Web 2.0 social software: an enabling suite of sociable technologies in health and health care education. *Health, Information and Libraries Journal*, 24, 2–23.

Boyd, D.M. & Ellison, N.B. (2007). *Social network sites: definition, history, and scholarship.* [Online]. *Journal of Computer-Mediated Communication*, 13(1), article 11. Available at: http://jcmc.indiana.edu/vol13/issue1/boyd.ellison.html [Accessed 13 October 2008].

Boyd-Barrett, O. (2004). Judith Miller, *The New York Times*, and the propaganda model. *Journalism Studies*, 5(4), 435–449.

Brachman, J.M. (2006). High-tech terror: Al-Qaeda's use of new technology. *The Fletcher Forum of World Affairs*, 30(2), 149–164.

Brady, H.E., Fishkin, J.S. & Luskin, R.C. (2003). *Informed public opinion about foreign policy.* [Online]. *The Brookings Review,* 21(3). Available at: http://cdd.standford.edu/research/papers.2003.informed.pdf [Accessed 26 June 2008].

Brockes, E. (2009). What happens in war happens. *The Guardian Weekend.* 3 January, 14–21.

Brooks, W. (2009). *Iraq's successful provincial elections auger well for Obama's troop withdrawal plan.* [Online] Brooks Foreign Policy Review. 8 February. Available at: http://brooksreview.wordpress.com/2009/02/ [Accessed 1 July 2009].

Brown, D. (2006). Joe Blogg's turn. *British Journalism Review,* 17, 15–19.

Bryan, D. (2007). *Abu Ghraib whistleblower's ordeal.* [Online] *BBC News Online,* 5 August. Available at: http://news.bbc.co.uk/1/hi/world/middle_east/6930197.stm [Accessed 20 February 2008].

Bunrs, J.F. & Santora, M. (2006). *Iraq Mainly Calm, Riveted by Video of Hussein Death.* [Online] *International Herald Tribune,* 30 December. Available at: http://www.iht.com/articles/2006/12/30/news/web.1230iraq.php [Accessed 16 December 2007].

Burgess, J. (2008). All your chocolate rain are belong to us? Viral video, *YouTube* and the dynamics of participatory culture. In G. Lovink & S. Niederer, eds *Video Vortex Reader: Responses to YouTube.* [e-book] Amsterdam: Institute of Network Cultures, pp. 101–119. Available at: http://networkcultures.org/wpmu/portal/publications/inc-readers/videovortex/ [Accessed 13 October 2008].

Bush, G.W. (2007). *President's address to the nation.* [Online] Washington, DC. The White House. (Updated 10 January 2007). Available at: http://www.whitehouse.gov/news/releases/2007/01/20070110–7.html [Accessed 13 January 2009].

—(2003). *President discusses the future of Iraq.* [Online] Washington, DC. The White House. (Updated 26 February 2003). Available at: http://www.whitehouse.gov/news/releases/2003/02/20030226–11.html [Accessed 11 January 2009].

—(2002). *The president's State of the Union address.* [Online] Washington, DC. The White House. (Updated 29 January 2002). Available at: http://www.whitehouse.gov/news/releases/2002/01/20020129–11.html [Accessed 12 July 2008].

—(2001). *Address to Congress.* [Online] Washington, DC. The White House. (Updated 20 September 2001). Available at: http:/www.whitehouse.gov/ews/eleases/001/9/0010920–8.html [Accessed 8 July 2008].

Butler Report. (2004). *Review of intelligence on weapons of mass destruction. Report of a committee of privy counsellors* [Online] House of Commons. (Published 14 July 2004). Available at: www.archive2.official-documents. co.uk/document/deps/hc/.../898.pdf [Accessed 29 October 2009].

Calabrese, A. (2005). Casus Belli. US media and the justification of the Iraq war. *Television and New Media*, 6(2), 153–175.

Callamard, A. (2009). *Protecting journalists in Iraq.* [Online] *Guardian. co.uk*, 28 August. Available at: http://www.guardian.co.uk/ commentisfree/2009/aug/28/iraq-draft-law-journalist-protection [Accessed 22 October 2009].

Canadian Forces General Order 136/06. (2006). *Guidance on blogs and other internet communications.* [Online]. Army.ca forums. Available at: http://forums.army.ca/forums/index.php/topic,51030.0.html [Accessed 22 August 2008].

Carpentier, N., Pruulmann-Vengerfeldt, P., Nordenstreng, K., Hartmann, M.,Vihalemm, P., Cammaerts, B. & Nieminen, H. (2007). *Media Technologies and Democracy in an Enlarged Europe. The Researching and Teaching Communication Series.* [e-book] Tartu: Tartu University Press. Available at: http://www.researchingcommunication.eu/reco_book3. pdf [Accessed 26 January 2009].

Carruthers, S.L. (2000). *The Media at War: Communication and Conflict in the Twentieth Century.* Basingstoke: Macmillan Press.

Cashmore, P. (2009). *#CNNfail: Twitter Blasts CNN Over Iran Election.* [Online] (Updated 14 June 2009). Available at: http://mashable. com/2009/06/14/cnnfail/ [Accessed 17 June 2009].

Castells, M. (2009). *Communication Power.* Oxford: Oxford University Press.

—(1996). *The Rise of the Network Society.* London: Blackwell.

Castells, M., Fernandez-Ardevol, M., Qui, J.L. & Sey, A. (2007). *Mobile Communication and Society: A Global Perspective.* Cambridge, MA: Massachusetts Institute of Technology.

CBC News. (2005). *In Depth: Iraq – Abu Ghraib Timeline.* [Online] CBC News online, 18 February. Available at: http://www.cbc.ca/news/ background/iraq/abughraib_timeline.html [Accessed 20 February 2008].

—(2004a). *Abuse at Abu Ghraib.* [Online] *CBS*, 5 May. Available at: http://www.cbsnews.com/stories/2004/05/05/60II/main615781. shtml [Accessed 11 August 2008].

—(2004b). *Abuse of Iraqi POWs by GIs probed: 60 Minutes II has exclusive report on alleged mistreatment. 60 minutes.* [Online] *CBS*, 28 April. Available at: http://www.cbsnews.com/stories/2004/04/27/60II/ main614063.shtml [Accessed 11 February, 2008].

Cellan-Jones, R. (2009). *Iran's internet dilemma.* [Online] BBC news. Dot.life, 19June.Availableat:http://www.bbc.co.uk/blogs/technology/2009/06/ irans_internet_dilemma.html [Accessed 11 October 2009].

CERN. (2003). *Ten years public domain for the original web software.* [Online] (Updated 30 April 1993). Available at: http://tenyears-www.web.cern. ch/tenyears-www/Declaration/Page2.html [Accessed 10 November 2008].

Chen, W., Boase, J. & Wellman, B. (2002). Comparing internet users and uses around the world. In C. Haythornthwaite & B. Wellman, eds *The Internet in Everyday Life.* Oxford: Blackwell, pp. 74–113.

Cherribi, S. (2006). From Baghdad to Paris: *al-Jazeera* and the veil. *The Harvard International Journal of Press/Politics*, 11(2), 121–128.

Chilcot, J. (2009). *The Iraq Inquiry.* [Online] (Updated 30 July 2009). Available at: http://www.iraqinquiry.org.uk/ [Accessed 29 October 2009].

Chouliaraki, L. (2006a). Towards an analytics of mediation. *Critical Discourse Studies*, 3(2), 153–178.

—(2006b). The aestheticization of suffering on television. *Visual Communication*, 5(3), 261–285.

Christensen, C. (2008). Uploading dissonance: *YouTube* and the US occupation of Iraq. *Media, War & Conflict*, 1(2), 155–175.

Chulov, M. (2009). *Reporters face violence as Iraq cracks down on media dissent.* [Online] guardian.co.uk, 5 November. Available at: http://www. guardian.co.uk/world/2009/nov/05/iraq-government-warn-media [Accessed 14 November 2009].

CID Report and Statements. (2004). *Annexes 25 and 26 to the Taguba Report.* [Online] (Updated 28 January 2004). Available at: http://www. publicintegrity.org/articles/entry/505/ [Accessed 5 August 2008].

Cirincione, J., Tuchman Mathews, J., Perkovich,G. & Orton, A. (2004). *WMD in Iraq: Evidence and Implications* [Online] Carnegie Endowment for International Peace. Available at: http://www.carnegieendowment. org/publications/index.cfm?fa=view&id=1435 [Accessed 14 April 2009].

Clark, A.M. & Christie, T.B. (2005). Ready . . . ready . . . drop! A content analysis of coalition leaflets used in the Iraq War. *Gazette: The International Journal For Communication Studies*, 67(2), 141–154.

Clifton, B. (2004). *Real or fake . . . a photograph allegedly taken while Saddam was dragged out of his bunker by US forces. The Daily Telegraph (Sydney).* [Online] *Thememoryhole.* (Updated 9 January 2004). Available at: http://www.thememoryhole.org/war/saddam-capture-unofficial. htm [Accessed 14 October 2009].

CNN. (2007). *More arrests expected from Hussein execution video* [Online] *CNN*, 3 January. Available at: http://edition.cnn.com/2007/WORLD/meast/01/03/saddam.execution/index.html [Accessed 19 April 2008].

—(2006). *Hussein Executed with 'Fear in his Face'* [Online] *CNN*, 30 December. Available at: http://edition.cnn.com/2006/WORLD/meast/12/29/hussein/index.html [Accessed 19 October 2007].

—(2003). *US releases photos said to show Saddam's sons' bodies.* [Online] *CNN*, 25 July. Available at: http://edition.cnn.com/2003/WORLD/meast/07/24/sprj.irq.sons/index.html [Accessed 29 June 2009].

Coalition Provisional Authority. (2003). *Public Notice: towards a responsible Iraqi media.* [Online]. Coalition Provisional Authority (Published 19 June 2003). Available at: http://www.cpa-iraq.org/regulations/ [Accessed 8 October 2009].

Coalition Provisional Authority. (n.d.). *CPA Official Documents.* [Online]. Available at: http://www.cpa-iraq.org/regulations/ [Accessed 8 October 2009].

Cockburn, A. (2007). *Rumsfeld: An American Disaster.* London: Verso.

Cohen, A. (2004a). *Special Report: The Abu Ghraib supplementary Documents.* [Online] 8 October. The Center for Public Integrity. Available at: http://www.publicintegrity.org/articles/entry/505/ [Accessed 28 February 2008].

—(2004b). *The Abu Ghraib supplementary Documents.* [Online] 31 October. The Center for Public Integrity. Available at: http://www.publicintegrity.org/articles/entry/506/ [Accessed 4 August 2008].

Cohen, B. (1963). *The Press and Foreign Policy.* Princeton: Princeton University Press.

Cohen, K.R. (2005). What does the photoblog want? *Media, Culture & Society,* 27, 883–901.

Conetta, C. (2003). *The wages of war: Iraqi combatant and noncombatant fatalities in the 2003 conflict.* [Online] Project on Defense Alternatives. Research Monograph # 8. (Updated 20 October 2003). Available at: http://www.comw.org/pda/0310rm8.html [Accessed 25 August 2009].

Cook, R. (2004). *The Point of Departure: Diaries from the Front Bench.* London: Pocket Books.

Cordesman, A.H. (1999). *Iraq and the War of Sanctions. Conventional threats and Weapons of Mass Destruction.* New York: Praeger.

Couldry, N. & Downey, J. (2004). War or peace? Legitimation, dissent and rhetorical closure in press coverage of the Iraq war build-up. In S. Allan & B. Zelizer, eds *Reporting War: Journalism in Wartime.* London: Routledge, pp. 266–282.

Cox, L. (2006). *Statement of Larry Cox, Executive Director, Amnesty International USA on the impending execution of Saddam Hussein. Amnesty International USA Press Release.* [Online] (Updated 29 December 2006). Available at: http://www.amnestyusa.org/document.php?lang=e&id=ENGUSA20061229001 [Accessed 14 October 2009].

Coyne, C. (2004). *Photos aren't the most shocking part of abuse story.* [Online] *Salt Lake Tribune,* 8 May. Available at: http://www.sltrib.com/ [Accessed 7 August 2008].

Crawford, D. (2004). *Television primary information source for most 2004 voters.* [Online] 21 May. International Information Programs. Available at: http://usinfo.state.gov/dhr/Archive/2004/May/21–752499.html [Accessed 18 February 2008].

Creative commons. (n.d.) *CC creative commons.* [Online]. Available at: http://creativecommons.org/ [Accessed 10 November 2008].

Crickett in LA. (2003). *Comment on 'Friday sermon in Kadhmia mosque'. Monday, 16-Jun-2003 00:00. Where is Raed? the photographic supplement [I am working my way up to Pax TV].* By Salam Pax. [Online]. Sent 30 June 2003, 19:02. Available at: http://salampax.fotopages.com/?entry=445&back=http://salampax.fotopages.com/?page=0#CommentsTop [Accessed 29 June 2009].

Cucolo, T. (2008). The military and the media: shotgun wedding, rocky marriage, committed relationship. *Media, War & Conflict,* 1(1), 84–89.

Cunningham, S. & Lavalette, M. (2004).'Active citizens' or 'irresponsible truants'? School student strikes against the war. *Critical Social Policy,* 24(2), 255–269.

Curtis, L. (1984). *Ireland: The Propaganda War. The British Media and the Battle for Hearts and Minds.* London: Pluto Press.

Curtis, N. (2007). The military, the media and mimesis. In S. Maltby & R. Keeble, eds *Communicating War: Memory, Media and Military.* Bury St Edmunds: Arima Publishing, pp.188–199.

Dahlberg, L. (2007). The internet and discursive exclusion: from deliberative to agonistic public sphere theory. In L. Dahlberg & E. Siapera, eds *Radical Democracy and the Internet: Interrogating Theory and Practice.* Basingstoke: Palgrave-Macmillan, pp. 128–145.

Dahlberg, L. & Siapera, E. (2007). *Radical Democracy and the Internet: Interrogating Theory and Practice.* Basingstoke: Palgrave-Macmillan.

Dahlgren, P. (2007). Civic identity and net activism: the frame of radical democracy. In L. Dahlberg & E. Siapera, eds *Radical Democracy and the Internet: Interrogating Theory and Practice.* Basingstoke: Palgrave-Macmillan, pp. 55–72.

Danner, M. (2005a). *Taking stock of the forever war.* [Online] (Updated 11 September 2005). Available at: http://www.markdanner.com/articles/show/2 [Accessed 15 August 2008].

——(2005b). *The secret way to war.* [Online] (Updated 9 June 2005). Available at: http://www.markdanner.com/articles/show/9 [Accessed 15 August 2008].

——(2005c). *Iraq: the real election.* [Online] (Updated 28 April 2005). Available at: http://www.markdanner.com/articles/show/10 [Accessed 15 August 2008].

——(2004). *Torture and Truth: America, Abu Ghraib and the War on Terror.* New York: New York Review Books.

Dao, J. & Lichtblau, E. (2004). *The struggle for Iraq: The images; soldier's family set in motion chain of events on disclosure.* [Online] *New York Times,* 8 May. Available at: http://query.nytimes.com/gst/fullpage. html?res=9B01E4D9143CF93BA35756C0A9629C8B63 [Accessed 10 February 2008].

Darby, J. (n.d). *Prisoner of conscience: for the first time since exposing the atrocities at Abu Ghraib, Joe Darby speaks out. As told to Wil S. Hylton.* [Online] GQ./Features. Men.Style.Com, Available at: http://men. style.com/gq/features/full?id=content_4785&pageNum=3 [Accessed 20 February 2008].

Davenport, C. (2004). *New prison images emerge: graphic photos may be more evidence of abuse.* [Online] *Washingtonpost.com,* 6 May. Available at: http://www.washingtonpost.com/ac2/wp-dyn/A5623–2004May5? language=printer [Accessed 10 February 2008].

Dawoody, A. (2006). The Kurdish quest for autonomy and Iraq's statehood. *Journal of Asian and African Studies,* 41(5/6), 483–505.

Dayan, D. & Katz, E. (1992). *Media Events: The Live Broadcasting of History.* Cambridge, MA: Harvard University Press.

De Quetteville, H. (2003). *Swaggering tyrant is pulled, groggy and dishevelled from his rat hole.* [Online] Telegraph, 14 December. Available at: http://www.telegraph.co.uk/news/main.jhtml?xml=/news/ 2003/12/15/wsad115.xml [Accessed 30 November 2007].

Dean, J., Anderson, J.W. & Lovink, G. (2006). *Reformatting Politics: Information Technology and Global Civil Society.* New York : Routledge.

Deleuze, G. (1995). *Negotiations.* New York: Columbia University Press.

——(1992). Postscript on the societies of control. *October,* 59, 3–7.

Deleuze, G. & Guattari, F. (1987). *A Thousand Plateaus: Capitalism and Schizophrenia.* Minneapolis: University of Minneapolis Press.

Department for Culture, Media and Sport. (2005). *Review of the BBC's Royal Charter: a strong BBC, independent of government.* [Online] London:

BBC Media Centre. Available at: www.bbccharterreview.org.uk/pdf_documents/bbc_cr_greenpaper.pdf [Accessed 16 March 2009].

Department of Defense. (2007). *Measuring stability and security in Iraq.* [Online] Report to Congress in accordance with the Department of Defense Appropriations Act 2007 (Section 9010, Public Law 109–289). Available at: www.defenselink.mil/pubs/.../FINAL-SecDef%20Signed-20071214.pdf [Accessed 6 August 2009].

—(2003). *Public Affairs Guidance (PAG) on embedding media during possible future operations/deployment in the U.S. Central Commands (CENT-COM) area of responsibility (AOR).* [Online] United States Department of Defense Defense Link. Available at: www.defenselink.mil/news/Feb2003/d20030228pag.pdf [Accessed 22 August 2008].

Dimitrova, D.V. & Neznanski, M. (2006). Online journalism and the war in cyberspace: a comparison between US and international newspapers. *Journal of Computer-Mediated Communication*, 12, 248–263.

Dimitrova, D.V., Kaid, L.L., Williams, A.P. & Trammell, K.D. (2005). War on the web: the immediate news framing of Gulf War II. *The Harvard International Journal of Press and Politics*, 10(1), 22–44.

Dodge, T. (2006). War and resistance in Iraq. In R. Fawn & R. Hinnebusch, eds *The Iraq War: Causes and Consequences*. London: Lynne Rienner, pp. 211–224.

—(2005). Iraqi transitions: from regime change to state collapse. *Third World Quarterly*, 26(4–5), 705–721.

Dorman, W. & Livingston, S. (1994). The establishing phase of the Persian Gulf policy debate. In W. Bennett and D. Paletz, eds *Taken by Storm: The Media Public Opinion and US Foreign Policy in the Gulf War*. Chicago: University of Chicago Press, pp. 63–81.

Dowmunt, T. & Coyer, K. (2007). Introduction. In K. Coyer, T. Dowmunt & A. Fountain, eds *The Alternative Media Handbook*. London: Routledge, pp. 1–12.

Duffy, B., Williams, M. & Hall, S. (2004). *Who Do You Believe? Trust in Government Information*. London: Ipsos MORI Publication.

Dworznik, G. (2006). Journalism and trauma. *Journalism Studies*, 7(4), 534–553.

Economist Intelligence Unit. (2006). *Global news analysis. Mobile fever in the Middle East. Global technology Forum*. [Online] (Updated 1 June 2006). Available at: http://www.ebusinessforum.com/index.asp?layout=rich_story&doc_id=8638&categoryid=&channelid=&search=arabia [Accessed 15 April 2009].

Edwards, D. & Cromwell, D. (2004). Mass deception: how the media helped the government deceive the people. In David Miller, ed. *Tell*

Me Lies; Propaganda and Media Distortion in the Attack on Iraq. London: Pluto Press, pp. 210–214.

Eid, G. (2007). *Arab activists and information technology; the internet: glimmer of light in dark tunnel. In Casa Arabe, Madrid 18–19 January 2007.* [Online] The Initiative for an Open Arab Net. Available at: http://www.openarab.net/en/node/268 [Accessed 14 April 2009].

Ēl Delilâh. (2007). *What I cannot help saying . . . My not-so-humble opinion.* [blog]. 1 January 2007. Available at: http://delilah-talks.blogspot.com/ [Accessed 18 November 2008].

El-Nawawy, M. & Gher, L.A. (2003). *Al Jazeera: bridging the East–West gap through public discourse and media diplomacy.* [Online]. *Journal of Transnational Broadcasting Studies,* 10(2). Available at: http://www.tbsjournal.com/Archives/Spring03/nawawy.html [Accessed 13 April 2009].

El-Nawawy, M. & Iskandar, A. (2002). *Al-Jazeera: How the Free Arab News Network Scooped the World and Changed the Middle East.* Cambridge, MA: Westview Press.

Engel, R. (2008). *War Journal: My Five years in Iraq.* New York: Simon & Schuster.

Engel, R. (2004). *A Fist in the Hornet's Nest: On the Ground in Baghdad Before, During and After the War.* New York: Hyperion.

Entman, R. (2004). *Projections of Power: Framing News, Public Opinion, and U.S. Foreign Policy.* Chicago: University of Chicago Press.

Entman, R. (1993). Framing: toward clarification of a fractured paradigm. *Journal of Communication,* 43, 51–58.

Fahmy, S. & Johnson, T.J. (2007). The caged bird sings: reliance on al Jazeera as a predictor of views regarding press freedom in the Arab world. In P. Seib, ed. *New Media and the New Middle East.* London: Palgrave Macmillan, pp. 81–100.

FAIR. (2003). *Media advisory: US media applaud bombing of Iraqi TV.* [Online] Fairness & Accuracy In Reporting. (Updated 27 March, 2003). Available at: http://www.fair.org/activism/iraqi-tv.html [Accessed 9 September 2008].

Falah, G.W., Flint, C. & Mamadouhz, V. (2006). Just War and extraterritoriality: the popular geopolitics of the United States' war on Iraq as reflected in newspapers of the Arab world. *Annals of the Association of American Geographers,* 96(1), 142–164.

Fandy, M. (1999). Cyber resistance: Saudi opposition between globalization and localization. *Comparative Studies in Society and History,* 41(1), 124–147.

Farhi, P. (2006). *Blogger takes aim at news media and makes a direct hit.* [Online] *Washingtonpost.com,* 9 August. Available at: http://www.

washingtonpost.com/wp-dyn/content/article/2006/08/08/
AR2006080801431.html [Accessed 10 November 2008].

Fathi, N. (2009). *Recount offer fails to quell political tumult in Iran.* [Online]
The New York Times, 16 June. Available at: http://www.nytimes.
com/2009/06/17/world/middleeast/17iran.html?_r=1&th&emc=th
[Accessed 17 June 2009].

Fawn, R. (2006). The Iraq war: unfolding and unfinished. In R. Fawn &
R. Hinnebusch, eds *The Iraq War: Causes and Consequences.* London:
Lynne Rienner, pp. 1–18.

Fawn, R. & Hinnebusch, R. (2006). *The Iraq War: Causes and Consequences.* London: Lynne Rienner.

Fay. G.R. (2004). *AR 15–6 Investigation of the Abu Ghraib detention facility
and 205th Military Intelligence Brigade.* [Online]. Available at: http://
www.salon.com/news/abu_ghraib/2006/03/14/investigations_
resources/index.html [Accessed 8 August 2008].

FDCH E-Media. (2004). *Rumsfeld Testifies Before Senate Armed Services
Committee.* [Online] Washingtonpost.com, 7 May. Available at: http://
www.washingtonpost.com/wp-dyn/content/article/2004/05/07/
AR2006021501327_5.html [Accessed 18 August 2008].

Feldstein, M. (2007). Dummies and ventriloquists: models of how
sources set the investigative agenda. *Journalism,* 8(5), 499–509.

Ferguson, R. & Griffiths, B. (2006). Hansard Society. Thin democracy?
Parliamentarians, citizens and the influence of blogging on political
engagement. *Parliamentary Affairs,* 59(2), 366–374.

Fernandez, L.A. & Huey, L. (2009). Editorial. Is Resistance Futile?
Thoughts on Resisting Surveillance. *Surveillance & Society,* 6(3), 198–
202. Available at: http://www.surveillance-and-society.org [Accessed
24 October 2009].

Field Manual (FM) 3–13. (2003). *Information operations: doctrine, tactics,
techniques, and procedures.* [Online] Washington DC: US Army (Published 28 November 2003). Available at: www.adtdl.army.mil/cgi-bin/
atdl.dll/fm/3–13/fm3_13.pdf [Accessed 9 June 2009].

Fiorina, C. (2002). *Imaging and invention in a digital age. Consumer Elec-
tronics Show (Ces). Las Vegas, Nevada.* [Online]. (Updated 8 January
2002). Available at: http://www.hp.com/hpinfo/execteam/speeches/
fiorina/ces_02.html [Accessed 17 September 2009].

Follman, M. & Clark-Flory, T. (2006). *Prosecutions and convictions.*
[Online] Salon.com. 14 March. Available at: http://www.salon.
com/news/abu_ghraib/2006/03/14/prosecutions_convictions/
index.html [Accessed 8 August 2008].

Fontenot, G., Degen, E.J. & Tohn, D. (2004). *On Point: The United States
Army in Operation Iraqi Freedom.* [Online]. Fort Leavenworth, Kansas:

Combat Studies Institute Press. Available at: http://www.globalsecurity. org/military/library/report/2004/onpoint/ [Accessed 10 July 2008].

Foucault, M. (1977). *Discipline and Punish: The Birth of the Prison.* Trans. A. Sheridan. New York: Vintage.

—(1965). *Madness and Civilization: a History of Insanity in the Age of Reason.* Trans. R. Howard. New York: Vintage Books.

FoxNews. (2006). *Saddam Hussein's Brutal Reign Ends in the Gallows.* [Online] FoxNews.com, 31 December. Available at: http://www.fox-news.com/story/0,2933,240117,00.html [Accessed 30 November 2007].

Fuchs, C. (2009). *Social Networking Sites and the Surveillance Society: A Critical Case Study of the Usage of studiVZ, Facebook, and MySpace by Students in Salzburg in the Context of Electronic Surveillance.* [e-book] Salzburg and Vienna, Austria: Forschungsgruppe Unified Theory of Information (Research Group Unified Theory of Information). Available at: fuchs. icts.sbg.ac.at/SNS_Surveillance_Fuchs.pdf [Accessed 15 November 2009].

Furedi, F. (1997). *Culture of Fear: Risk-taking and the Morality of Low Expectation.* London: Cassell.

G. (2003). *Geeinbaghdad.* [blog]. 25 June 2003. Available at: http:// geeinbaghdad.blogspot.com/ [Accessed 25 June 2009].

Gamson, W.A., Croteau, D., Hoynes, W. & Sasson, T. (1992). Media images and the social construction of reality. *Annual Review of Sociology*, 18, 373–393.

Gandy, O.H. (2003). Data mining and surveillance in the post-9/11 environment. In K. Ball & F. Webster, eds *The Intensification of Surveillance: Crime, Terrorism and Warfare in the Information Age.* London: Pluto, pp. 26–41.

Garcia, D. (2008). (Un)real-time media – 'Got live if you want it'. In G. Lovink & S. Niederer, eds *Video Vortex Reader: Responses to YouTube.* [e-book] Amsterdam: Institute of Network Cultures, pp. 293–296. Available at: http://networkcultures.org/wpmu/portal/publications/ inc-readers/videovortex/ [Accessed 13 October 2008].

Garfinkel, H. (1967). *Studies in Ethnomethodology.* Cambridge: Polity.

Geneva Convention. (1950a). *Geneva Convention relative to the Protection of Civilian Persons in Time of War.* [Online] Office of the High Commission for Human Rights. Geneva, Switzerland. Available at: http://www.unh-chr.ch/html/menu3/b/92.htm [Accessed 19 April 2008].

—(1950b). *Geneva Convention relative to the Treatment of Prisoners of War.* [Online] Office of the High Commission for Human Rights. Geneva, Switzerland. Available at: http://www.unhchr.ch/html/menu3/b/91. htm [Accessed 19 April 2008].

Gerth, J. & Shane, S. (2005). *US is said to pay to plant articles in Iraq papers.* [Online] *The New York Times,* 1 December. Available at: http://www. nytimes.com/2005/12/01/politics/01propaganda.html?ex=129109 3200&en=15a816ad2c204281&ei=5088&partner=rssnyt&emc=rss [Accessed 30 June 2009].

Gher, L.A. & Amin, H.Y. (1999). New and old media access and ownership in the Arab world. *International Communication Gazette,* 61(1), 59–88.

Gibbs, N. (2003). *Person of the year 2003: the American soldier.* [Online] *Time,* 21 December. Available at: http://www.time.com/time/subscriber/ personoftheyear/2003/story.html [Accessed 16 October 2009].

Gilboa, E. (2002). *The Global News Networks and US Policymaking in Defense and Foreign Affairs.* [e-book] The Joan Shorenstein center on the press, politics and public policy. Harvard University. Available at: www.hks.harvard.edu/presspol/publications/.../2002_06_gilboa. pdf [Accessed 21 June 2009].

—(2000). Mass communication and diplomacy: A theoretical framework. *Communication Theory,* 10(3), 275–309.

Gill in London. (2003). *Comment on 'Friday sermon in Kadhmia mosque. Monday, 16-Jun-2003 00:00.' Where is Raed? the photographic supplement [I am working my way up to Pax TV].* By Salam Pax. [Online] 9 July 2003, 10:14. Available at: http://salampax.fotopages.com/?entry=445&back=http://salampax. fotopages.com/?page=0#CommentsTop [Accessed 29 June 2009].

Global Operations Panel (2008). Global Operations: Sourcing Globally, Reporting Globally. In *investigative journalism goes global conference.* London, UK. 13 June 2008. University of Westminster.

Goddard, P. (2006). 'Improper liberties.' Regulating undercover journalism on *ITV,* 1967–1980. *Journalism,* 7(1), 45–63.

Goddard, P., Robinson, P. & Parry, K. (2008). Patriotism meets plurality: reporting the 2003 Iraq War in the British press. *Media, War & Conflict,* 1(1), 9–30.

Goggin, G. (2006). *Cell Phone Culture: Mobile Technology in Everyday Life.* London: Routledge.

Gopsill, T. (2004). Target the media. In D. Miller, ed. *Tell Me Lies: Propaganda and Media Distortion in the Attack on Iraq.* London: Pluto, pp. 251–261.

Phillis, B. (2003). *Government Communication Review Group Interim Report.* [Online] September 2003. Available at: http://www.gics.gov.uk/ access/review/interimreport.htm [Accessed 2 July 2006].

Graves, L. (2007). The affordances of blogging. A case study in culture and technological effects. *Journal of Communication Inquiry,* 31(4), 331–346.

Greene, R.A. (2006). *Pentagon keeps eye on war videos.* [Online] *BBC News Online,* 29 July. Available at: http://news.bbc.co.uk/2/hi/ technology/5226254.stm [Accessed 8 March 2009].

Griffin, M. (2004). Picturing America's 'War on Terrorism' in Afghanistan and Iraq: photographic motifs as news frames. *Journalism,* 5(4), 381–402.

Grossman, L. (2006). *Time's Person of the Year: You.* [Online] *TIME,* 13 December. Available at: http://www.time.com/time/magazine/ article/0,9171,1569514,00.html [Accessed 8 October 2008].

Grossman, L.K. (1995). *The Electronic Republic: Reshaping Democracy in the Information Age.* New York: Viking.

Guardian.co.uk (n.d.). *Torture scandal: the images that shamed America.* [Online] Guardian.co.uk, (Updated 2009). Available at: http:// www.guardian.co.uk/gall/0,,1211872,00.html [Accessed 18 August 2008].

Gumpert, G. & Drucker, S.J. (2007). The technology of distrust. In V. Bakir & D. Barlow, eds *Communication in the Age of Suspicion: Trust and the Media.* London: Palgrave-Macmillan, pp. 189–201.

Gunther, R. & Mughan, A. (2000). *Democracy and the Media: A Comparative Perspective.* Cambridge: Cambridge University Press.

Guntzel, J.S. (2007). *The US and Iraq's 'free' media: delusion or prophecy?* [Online] Electroniciraq.net, 8 May. Available at: http://electroniciraq. net/news/war-every-day-blog/The_US_and_Iraq_s_Free_Media_ Delusion_or_Prophecy_3056–3056.shtml [Accessed 22 July 2009].

Habermas, J. (1996 [1962]).*The Structural Transformation of the Public Sphere: An Inquiry into a Category of Bourgeois Society.* Trans. T. Burger & F. Lawrence. Cambridge: Polity Press.

—(1995 [1981]). *Theory of Communicative Action.* Trans. T. McCarthy. Cambridge: Polity Press.

Haggerty, K.D., & Ericson, R.V. (2000).The surveillant assemblage. *British Journal of Sociology,* 51(4), 605–622.

Hall, T. (2007). *Review of Media Access to Personnel.* [Online]. (Updated 19 June 2007). Available at: http://www.mod.uk/DefenceInternet/ AboutDefence/CorporatePublications/MediaandPublicCommunicationPublications/MediaRelations/ReportByTonyHallOnReview OfMediaAccessToPersonnel.htm [Accessed 12 September 2008].

Hallin, D. & Gitlin, T. (1994). The Gulf War as popular culture and television drama. In W. Bennett & D. Paletz, eds *Taken by Storm: The Media, Public Opinion and US Foreign Policy in the Gulf War.* Chicago: University of Chicago Press, pp. 149–163.

Hamilton, J. (2004). *War in Iraq: Real-time Reporting.* Minnesota: Abdo.

Hamm, H.I. (2007).'High crimes and misdemeanors': George W. Bush and the sins of Abu Ghraib. *Crime, Media, Culture*, 3(3), 259–284.

Hamza, K. (2000). *Saddam's Bombmaker: The Terrifying Story of the Iraqi Nuclear and Biological Weapons Agenda.* New York: Scribner.

Harnden, T. (2006). *Humiliated and hooded, the tyrant faces his fate on the steel scaffold.* [Online] Telegraph, 30 December. Available at: http://www.telegraph.co.uk/news/main.jhtml?xml=/news/2006/12/30/wsaddam130.xml [Accessed 17 December 2007].

Hartnett, S.J. & Stengrim, L.A. (2004). The whole operation of deception: reconstructing President Bush's rhetoric of weapons of mass destruction. *Cultural Studies <=> Critical Methodologies*, 4(2), 152–197.

Haugbolle, S. (2007). *From A-lists to webtifadas: developments in the Lebanese blogosphere 2005–2006.* [Online] *Arab Society and Media*, February. Available at: *http://www.arabmediasociety.com/?article=40* [Accessed 14 April 2009].

Hayes, G. (2009). *Letting audiences play with your pieces – participatory film & music.* [Online] 21 March. Available at: http://www.personalizemedia.com/letting-audiences-play-with-your-pieces-participatory-film-music/ [Accessed 17 September 2009].

Haynes, D. (2008). *Saddam Hussein's body was stabbed in the back, says guard.* [Online] *The Times*, 1 November. Available at: http://www.timesonline.co.uk/tol/news/world/iraq/article5058550.ece [Accessed 16 October 2009].

Haythornthwaite, C. & Wellman, B. (2002). The internet in everyday life: an introduction. In C. Haythornthwaite & B. Wellman, eds *The Internet in Everyday Life.* Oxford: Blackwell, pp. 3–41.

Heaney, M.T. (2008). Blogging congress: technological change and the politics of the congressional press galleries. *PS: Political Science and Politics*, April, 422–426.

Helmond, A. (2008). *How many blogs are there? Is someone still counting?* [Online] *The Blog Herald*, 11 February. Available at: http://www.blogherald.com/2008/02/11/how-many-blogs-are-there-is-some-one-still-counting/ [Accessed 13 October 2008].

Helmore, E. (2007). *Saddam 'Snuff Video' Signals the End of Editorial Control.* [Online] *The Observer*, 7 January. Available at: http://www.guardian.co.uk/Iraq/Story/0,,1984322,00.html [Accessed 17 December 2007].

Hendelman-Baavur, L. (2007). Promises and perils of weblogistan: online media and Iran. *MERIA Journal*, 11(2). Available at: http://www.meriajournal.com/en/asp/journal/2007/june/baavur/index.asp [Accessed 15 April 2009].

Herman, E.S. & Chomsky, N. (1988). *Manufacturing Consent. The Political Economy of the Mass Media.* New York: Pantheon Books.

Hersh, S.M. (2004a). *Torture at Abu Ghraib.* [Online] *The New Yorker,* 10 May. Available at: http://www.newyorker.com/archive/2004/05/10/040510fa_fact [Accessed 21 February 2008].

—(2004b). *Chain of Command.* [Online] *The New Yorker,* 17 May. Available at: http://www.newyorker.com/archive/2004/05/17/040517fa_fact2 [Accessed 14 August 2008].

—(2004c). *The Gray Zone.* [Online] *The New Yorker,* 24 May. Available at: http://www.newyorker.com/archive/2004/05/24/040524fa_fact [Accessed 14 August 2008].

—(2004d). *Chain of Command: The Road from 9/11 to Abu Ghraib.* New York: Harper Perennial.

Hesford, W. (2006). Staging terror. *TDR: The Drama Review,* 50(3), 29–41.

Hiebert, R.E. (2003). Public relations and propaganda in framing the Iraq War: a preliminary review. *Public Relations Review,* 29(2), 243–255.

Hill, A. (2009). *Re-Imagining the War on Terror: Seeing, Waiting, Travelling.* Basingstoke: Palgrave-Macmillan.

—(2008). Hostage videos in the War on Terror. In K. Randell & S. Redmond, eds *The War Body on Screen.* New York: Continuum, pp. 251–265.

Hinnebusch, R. (2006). Hegemonic stability theory reconsidered: implications of the Iraq war. In R. Fawn & R. Hinnebusch, eds *The Iraq War: Causes and Consequences.* London: Lynne Rienner, pp. 283–322.

Hirji, F. (2006). Common concerns and constructed communities: Muslim Canadians, the internet, and the war. *Journal of Communication Inquiry,* 30(2), 125–141.

Hochschild, A. (2004). *Op-Ed. What's in a word? Torture.* [Online] *The New York Times,* 23 May. Available at: http://www.nytimes.com/2004/05/23/opinion/23HOCH.html?ex=1202965200&en=b7e7dab8a630d657&ei=5070 [Accessed 12 February 2008].

Hockenberry, J. (2005). *The blogs of War.* [Online] *Wired,* August. Available at: http://www.wired.com/wired/archive/13.08/milblogs.html [Accessed 4 July 2008].

Hoffmann, B. (2006a). *The Use of the Internet by Islamic Extremists.* Santa Monica: RAND Corporation. May, 1–20.

Hoffmann, J. (2006b). *Sousveillance.* [Online] *The New York Times,* 10 December. Available at: http://www.nytimes.com/2006/12/10/magazine/10section3b.t-3.html [Accessed 7 September 2009].

Holahan, C. (2007). *Video sharing: thinning the pack.* [Online] *BusinessWeek,* 1 February. Available at: http://www.businessweek.com/technology/

content/feb2007/tc20070201_344549.htm?campaign_id=rss_daily [Accessed 16 October 2008].

Hollis, R. (2006). The United Kingdom: fateful decision, divided nation. In R. Fawn & R. Hinnebusch, eds *The Iraq War: Causes and Consequences.* London: Lynne Rienner, pp. 37–47.

Horrocks, P. (2008). *Value of citizen journalism.* [Online] *BBC News Online,* 7 January. Available at: http://www.bbc.co.uk/blogs/theeditors/2008/01/value_of_citizen_journalism.html [Accessed 4 October 2008].

House of Commons Defence Committee. (2005). *Iraq: An Initial Assessment of Post Conflict Operations.* [Online] Government response to the Committee's Sixth Report of Session 2004–05. (Published 20 July 2005). Available at: http://www.mod.uk/DefenceInternet/AboutDefence/CorporatePublications/DoctrineOperationsandDiplomacyPublications/OperationsInIraq/IraqAnInitialAssessmentOfPostConflictOperations.htm [Accessed 12 September 2008].

Human Rights Watch. (2006). *No blood, no foul,* [Online] July. Available at:http://www.hrw.org/en/reports/2006/07/22/no-blood-no-foul-0 [Accessed 8 October 2009].

Hume, M. (2004). *Is Abu Ghraib the military version of reality TV?* [Online] 28 May. Available at: http://www.spiked-online.com/Printable/0000000CA551.htm [Accessed 7 August 2008].

Ibrahim, Y. (2007). *The emergence of audience as victims: the issue of trust in an era of phone scandals.* [Online]. *M/C Journal: A Journal Of Media And Culture* 10(5). Available at: http://journal.media-culture.org.au/0710/09-ibrahim.php [Accessed 20 March 2009].

icasualties.org. (2009). *Iraq coalition casualty count.* [Online]. Available at: http://icasualties.org/oif/ [Accessed 14 November 2009].

ICM. (2008). *ICM poll for the Sunday Telegraph (12–13 March 2008).* [Online]. Available at: http://www.icmresearch.co.uk/pdfs/2008_mar_sun_tele_iraq_poll.pdf [Accessed 30 October 2009].

ICRC. (2004). *Report of the International Committee of the Red Cross (ICRC) on the treatment by the Coalition forces of prisoners of war and other protected persons by the Geneva Conventions in Iraq during arrest, internment and interrogation.* [Online]. Available at: http://www.globalsecurity.org/military/library/report/2004/icrc_report_iraq_feb2004.htm [Accessed 11 August 2008].

International Crisis Group. (2006). *In their own words: reading the Iraqi insurgency.* [Online]. *Middle East Report,* 50. Available at: http://www.crisisgroup.org/home/index.cfm?id=3953 [Accessed 12 September 2008].

International Telecommunication Union. (2009). *The world in 2009; ICT facts and figures.* [Online]. Available at: www.itu.int/ITU-D/ict/material/Telecom09_flyer.pdf [Accessed 1 November 2009].

Internet World Stats Usage and Population Statistics. (2009). *United States of America. Internet usage and broadband usage report.* [Online]. Available at: http://www.internetworldstats.com/am/us.htm [Accessed 14 October 2009].

Ipsos MORI. (2007). *War With Iraq – Trends (2002–2007).* [Online]. Ipsos MORI Publication. Available at: http://www.ipsos-mori.com/research-publications/researcharchive/poll.aspx?oItemID=55&view=wide [Accessed 15 October 2009].

Iraqbodycount. (2009). *Database. Documented civilian deaths from violence.* [Online]. Available at: http://www.iraqbodycount.org/database/ [Accessed 14 November 2009].

Iraqi Constitution. (2005). *United Nations assistance mission for Iraq.* [Online]. Available at: http://www.uniraq.org [Accessed 14 November 2009].

Is This the Way to Amarillo. (1971) [song]. Recorded by Tony Christie. Written by Neil Sedaka and Howard Greenfield.

(Is This the Way to) Amarillo (2005) [Online video]. Directed by David Mallet. Available at: http://www.youtube.com/watch?v=rFguq39y99E [Accessed 12 November 2009].

Is this the Way to Armadillo? (2005) [Online video]. Directed by The Munganator. Available at: http://www.youtube.com/watch?v=tN1mIerM1BQ [Accessed 12 February 2008].

Iskandar, A. & El-Nawawy, M. (2004). *Al-Jazeera* and war coverage in Iraq: the media's quest for contextual objectivity. In S. Allan & B. Zelizer, eds *Reporting War: Journalism in Wartime.* London: Routledge, pp. 315–332.

Israel, S. (2009). *SM Global Report: Howard Rheingold, Part 1. Where we've been. Global neighbourhoods: following social media wherever it leads.* [Online]. Available at: http://redcouch.typepad.com/weblog/2009/10/sm-global-report-howard-rheingold.html [Accessed 28 October 2009].

Ito. J. (2004). *Joi Ito's moblogging, blogmapping and moblogmapping related resources as of 6/10/2003. Joi Ito's radio outline.* [Online]. Available at: http://radio.weblogs.com/0114939/outlines/moblog.html [Accessed 3 September 2009].

Jabar, F.A. (2007). *Iraq four years after the US-led invasion: assessing the crisis and searching for a way forward.* [Online]. *Policy Outlook,* 37 (July). Carnegie Middle East Center, Carnegie Endowment for International Peace, 1–14. Available at: http://www.carnegieendowment.

org/publications/index.cfm?fa=view&id=19420&prog=zgp&proj=z me [Accessed 1 December 2007].

Jackson, P., Jervis, R. & Johnson, L.K. (2008). The Butler Report, 2004. In R. G.Hughes, P. Jackson & L. Scott, eds *Exploring Intelligence Archives: Enquiries into the Secret State.* Oxford: Routledge, pp. 277–309.

Jamail, D. (2007). *Beyond the Green Zone: Dispatches from an Unembedded Journalist in Occupied Iraq.* Chicago: Haymarket.

Jamail, D. & al-Fadhily, A. (2007). *Media under siege.* [Online] *Electroniciraq.net,* 11 January. Available at: http://electroniciraq.net/news/themedia/Media_Under_Siege_2814–2814.shtml [Accessed 22 July 2009].

Jenkins, H. (2007). *Slash me, mash me, spread me . . . confessions of an ACA-fan.* [Online]. The official weblog of Henry Jenkins. Available at: http://www.henryjenkins.org/2007/04/slash_me_mash_me_but_please_sp.html [Accessed 16 October 2008].

—(2006a). *Convergence Culture.* New York: New York University.

—(2006b). *Fans, Bloggers and Gamers: Exploring Participatory Culture.* New York and London: New York University Press.

—(2004), The cultural logic of media convergence. *International Journal of Cultural Studies,* 7(1), 33–43.

Jenkins, H. & Thorburn, D. (2003). *Democracy and New Media.* Cambridge, MA: MIT Press.

Jervis, R.L. (2008). Commentary: the Butler Report. In R.G. Hughes, P. Jackson & L. Scott, eds *Exploring Intelligence Archives: Enquiries into the Secret State.* Oxford: Routledge, pp. 309–313.

JIC. (2002). *Iraq's weapons of mass destruction: the assessment of the British government.* [Online]. Available at: http://www.number10.gov.uk/Page281 [Accessed 9 March 2009].

Johnson Jr., R.J. (2005). *DOD public affairs strategies and means during OIF: were they effective?* [Online] USAWC strategy research project. Available at: http://www.strategicstudiesinstitute.army.mil/pdffiles/ksil172.pdf [Accessed 24 August 2008].

Johnson, S. (2007). *We're Losing the Infowar.* [Online] *Newsweek,* 15 January. Available at: http://www.newsweek.com/id/56592 [Accessed 9 March 2009].

Johnson, T. & Kaye, B. (2004). Wag the blog: how reliance on traditional media and the internet influence credibility perceptions of weblogs among blog users. *Journalism and Mass Communication Quarterly,* 81, 622–644.

Jones, A.R. (2004). *Army Regulation 15–6 Investigation of the Abu Ghraib prison and 205th Military Intelligence Brigade.* [Online] Available at:

http://www.salon.com/news/abu_ghraib/2006/03/14/investiga-tions_resources/index.html [Accessed 8 August 2008].

Jones, J. (2007). Branding trust: the ideology of making truth claims through interactive media. In V. Bakir & D. Barlow, eds *Communication in the Age of Suspicion: Trust and the Media*. London: Palgrave-Macmillan, pp. 177–188.

Kalb, M. & Saivetz, C. (2007). The Israeli-Hezbollah war of 2006: the media as a weapon in an asymmetrical conflict. *The Harvard International Journal of Press and Politics*, 12(3), July, 43–66.

Kalyvas, S.N. & Kocher, M.A. (2007). Ethnic cleavages and irregular war: Iraq and Vietnam. *Politics & Society*, 35(2), June, 183–223.

Kambouri, N. & Hatzopoulos, P. (2008). Making violent practices public. In G. Lovink and S. Niederer, eds *Video Vortex Reader: Responses to YouTube*. [e-book]. Amsterdam: Institute of Network Cultures, pp. 125–131. Available at: http://networkcultures.org/wpmu/portal/publications/inc-readers/videovortex/ [Accessed 13 October 2008].

Katovsky, B. & Carlson, T. (2003). *Embedded: The Media at War in Iraq. An Oral History*. Connecticut: The Lyons Press.

Katz, I. (2003). Introduction. In S. Pax ed. *The Baghdad Blog*. London: Atlantic Books.

Kean, T.H. (2004). *The 9/11 commission report: final report of the national commission on terrorist attacks upon the United States*. [Online]. (Published 22July2004).Availableat:www.9–11commission.gov/report/911Report.pdf [Accessed 2 November 2009].

Keesing's Record of World Events. (2006). Dec 2006 – Execution of Saddam Hussein. *Keesing's Worldwide*, 52, December. London: Longman, p. 47657.

Kellner, D. (2007). Lying in politics: The case of George W. Bush and Iraq. *Cultural Studies <=> Critical Methodologies*, 7(2), 132–144.

—(2004). Media propaganda and spectacle in the war on Iraq: A critique of U.S. broadcasting networks. *Cultural Studies <=> Critical Methodologies*, 4(3), 329–338.

—(1995). *Media Culture: Cultural Studies, Identity and Politics Between the Modern and the Postmodern*. London and New York: Routledge.

—(1992). *The Persian Gulf TV War*. Oxford: Westview Press.

Kerbel, M.R. & Bloom, J.D. (2005). Blog for America and civic involvement. *The Harvard International Journal of Press/Politics*, 10(4), 3–27.

Kets de Vries, M.F.R. (2006). The spirit of despotism: understanding the tyrant within. *Human Relations*, 59(2), 195–220.

Kewney, G. (2004). *Did Rumsfeld ban Iraq camera phones?* [internet] *The Register*, 25 May. Available at: http://www.theregister.co.uk/2004/05/25/iraq-camera_phone_ban/ [Accessed 8 August 2008].

Khoury-Machool, M. (2007). Kidnap videos: setting the power relations of new media. In S. Maltby & R. Keeble, eds *Communicating War: Memory, Media and Military*. Bury St Edmunds: Arima Publishing, pp. 163–176.

Kinder, M. (2008). The conceptual power of on-line video: 5 easy pieces. In G. Lovink & S. Niederer, eds *Video Vortex Reader: Responses to YouTube*. [e-book] Amsterdam: Institute of Network Cultures, pp. 53–62. Available at: http://networkcultures.org/wpmu/portal/publications/inc-readers/videovortex/ [Accessed 13 October 2008].

Klein, N. (2007). *The Shock Doctrine: The Rise of Disaster Capitalism*. London: Penguin.

Knight, A. (2008). Debate – Who is a journalist? Journalism in the age of blogging. *Journalism Studies*, 9(1), 117–131.

Knightley, P. (2004.) History or bunkum? In D. Miller, ed. *Tell Me Lies: Propaganda and Media Distortion in the Attack on Iraq*. London: Pluto, pp. 100–107.

—(2003). *The First Casualty: The War Correspondent as Hero, Propagandist and Myth Maker from the Crimea to Iraq*. London: Andre Deutsch.

—(2000). *The First Casualty: The War Correspondent as Hero, Propagandist and Myth Maker from the Crimea to Kosovo*. London: Prion Books.

Kohut, A. (2003). *Anti-Americanism: Causes and Characteristics*. [Online]. Philadelphia, PA: Pew Center for the People and the Press. December 10, 2003. Available at: http://people-press.org/commentary/?analysisid=%2077 [Accessed 13 April 2008].

Kraidy, M.M. (2006). *Hypermedia and governance in Saudi Arabia*. [Online]. *First Monday*, 7, September. Available at: http://firstmonday.org/htbin/cgiwrap/bin/ojs/index.php/fm/article/view/1610/1525 [Accessed 17 April 2009].

Kulikova, S.V. & Perlmutter, D.D. (2007). Blogging down the dictator? The Kyrgyz revolution and Samizdat websites. *International Communication Gazette*, 69(1), 29–50.

Kull, S., Ramsay, C., Subias, S. & Lewis, E. (2003–2004). Misperceptions, the Media, and the Iraq War. *Political Science Quarterly*, 118(4), 568–598.

Kumar, R. (2005). *Research Methodology: A Step by Step Guide for Beginners*. London: Sage.

Kyrke-Smith, L. (2007). *Information intervention and the case of Kosovo: realising the responsibility to protect*. [Online]. *Knowledge Politics Quarterly*,

1(1). Available at: http://www.knowledgepolitics.org.uk/journal_V1_1.html [Accessed 14 April 2009].

Lang, G.E. & Lang, K. (1983). *The Battle for Public Opinion: The President, the Press, and the Polls during Watergate.* New York: Columbia University Press.

Larson, E.V. & Savych, B. (2006). *Misfortunes of war. Press and public reactions to civilian deaths in wartime.* [online]. Aerospace Force Development Program of RAND Project AIR FORCE. Santa Monica, CA: RAND Corporation. Available at: www.rand.org/pubs/monographs/2006/RAND_MG441.sum.pdf [Accessed 14 April 2009].

Larson, R.P. (2004). Anatomy of a bonding: an embedded reporter's account of the bonding process with the soldiers. In Y. Kamalipour & N. Snow, eds *War, Media And Propaganda: A Global Perspective.* Lanham, MD: Rowman & Littlefield, pp. 125–130.

Lasswell, H.D. (1971 [1927]). *Propaganda Technique in the World War.* London: The MIT Press.

Lazar, A. & Lazar, M.M. (2004). The discourse of the New World Order: 'Out-casting' the double face of threat. *Discourse and Society,* 15(2–3), 223–242.

Lazzarato, M. (1996). Immaterial labour. In P. Virno & M. Hardt, eds *Radical Thought in Italy.* Minneapolis: University of Minnesota Press, pp. 132–146.

Leigh, D. (2009). *Trafigura drops bid to gag Guardian over MP's question.* [Online] Guardian.co.uk, 13 October. Available at: http://www.guardian.co.uk/media/2009/oct/13/trafigura-drops-gag-guardian-oil [Accessed 30 October 2009].

Leonard, M. (2002). *Public Diplomacy.* London: Foreign Policy Centre.

Lévy, P. (1997). *Collective Intelligence: Mankind's Emerging World in Cyberspace.* Cambridge, MA: Perseus Books.

Levy, S. (2009). *Booting up Baghdad: tech execs take a tour in Iraq.* [Online]. *Wired,* 20 July. Available at: http://www.wired.com/politics/security/magazine/17–08/ff_iraq?currentPage=1 [Accessed 30 July 2009].

Lewis, J. & Brookes, R. (2004). How British television news represented the case for the war in Iraq. In S. Allan & B. Zelizer, eds *Reporting War: Journalism in Wartime.* London: Routledge, pp. 283–300.

Lewis, J., Cushion, S. & Thomas, J. (2005). Immediacy, convenience or engagement? An analysis of 24-hour news channels in the UK. *Journalism Studies,* 6(4), 461–477.

Lewis, J., Threadgold, T., Brookes, R., Mosdell, N., Brander, K., Clifford, S., Bessaiso, E. & Harb, Z. (2004). *Too Close for Comfort? The Role of Embedded Reporting in the Media Coverage Of The 2003 Iraq War.*

Commissioned by the BBC. Cardiff: School of Journalism, Media and Cultural Studies.

Lewis, T., Kwon, P. & Lange, P. (2008). *2008 Middle East – telecoms, internet, broadband and mobile statistics.* [Online]. September 2008 (7th Edition) Available at: https://www.budde.com.au/Research/2008-Middle-East-Telecoms- [Accessed 21 October 2009].

Library of Congress. (2006). *Country profile: Republic of Iraq, August 2006.* [Online]. Federal Research Division. Available at: http://lcweb2.loc.gov/frd/cs/profiles/Iraq.pdf [Accessed 7 January 2008].

Limbaugh, R. (2004). *Statements aired on WNBC.* [Online] Available at: http://clips.mediamatters.org/static/audio/limbaugh-20040504.mp3 [Accessed 19 February 2008].

Live leak. (n.d.). *Full Saddam execution video leaked from cellphone.* [Online video] Available at: http://www.liveleak.com/view?i=863ce7d4a3 [Accessed 17 January 2008].

Livingston, S. (1997). *Clarifying the CNN effect: an examination of media effects according to type of military intervention.* [Online]. Research paper R-18 (June). Cambridge, MA: The Joan Shorenstein Center Research on the Press, Politics, and Public Policy, John F Kennedy School of Government, Harvard University. Available at: http://www.hks.harvard.edu/presspol/publications/papers.html#1 [Accessed 19 May 2009].

Losh, E. (2008). Government *YouTube.* Bureaucracy, surveillance, and legalism in state-sanctioned online video channels. In G. Lovink & S. Niederer, eds *Video Vortex Reader: Responses to YouTube.* [e-book] Amsterdam: Institute of Network Cultures, pp. 111–124. Available at: http://networkcultures.org/wpmu/portal/publications/inc-readers/videovortex/ [Accessed 13 October 2008].

Loughlin, S. (2003). *Rumsfeld on looting in Iraq: 'Stuff happens'.* [Online] CNN.com, 12 April. Available at: http://edition.cnn.com/2003/US/04/11/sprj.irq.pentagon/ [Accessed 6 January 2009].

Louw, P.E. (2003). The 'War Against Terrorism': a public relations challenge for the Pentagon. *International Communication Gazette,* 65(3), 211–230.

Lovink, G. (2008). The art of watching databases: introduction to the Video Vortex Reader. In G. Lovink & S. Niederer, eds *Video Vortex Reader: Responses to YouTube.* [e-book] Amsterdam: Institute of Network Cultures, pp. 9–12. Available at: http://networkcultures.org/wpmu/portal/publications/inc-readers/videovortex/ [Accessed 13 October 2008].

Lowenthal, A. (2008). Pixelate or perish. Networking developers and video activists at Transmission Asia-Pacific. In G. Lovink & S. Niederer, eds *Video Vortex Reader: Responses to YouTube.* [e-book] Amsterdam:

Institute of Network Cultures, pp. 297–300. Available at: http://networkcultures.org/wpmu/portal/publications/inc-readers/videovortex/ [Accessed 13 October 2008].

Lowrey, W. (2006). Mapping the journalism-blogging relationship. *Journalism*, 7(4), 477–500.

Lowrey, W. & Mackay, J.B. (2008). Journalism and blogging. *Journalism Practice*, 2(1), 64–81.

Loyn, D. (2007). Local heroes: risk-taking in Iraq. *British Journalism Review*, 18(2), 21–25.

Luana in Washington State. (2003). *Comment on 'Friday sermon in Kadhmia mosque. Monday, 16-Jun-2003 00:00.' Where is Raed? the photographic supplement [I am working my way up to Pax TV]. By Salam Pax.* [Online]. 26 June 2003, 23:38 Available at: http://salampax.fotopages.com/?entry=139 [Accessed 2 July 2009].

Luckhurst, T. (2007). Now we can all set the agenda. [Online]. *The Independent on Sunday, suppl. Business,* 7 January. Available at: http://news.independent.co.uk/media/article2132469.ece [Accessed 16 December 2007].

Lynch, M. (2007). *Blogging the new Arab public.* [Online]. *Arab Media and Society,* February. Available at: http://www.arabmediasociety.com/?article=10 [Accessed 17 April 2009].

—(2006). *Voices of the New Arab Public: Iraq, al-Jazeera, and Middle East Politics Today.* New York: Columbia University Press.

—(2003). Beyond the Arab street: Iraq and the Arab public sphere. *Politics & Society*, 31(1), 55–91.

Lyon, D. (2003). *Surveillance after September 11.* Cambridge: Polity.

—(2001). *Surveillance Society: Monitoring Everyday Life.* Buckingham: Open University Press.

MacDonald, N. (2005). Iraqi reality-TV hit takes fear factor to another level. [Online]. *The Christian Science Monitor,* 7 June. Available at: http://www.csmonitor.com/2005/0607/p01s03-woiq.html [Accessed 5 October 2009].

MacFarquhar, N. & Burns. J.F. (n.d). *Death of the Iraqi tyrant. Interactive feature.* [Online]. *New York Times,* Available at: http://topics.nytimes.com/top/reference/timestopics/people/h/saddam_hussein/index.html?inline=nyt-per [Accessed 19 October 2007].

Machin, D. & Suleiman, U. (2006). Arab and American computer war games: the influence of a global technology on discourse. *Critical Discourse Studies*, 3(1), 1–22.

MacLeod, S. (2009). *How al-Arabiya got the Obama interview.* [Online]. *Time,* 28 January. Available at: http://www.time.com/time/world/article/0,8599,1874379,00.html?imw=Y [Accessed 29 January 2009].

Madden, M. (2008). *2008 Elections: Barack Obama's super marketing machine.* [Online]. Salon.com, 16 July. Available at: http://www.salon.com/news/feature/2008/07/16/obama_data/ [Accessed 22 July 2009].

Makiya, K. (1998). *Republic of Fear: The Politics of Modern Iraq.* Berkeley: University of California Press. (Originally written under pseudonym al-Khalil, S. (1989).)

—(1991). *The Monument: Art, Vulgarity, and Responsibility in Iraq.* Berkeley: University of California Press. (Originally written under pseudonym al-Khalil, S. (1989).)

Maluf, R. (2007). Review article. *European Journal of Communication,* 22, 229–235.

Mandaville, P. (2007). *Global Political Islam.* London: Routledge.

Manheim, J.B. (1991). *All of the People, All of the Time: Strategic Communication and American Politics.* Armonk, NY: M.E. Sharpe.

Manjoo, F. (2004). *Horror show.* [Online]. Salon.com, 12 May. Available at: http://dir.salon.com/story/tech/feature/2004/05/12/beheading_video/index.html [Accessed 25 June 2008].

Mann, S. (2005). Sousveillance and cyberglogs. A 30-year empirical voyage through ethical, legal and policy issues. *Presence: Teleoperators and Virtual Environments,* 14(6), 625–646.

—(2004a). Continuous lifelong capture of personal experience with EyeTap. *Carpe'04,* October 15, 1–21.

—(2004b). 'Sousveillance': Inverse surveillance in multimedia imaging. In *international multimedia conference: proceedings of the 12th annual ACM international conference on Multimedia,* New York 10–16 October 2004. ACM Press, 620–627. Available at: http://idtrail.org/content/view/135/42/ [Accessed 23 October 2008].

—Mann, S. (2003a). Cyborg logs and collective stream of (de)consciousness capture for producing attribution-free informatic content such as cyborglogs. *First Monday,* 8(2). Available at: http://131.193.153.231/www/issues/issue8_2/mann/index.html [Accessed 3 September 2009].

—(2003b). Existential technology: wearable computing is not the real issue! *Leonardo,* 36(1), 19–26. Available at: http://www.eyetap.org/papers/docs/id_leonardo_36_1_19_0/ [Accessed 28 October 2009].

—(2002). *Sousveillance.* [Online]. Available at: http://wearcam.org/sousveillance.htm [Accessed 23 October 2008].

—(2001). *Cyborg: Digital Destiny and Human Possibility in the Age of the Wearable Computer.* With H. Niedzviecki. Canada: Doubleday Canada.

—(1997). Wearable computing: a first step toward personal imaging. *IEEE Computer,* 30(2), 25–32.

—(1995). *The gas-stove analogy: pseudo privacy versus true privacy.* [Online]. (Updated 16 February 1995). Available at: http://wearcam.org/gas_stove_analogy.htm [Accessed 28 October 2009].

Mann S., Fung, J. & Lo R. (2006). Cyborglogging with camera phones: steps toward equiveillance. In *International Multimedia Conference archive. Proceedings of the 14th annual ACM international conference on Multimedia.* Santa Barbara, CA, USA. 23–27 October, 167–170.

Mann, S., Nolan, J. & Wellman, B. (2003). Sousveillance: inventing and using wearable computing devices for data collection in surveillance environments. *Surveillance & Society,* 1(3), 331–355. Available at: http://www.surveillance-and-society.org/journal.htm [Accessed 19 October 2007].

Manovich, L. (2008). The practice of everyday (media) life. In G. Lovink & S. Niederer, eds *Video Vortex Reader: Responses to YouTube.* [e-book] Amsterdam: Institute of Network Cultures, pp. 33–44. Available at: http://networkcultures.org/wpmu/portal/publications/inc-readers/videovortex/ [Accessed 13 October 2008].

Marshall, T. & Project for Excellence in Journalism. (2008). *Special reports: the changing newspaper newsroom. The state of the news media 2008: an annual report on American journalism.* [online]. Available at: http://www.stateofthenewsmedia.org/2008/ [Accessed 13 October 2009].

Matheson, D. (2004). Weblogs and the epistemology of the news: some trends in online journalism. *New Media and Society,* 6, 443–438.

Matheson, D. & Allan, S. (2007). Truth in a warzone: the role of war-blogs in Iraq. In S. Maltby & R. Keeble, eds *Communicating War: Memory, Media and Military.* Bury St Edmunds: Arima Publishing, pp. 75–89.

Mathiesen, T. (1997). The viewer society: Michel Foucault's 'panopticon' revisited. *Theoretical Criminology,* 1(2), 215–234.

McCarthy, K. (2003a). *Iraq, its domain and the 'terrorist-funding' owner.* [Online]. *The Register,* 9 April. Available at: http://www.theregister.co.uk/2003/04/09/iraq_its_domain/ [Accessed 19 June 2008].

McCarthy, R. (2003b). *Salam's story.* [Online]. *The Guardian,* 30 May. Available at: http://www.guardian.co.uk/world/2003/may/30/iraq.digitalmedia [Accessed 25 June 2009].

McCarthy, R. (2003c). *'I am Saddam Hussein the president of Iraq and I am willing to negotiate'.* [Online]. *The Guardian,* 16 December. Available at: http://www.guardian.co.uk/world/2003/dec/16/iraq.rorymccarthy [Accessed 14 October 2009].

McCary, J. A. (2009). The Anbar Awakening: an alliance of incentives. *The Washington Quarterly,* 32(1), 43–59.

McClellan, S. (2008). *What Happened: Inside the Bush White House and Washington's Culture of Deception.* New York: Public Affairs.

McCormick, N. (2008). *Barack Obama's 'Yes We Can' video.* [Online]. Telegraph.co.uk, 21 February. Available at: http://www.telegraph. co.uk/culture/music/3671190/Barack-Obama%27s-%27Yes-We-Can%27-video.html [Accessed 29 January 2009].

McElroy, D. (2007). *Execution 'turned Saddam into Martyr'.* [Online]. Telegraph.co.uk, 6 January. Available at: http://www.telegraph.co. uk/news/main.jhtml?xml=/news/2007/01/05/usaddam105.xml [Accessed 14 December 2007].

McKelvey, F. (2007). *YouTube* and Canada in Afghanistan. In *internet research 8.0: let's play! International and interdisciplinary conference of the association of internet researchers,* Vancouver, Canada 18–20 October 2007.

McLaren, P. & Martin, G. (2004). The legend of the Bush gang: imperialism, war, and propaganda. *Cultural Studies <=> Critical Methodologies,* 4(3), 281–303.

McNair, B. (2007). *An Introduction to Political Communication.* London: Routledge (4th edition).

—(2006). *Cultural Chaos: Journalism, News And Power in a Globalised World.* London: Routledge.

—(2003). From control to chaos: towards a new sociology of journalism. *Media, Culture & Society,* 25, 547–555.

McStay, A. (2009). *Digital Advertising.* Basingstoke: Palgrave-Macmillan.

—(2007). Regulating the suicide bomber: a critical examination of online viral advertising and simulations of self-broadcasting. *Ethical Space: The International Journal of Communication Ethics,* 4(1–2), 40–48.

McStay, A. & Bakir, V. (2006). Privacy, online advertising and marketing techniques: the paradoxical disappearance of the user. *Ethical Space: The International Journal of Communication Ethics,* 3(1), 24–31.

Media Monitor. (2003). The media go to war: TV news coverage of the war in Iraq. *Media Monitor,* XVII (2) July/August, 1–8. [Online] www.cmpa.com/files/media_monitor/03julaug.pdf [Accessed 14 February 2010].

Mellor, N. (2007). *Modern Arab Journalism: Problems and Prospects.* Edinburgh: Edinburgh University Press.

Mermin, J. (1999). *Debating War and Peace. Media Coverage of U.S. Intervention in the Post-Vietnam Era.* Princeton: Princeton University Press.

Metz, C. (2007). *Web 3.0.* [Online]. PCmag.com, 14 March. Available at: http://www.pcmag.com/article2/0,2817,2102852,00.asp [Accessed 28 October 2009].

Miles, H. (2005a). *Al Jazeera: The Inside Story of the Arab News Channel that is Challenging the West.* New York: Grove Press.

Miles, H. (2005b). *Al-Jazeera: How Arab TV News Challenged the World.* London: Abacus.

Militant Islam Monitor.org. (n.d.). *Saddam Hussein shouts encouragement to PA terrorists before hanging – uncut execution video,* [Online video]. Available at: http://www.militantislammonitor.org/article/id/2646 [Accessed 17 January 2008].

Miller, D. (2004a). The propaganda machine. In D. Miller, ed. *Tell Me Lies: Propaganda and Media Distortion in the Attack on Iraq.* London: Pluto Press, pp. 80–99.

—(2004b). Information dominance: the philosophy of total propaganda control? In Y. R. Kamalipour & N. Snow, eds *War, Media, and Propaganda: A Global Perspective.* Lanham, MD: Rowman & Littlefield, pp. 7–16.

—(1994). *Don't Mention the War: Northern Ireland, Propaganda and the Media.* London: Pluto Press.

Miller, G. & Barnes, J.E. (2008). *Rumsfeld blamed in detainee abuse scandals.* [Online]. *Los Angeles Times,* 12 December. Available at: http://www.latimes.com/news/nationworld/nation/la-na-interrogate-abuse 12–2008dec12,0,2238629.story [Accessed 3 January 2009].

Miller, L., Stauber, J. & Rampton, S. (2004). War is sell. In D. Miller, ed. *Tell Me Lies, Propaganda and Media Distortion in the Attack on Iraq.* London: Pluto, pp. 41–51.

Ministry of Defence. (2008). *Contact with the media and communicating in public. Defense instructions and notices,* [Online]. Directorate of Communication and Planning. Defence: Media Relations. Available at: http://www.mod.uk/DefenceInternet/AboutDefence/CorporatePublications/MediaandPublicCommunicationPublications/MediaRelations/Din2007din03006ContactWithTheMediaAndCommunicatingInPublic.htm [Accessed 2 November 2009].

—(2007). *Contact with the media and communicating in public. Defense instructions and notices,* [Online]. Directorate of Communication and Planning. Defence: Media Relations. Available at: http://www.mod.uk/DefenceInternet/AboutDefence/CorporatePublications/MediaandPublicCommunicationPublications/MediaRelations/August 2007 [Accessed 12 September 2008].

—(2004). *Ministry of Defence memo (Jan 2004) on Media Operations in Iraq 2003,* [Online]. Select Committee on Defence Written Evidence. Available at: http://ics.leeds.ac.uk/papers/vp01.cfm?outfit=pmt&requesttimeout=500&folder=34&paper=2599 [Accessed 12 September 2008].

—(2003a). *Operations in Iraq: first reflections*, [Online]. July 2003. Available at: http://www.mod.uk/DefenceInternet/AboutDefence/CorporatePublications/DoctrineOperationsandDiplomacy Publications/OperationsInIraq/OperationInIraqFirstReflections.htm [Accessed 12 September 2008].

—(2003b). *The information campaign.* [Online]. In *Operations in Iraq: Lessons for the Future,* 18 December 2003. Available at: http://webarchive.nationalarchives.gov.uk/20060130194436/http://www.mod.uk/publications/iraq_futurelessons/chap10.htm [Accessed 9 June 2009].

—(2001). *Media operations, joint warfare publication 3–45.* [Online]. The Joint Doctrine and Concepts Centre. November 2001. Available at: http://ics.leeds.ac.uk/papers/vp01.cfm?outfit=pmt&requesttimeout=500&folder=34&paper=2268 [Accessed 12 September 2008].

—(n.d.). MOD working arrangements with the media for use throughout the full spectrum of military operations. Defence: The Green Book. [Online]. Available at: http://www.mod.uk/DefenceInternet/About Defence/CorporatePublications/DoctrineOperationsandDiplomacy-Publications/TheGreenBook/ [Accessed 12 September 2008].

Miracle, C.T.L. (2003). The army and embedded media. *Military Review,* September–October, 41–45.

Miskin, A. (1991). Mediations. No place to hide. *Middle East Report,* 168, (Jan–Feb), 33, 35.

Miskin, S., Rayner, L. & Lalic, M. (2003). *Media under fire: reporting conflict in Iraq* [Online]. (Current issues brief index). Department of the Parliamentary Library, Parliament of Australia, pp. 1–26. Available at: http://www.aph.gov.au/library/pubs/CIB/2002–03/03cib21.htm [Accessed 22 August 2008].

Mitchem, M. (2008). Video social: complex parasitical media. In G. Lovink & S. Niederer, eds *Video Vortex Reader: Responses to YouTube.* [e-book] Amsterdam: Institute of Network Cultures, pp. 273–281. Available at: http://networkcultures.org/wpmu/portal/publications/inc-readers/videovortex/ [Accessed 13 October 2008].

MixMax. (2008). Iraqi TV after 2003 [blog] 12 January. Available at: http://mixmode.blogspot.com/2008/01/iraqi-tv-after-2003.html [Accessed 20 April 2009].

Molotch, H. & Lester, M. (1975). Accidental news: the great oil spill as local occurrence and national event. *American Journal of Sociology,* 81, 235–260.

Morrison, D. & Tumber, H. (1988). *Journalists at War: The Dynamics of News Reporting during the Falklands Conflict.* London: Sage.

Mosco, V. (2000). Learning to be a citizen of cyberspace. In K. Rubenson and H.G. Schuetze, eds *Transition to the Knowledge Society: Policies and Strategies for Individual Participation and Learning.* University of British Columbia: UBC Institute for European Studies, pp. 377–392.

Mouffe, C. (2005). *On the Political.* London: Routledge.

—(2000). Deliberative democracy or agonistic pluralism? *Political Science Series Number, 72,* 1–17.

MSNBC. (2007). *Iraqis arrest men over Saddam hanging video.* [Online]. *MSNBC,* 23 January. Available at: http://www.msnbc.msn.com/id/13259309 [Accessed 17 April 2008].

—(2003). *Saddam captured without a shot fired.* [Online]. *MSNBC,* 15 December. Available at: http://www.msnbc.msn.com/id/3708711/ [Accessed 7 January 2008].

Mudhai, O.F. (2006). Exploring the potential for more strategic civil society use of mobile phones. In J. Dean, J.W. Anderson & G. Lovink, eds *Reformatting Politics: Information Technology and Global Civil Society.* New York: Routledge, pp. 107–120.

Multi-National Force – Iraq. (2007). *YouTube* channel [Online]. Available at: http://www.youtube.com/mnfiraq [Accessed 20 October 2008].

Munson, H. (2006). Islamic militancy. In R. Fawn & R. Hinnebusch, eds *The Iraq War: Causes and Consequences.* London: Lynne Rienner, pp. 235–246.

Naim, M. (2007). The *YouTube* effect. *Foreign Policy,* January/February, 103–104.

Nakash, Y. (2006). *Reaching for Power: The Shi'a in the Modern Arab World.* Princeton and Oxford: Princeton University Press..

Nana. (2003). *Comment on 'Friday sermon in Kadhmia mosque. Monday, 16-Jun-2003 00:00.' Where is Raed? the photographic supplement [I am working my way up to Pax TV].* [Online]. By Salam Pax., 27 June 2003, 02:45. Available at: http://salampax.fotopages.com/?entry=445&back=http://salampax.fotopages.com/?page=0#CommentsTop [Accessed 29 October 2009].

Nasaw, D. (2009). Report vindicates soldiers prosecuted over Abu Ghraib abuses, lawyers say. [Online]. guardian.co.uk, 22 April. Available at: http://www.guardian.co.uk/world/2009/apr/22/abu-ghraib-iraq-torture-senate [Accessed 19 May 2009].

Nashashibi, S.H., Boulos, Z. & Gabriel, G. (2007). *Monitoring study: media portrayals of the Arab Gulf states.* [Online]. Available at: http://www.arabmediawatch.com/amw/ [Accessed 1 May 2009].

Negroponte, N. (1995). *Being Digital.* New York: Knopf.

Nelson, H. (2004). *AR 15–6 Investigation – Allegations of detainee abuse at Abu Ghraib, Psychological Assessment, Taguba Report, Annex 1*, [Online]. Available at: http://www.publicintegrity.org/articles/entry/506/ [Accessed 5 August 2008].

Nisbet, E.C., Nisbet, M.C., Scheufele, D.A. & Shanahan, J.E. (2004). Public diplomacy, television news, and Muslim opinion. *The Harvard International Journal of Press and Politics*, 9(2), 11–37.

Nye, J.S. (2004). *Soft Power: The Means to Success in World Politics*. New York: Public Affairs.

Obama, B. (2008). *Change We Can Believe In: Barack Obama's Plan to Renew America's Promise*. New York: Random House.

Ofcom. (2007). *Ofcom broadcast bulletin*, [Online]. 84(8 May). Available at: http://www.ofcom.org.uk/tv/obb/prog_cb/obb84/ [Accessed 30 December 2007].

—(2006a). *Audience research*, [Online]. 1, Doc. 3 Available at: http://www.ofcom.org.uk/consult/condocs/psb/psb/sup_vol_1/audience/ [Accessed 18 February 2008].

—(2006b). *The communications market 2006: 3 telecommunications*, [Online]. 10 August. Available at: http://www.ofcom.org.uk/research/cm/cm06/cmr06_print/ [Accessed 28 October 2009].

Office of the High Commissioner for Human Rights. (1984). *Convention against torture and other cruel, inhuman or degrading treatment or punishment*, [Online]. Geneva, Switzerland: United Nations. Available at: http://www.unhchr.ch/html/menu3/b/h_cat39.htm [Accessed 28 January 2009].

Ogrish.com. (2006). *OGRISH F.A.Q.*, [Online]. Available at: http://web.archive.org/web/20061023065518/www.ogrish.com/faq.html [Accessed 28 January 2009].

O'Reilly, T. (2005). *What is Web 2.0? Design patterns and business models for the next generation of software*, [Online]. (Published 30 September 2005). Available at: http://www.oreillynet.com/pub/a/oreilly/tim/news/2005/09/30/what-is-web-20.html?page=2 [Accessed 10 January 2008].

O'Reilly, T. & Battelle, J. (2009). *Web squared: Web 2.0 five years on. Web 2.0 summit*. [Online]. Co-produced by O'Reilly Media, Inc. and TechWeb. Available at: http://www.web2summit.com/web2009 [Accessed 21 September 2009].

O'Rourke, R. (2003). *Iraq War: defense program implications for Congress*. [Online]. Congressional Research Service, Library of Congress. Available at: www.au.af.mil/au/awc/awcgate/crs/rl31946.pdf [Accessed 1 January 2008].

Owen, G. (2006). *'Don't be Afraid', Saddam told himself at the Gallows.* [Online]. *Daily Mail,* 30 December. Available at: http://www.dailymail. co.uk/pages/live/articles/news/news.html?in_article_id= 425585&in_page_id=1770 [Accessed 12 December 2007].

Oxford Research International. (2004). *National survey of Iraq* [Online]. Available at: http://news.bbc.co.uk/nol/shared/bsp/hi/pdfs/15_03_04_ iraqsurvey.pdf [Accessed 30 June 2009].

Paletz, D. & Schmid, A. (1992). *Terrorism and the Media.* London: Sage.

Palmer, J. & Fontan, V. (2007). 'Our ears and our eyes': Journalists and fixers in Iraq. *Journalism,* 8(1), 5–24.

Pantic, D. (2006). Anybody can be TV: How P2P home video will challenge the network news. In J. Dean, J.W. Anderson & G. Lovink, eds *Reformatting Politics: Information Technology and Global Civil Society.* New York: Routledge, pp. 55–65.

Parker, N. & Colvine, M. (2006). *Saddam Hussein is hanged, defiant to the last.* [Online]. *Timesonline,* 30 December. Available at: http://www. timesonline.co.uk/tol/news/world/middle_east/article1265314. ece [Accessed 16 December 2007].

Parker, N. & Hamdani, A. (2007). *How one mobile phone made Saddam's hanging a very public execution.* [Online]. *Timesonline,* 1 January. Available at: http://www.timesonline.co.uk/tol/news/world/iraq/ article1265619.ece [Accessed 16 December 2007].

Paul, C. & Kim, J.J. (2004). *Reporters on the battlefield: the embedded press system in historical context.* [Online]. Arlington, VA: Rand National Security Research Division, RAND Corporation. Available at: http:// ics.leeds.ac.uk/papers/vf01.cfm?folder=34&outfit=pmt [Accessed 9 September 2008].

Paul, J. & Nahory, C. (2007). *War and occupation in Iraq.* [Online]. Global Policy Forum. Available at: www.usawatch.org/docs/warin-iraq.pdf [Accessed 7 October 2009].

Pax, S. (2004). *Where is Raed?* [blog]. 26 January 2004. Available at: http://dear_raed.blogspot.com/ [Accessed 30 June 2009].

—(2003a). *The Baghdad Blog.* London: Atlantic Books.

—(2003b). *I became the profane pervert Arab blogger.* [Online]. *The Guardian,* 9 September. Available at: http://www.guardian.co.uk/ world/2003/sep/09/iraq.biography [Accessed 25 June 2009].

—(2003c). *Webchat transcript: Baghdad War diary.* [Online]. Today. Radio 4 9 September. Available at: http://www.bbc.co.uk/radio4/ today/webchat/webchat_iraq.shtml [Accessed 25 June 2009].

—(2003d). *Where is Raed?* [blog]. 23 December 2003. Available at: http://dear_raed.blogspot.com/ [Accessed 25 June 2009].

—(2003e). *Where is Raed?* [blog]. October 18 2003 8:50 PM. Available at: http://dear_raed.blogspot.com/ [Accessed 25 June 2009].

—(2003f). *Where is Raed?* [blog]. 24 July 2003. Available at: http://dear_raed.blogspot.com/ [Accessed 25 June 2009].

—(2003g). *Where is Raed?* [blog]. 18 June 2003. Available at: http://dear_raed.blogspot.com/ [Accessed 25 June 2009].

—(2003h). *Where is Raed?* [blog]. 7 April 2003, 11:30am posted on 7 May 2003. Available at: http://dear_raed.blogspot.com/ [Accessed 25 June 2009].

—(2003i). *Where is Raed?* [blog]. 23 March 2003, 8.30pm, posted 24 March 2003, 4:41 PM. Available at: http://dear_raed.blogspot.com/ [Accessed 25 June 2009].

—(2003j). *Where is Raed?* [blog]. 22 March 2003, 4:30pm posted on 24 March 2003. Available at: http://dear_raed.blogspot.com/ [Accessed 25 June 2009].

—(2003k). *Where is Raed?* [blog]. 20 March 2003, 12:21 AM. Available at: http://dear_raed.blogspot.com/ [Accessed 25 June 2009].

—(2003l). *Where is Raed?* [blog]. 20 March 2003, 4:28 PM. Available at: http://dear_raed.blogspot.com/ [Accessed 25 June 2009].

—(2002). *Where is Raed?* [blog]. 22 December 2002, 10:42 AM. Available at: http://dear_raed.blogspot.com/ [Accessed 25 June 2009].

Perry, W.L., Johnson, S.E., Crane, K., Gompert, D.C., Gordon IV, J., Hunter, R.E., Kaye, D.D., Kelly, T.K., Peltz, E. & Shatz, H.J. (2009). *Withdrawing from Iraq: alternative schedules, associated risks, and mitigating strategies.* [Online]. Santa Monica, CA: Rand Corporation. Available at: www.rand.org/pubs/monographs/MG882/ [Accessed 30 October 2009].

Peterson, H. (1939). *Propaganda for War: The Campaign against American Neutrality, 1914–17.* Norman: University of Oklahoma Press.

Petley, J. (2004). Let the atrocious images haunt us. In D.Miller, ed. *Tell Me Lies; Propaganda and Media Distortion in the Attack on Iraq.* London: Pluto Press, pp. 165–175.

Pew Research Centre. (2007). *Pew weekly news interest index poll. Iraq news: less dominant, still important: public wants more coverage of US troops.* [Online]. The Pew Research Centre for the People and the Press. Available at: http://people-press.org/reports/display.php3?ReportID= 370 [Accessed 14 November 2008].

Pew Research Centre for the People and the Press. (2004). *Survey reports: cable and internet loom large in fragmented political news universe.* [Online]. Washington D.C.: Pew Research Centre. Available at:

http://people-press.org/report/200/cable-and-internet-loom-large-in-fragmented-political-news-universe [Accessed 26 June 2008].

Pfau, M., Haigh, M., Gettle, M., Donnelly, M., Scott, G., Warr, D. & Wittenberg, E. (2004). Embedding journalists in military combat units: impact on newspaper story frames and tone. *Journalism & Mass Communication Quarterly*, 81(1), 74–88.

Pfau, M., Haigh, M., Logsdon, L., Perrine, C., Baldwin, J.P., Breitenfeldt, R.E., Cesar, J., Dearden, D., Kuntz, G., Montalvo, E., Roberts, D. & Romero, R. (2005). *Embedded reporting during the invasion and occupation of Iraq: how the embedding of journalists affects television news reports.* [Online]. *Journal of Broadcasting & Electronic Media*, Dec, 1–17. Available at: http://findarticles.com/p/articles/mi_m6836/is_4_49/ai_n25120983/?tag=content;col1 [Accessed 18 November 2008].

Pincus, W. (2009). *Solicitation for media team in Iraq hints at contracting-overhaul snags.* [Online]. *Washingtonpost.com*, 8 March, p. A14. Available at: http://www.washingtonpost.com/wp-dyn/content/article/2009/03/07/AR2009030701795.html [Accessed 18 March 2009].

Poole, O. (2003). *Black Knights: On the Bloody Road to Baghdad.* London: Reportage Press.

Post, J.M. & Panis, L.D. (2005). Tyranny on trial: personality and courtroom conduct of defendants Slobodan Milosevic and Saddam Hussein. *Cornell International Law Journal*, 38, 823–836.

Poster, M. (1997). *The Second Media Age.* Cambridge: Polity Press.

Price, M. & Thompson, M. (2002). *Forging Peace: Intervention, Human Rights and the Management of Media Space.* Edinburgh: Edinburgh University Press.

Project for Excellence in Journalism. (2008). *The state of the news media 2008: an annual report on American journalism.* [Online]. Journalism. org. Available at: http://www.stateofthenewsmedia.org/2008/ [Accessed 12 November 2009].

—(2007). *The state of the news media 2007: an annual report on American journalism.* [Online]. Available at: http://www.stateofthemedia.org/2007/narrative_overview_intro.asp?cat=1&media=1 [Accessed 16 November 2008].

—(2006). *The state of the news media 2006: an annual report on American journalism.* [Online]. Available at: http://www.stateofthemedia.org/2006/ [Accessed 16 November 2009].

—(2003). *Embedded reporters. What are Americans getting?* [Online]. Journalism.org. Available at: http://journalism.org/node/211 [Accessed 16 November 2008].

Purvis, S. (2007). Tony Blair's 'Media' speech: the commentators. It's the technology, stupid. *The Political Quarterly*, 78(4), 495–497.

Quiggin, J. (2006). Blogs, wikis and creative innovation. *International Journal of Cultural Studies*, 9(4), 481–496.

Quinn, S. (2005). Convergence's fundamental question. *Journalism Studies*, 6(1), 29–38.

Raab, C.D. (2003). Joined-up surveillance: the challenge to privacy. In K. Ball & F. Webster, eds *The Intensification of Surveillance: Crime, Terrorism and Warfare in the Information Age*. London: Pluto, pp. 42–61.

Raaman, A., Damon, A., Chilcote, R., Dagher, S., Karadsheh, J. & Henry, E. (2006). *Witness: Saddam Hussein argued with guards moments before death.* [Online]. CNN.com, 30 December. Available at: http://edition.cnn.com/2006/WORLD/meast/12/30/hussein/index.html [Accessed 19 October 2007].

Rachel. (June, 2003). *Comment on "Friday sermon in Kadhmia mosque. Monday, 16-Jun-2003 00:00." Where is Raed? the photographic supplement [I am working my way up to Pax TV].* [Online]. By Salam Pax. 26 June 2003, 19:43. Available at: http://salampax.fotopages.com/?entry=445&back=http://salampax.fotopages.com/?page=0#CommentsTop [Accessed 1 July 2009].

Ramesh, R. (2003). *The War We Could Not Stop: The Real Story of the Battle for Iraq. The Guardian.* London: Faber & Faber.

Rampton, S. & Stauber, J. (2004). *Weapons of Mass Deception: The Uses of Propaganda in Bush's War on Iraq.* New York: Penguin.

Ravi, N. (2005). Looking beyond flawed journalism: how national interests, patriotism, and cultural values shaped the coverage of the Iraq War. *The Harvard International Journal of Press/Politics*, 10(1), 45–62.

Reporters without borders. (2005). *The 15 enemies of the internet and other countries to watch. Press freedom day by day.* [Online]. Available at: http://www.rsf.org/article.php3?id_article=15613 [Accessed 15 April 2009].

Reuters. (2009a). *Suicide bomber in west Iraq kills 7, wounds 16.* [Online]. *Reuters*, 7 September. Available at: http://www.reuters.com/article/latestCrisis/idUSL7532800 [Accessed 8 September 2008].

—(2009b). *Obama team drops 'war on terror' rhetoric.* [Online]. *Reuters*, 31 March. Available at: http://uk.reuters.com/article/idUKTRE52T7N920090330 [Accessed 3 November 2009].

Rheingold, H. (2003). *Moblogs seen as a crystal ball for a new era in online journalism.* [Online]. Online Journalism Review, USC, Available at: http://www.ojr.org/ojr/technology/1057780670.php [Accessed 10 January 2007].

—(2002). *Smart Mobs: The Next Social Revolution.* New York: Basic Books.

—(1993). *The Virtual Community: Homesteading on the Electronic Frontier.* New York: HarperCollins.

Rhoads, C. & Chao, L. (2009). *Iran's web spying aided by western technology.* [Online]. *The Wall Street Journal,* 23 June. Available at: http://online.wsj. com/article/SB124562668777335653.html [Accessed 26 June 2009].

Ricchiardi, S. (2004). *Missed signals.* [Online]. *American Journalism Review,* August/September. Available at: http://www.ajr.org/Article. asp?id=3716 [Accessed 14 August 2008].

—(2003). *Preparing for war.* [Online]. *American Journalism Review,* March. Available at: http://www.ajr.org/Article.asp?id=2794 [Accessed 9 September 2008].

Richard, B. (2008). Media masters and grassroot art 2.0 on *Youtube.* In G. Lovink & S. Niederer, eds *Video Vortex Reader: Responses to YouTube.* [e-book] Amsterdam: Institute of Network Cultures, pp. 141–152. Available at: http://networkcultures.org/wpmu/portal/publications/ inc-readers/videovortex/ [Accessed 13 October 2008].

Richards, E. (2007). *IPPR media convention.* [Online]. (Updated 18 January 2007). Available at: http://www.ofcom.org.uk/media/speeches/2007/01/ ippr [Accessed 9 March 2009].

Ricks, T.E. (2006). *Fiasco: The American Military Adventure in Iraq.* New York: Penguin.

Ridley, Y. (2008). Introductory Panel. In CAMMRO (Centre for Arab and Muslim Media Research) *4th international conference on new media and social change in the Arab and Muslim world.* London, UK. 16 June 2008. King's College, University of London.

—(2004). Turning my back on the mainstream. In D. Miller, ed. *Tell Me Lies: Propaganda and Media Distortion on the Attack on Iraq.* London: Pluto, pp. 262–268.

Riegert, K. & Johansson, A. (2005). The struggle for credibility during the Iraq War. In J. Hallenberg & H. Karlsson, eds *The Iraq War: European Perspectives on Politics, Strategy, and Operations.* London: Frank Cass, pp. 210–228.

Riverbend. (2006). *A Lynching . . . Baghdad Burning.* [blog]. 31 December 2006. Available at: http://riverbendblog.blogspot.com/2006_12_01_ riverbendblog_archive.html [Accessed 26 June 2009].

—(2005). *Baghdad Burning: Girl Blog from Iraq.* London and New York: Marion Boyars.

Rob. (June 26, 2003 18:08). *Comment on 'New York Times House in Baghdad. Thursday, 26-Jun-2003 00:00.' Where is Raed? the photographic supplement [I am working my way up to Pax TV].* [Online]. By Salam Pax.Availableat:http://salampax.fotopages.com/?entry=445&back= http://salampax.fotopages.com/?page=0#CommentsTop [Accessed 29 June 2009].

Robertson, L. (2008). Baghdad ER. Subverting the mythic gaze upon the wounded and the dead. In K. Randell & S. Redmond, eds *The War Body on Screen.* New York: Continuum, pp. 64–78.

Robinson, P. (2002). *The CNN Effect: The Myth of News, Foreign Policy and Intervention.* London: Routledge.

Robinson, S. (2006). The mission of the J-blog: recapturing journalistic authority online. *Journalism,* 7, 65–83.

Robinson, W. & Robinson, D. (2006). Tsunami mobilizations: considering the role of mobile and digital communication devices, citizen journalism and the mass media. In A. Kavoori & N. Arceneaux, eds *The Cell Phone Reader: Essays in Social Transformation.* New York: Peter Lang, pp. 85–104.

Rogers, E.M. & Dearing, J.W. (1988). Agenda-setting research: where has it been, where is it going? In J.A. Anderson, ed. *Communication Yearbook 11,* London: Sage, pp. 555–594.

Rohrer, F. (2009). *When all video all.* [Online]. *BBC News Magazine,* 21 April.Availableat:http://news.bbc.co.uk/1/hi/magazine/8010098. stm [Accessed 28 October 2009].

Rowell, A. (2004). No blood for oil? In D. Miller, ed. *Tell Me Lies: Propaganda and Media Distortion on the Attack on Iraq.* London: Pluto, pp. 115–125.

Roy, S. (2004). *Al-Jazeera closure a warning to other Arab media: Q&A.* [Online]. Pacific News Service, 16 August. Available at: http:// news.pacificnews.org/news/view_article.html?article_id=9fea8a87b ae4af86b45fdac6947e940a [Accessed 21 May 2009].

Rubin, A.J. & Cave, D. (2007). *In a force for Iraqi calm, seeds of conflict.* [Online]. *The New York Times,* 23 December. Available at: http:// www.nytimes.com/2007/12/23/world/middleeast/23awakening. html?_r=1&pagewanted=all [Accessed 21 May 2009].

Ryan, M. & al-Ansary, K. (2009). *Iraq media booming, yet still in sectarian grip.* [Online]. *Reuters,* 10 March. Available at: http://www.reuters. com/article/worldNews/idUSTRE52A05R20090311?feedType= RSS&feedName=worldNews [Accessed 22 May 2009].

Ryder, D. (2003). *Report on detention and corrections operations in Iraq.* [Online]. Department of the Army, Office of the Provost Marshal General, Washington D.C. 5 November 2003. (Annex 19 of Taguba

Report, 2004). Available at: http://www.publicintegrity.org/articles/entry/505/ [Accessed 5 August 2008].

Saad, L. (2006). *Military still tops in public confidence.* [Online] The Gallup Poll, 7 June. Available at: http://poll.gallup.com/content/?ci=23227 [Accessed 5 May 2006].

Sabatino, R. (2004). *Testimony of Colonel Ralph Sabatino, CFLCC Staff Judge Advocate's office. (Annex 47).* [Online]. Available at: http://www.publicintegrity.org/articles/entry/505/ [Accessed 5 August 2008].

Sakr, N. (2001). *Satellite Realms: Transnational Television, Globalization and the Middle East.* London: I.B. Tauris.

Salama, V. (2007). *Death by video phone: coverage of Saddam Hussein's execution.* [Online]. *Arab Media & Society,* March: 1–13. Available at: www.arabmediasociety.com/.../20070327122124_AMS2_Vivian_Salama.pdf [Accessed 5 August 2009].

Sante, L. (2004). *The Abu Ghraib photos.* [Online]. Available at: http://www.black-international-cinema.com/XIX.BlackInternationalCinema2004/article_33.html [Accessed 9 August 2008].

Santora, M., Glanz, J. & Tavernise, S. (2006). *Dictator who ruled Iraq for 30 years is hanged for crimes against humanity.* [Online]. *International Herald Tribune,* 29 December. Available at: http://www.iht.com/articles/2006/12/30/africa/web.1230saddam.php [Accessed 11 December 2007].

Sass, E. (2007). *Mainstream media eschews execution footage, links to web videos.* [Online]. Available at: http://www.frankwbaker.com/hussein_media.htm [Accessed 25 October 2009].

Schleifer, R. (2007). A century of psyops: psychological warfare from the First World War to Lebanon. In S. Maltby & R. Keeble, eds *Communicating War: Memory, Media and Military.* Bury St Edmunds: Arima Publishing, pp. 151–162.

Schlesinger, J.R. (2004). *Final Report of the Independent Panel to Review DoD Detention Operations.* [Online]. Washington, DC: US Department of Defense. Available at: http://www.salon.com/news/abu_ghraib/2006/03/14/investigations_resources/index.html [Accessed 8 August 2008].

Schlesinger, P. (1990). Rethinking the sociology of journalism: source strategies and the limits of media-centrism. In M. Ferguson, ed. *Public Communications: The New Imperatives – Future Directions for Media Research,* London: Sage, pp. 61–83.

Schmid, A. & de Graaf, J. (1982). *Violence as Communication: Insurgent Terrorism and the Western News Media.* London: Sage.

Scott, J.C. (1990). *Domination and the Arts of Resistance.* New Haven, CT: Yale University Press.

Seib, P. (2005). *Reconnecting the world: how new media technologies may help change Middle East politics.* [Online]. Transnational Broadcasting Studies, 15. Available at: http://www.tbsjournal.com/Archives/Fall05/Seib.html [Accessed 6 April 2009].

Senanayake, S. (2007). *Iraq: Hussein execution video proves damaging for premier.* [Online]. Radio Free Europe, Radio Liberty, 4 January. Available at: http://www.rferl.org/featuresarticle/2007/01/2BE17EEF-DE32–421D-9F21–5D638F0953F7.html [Accessed 11 December 2007].

Seymour, M. (2004). Ancient Mesopotamia and modern Iraq in the British press, 1980–2003. *Current Anthropology,* 45(3), 351–363.

Shanker, T. (2004). *The struggle for Iraq: civil society. US team in Baghdad fights a persistent enemy: rumors.* [Online]. *New York Times,* 23 March. Available at: http://www.nytimes.com/2004/03/23/world/struggle-for-iraq-civil-society-us-team-baghdad-fights-persistent-enemy-rumors.html [Accessed 11 December 2007].

Sharkey, J.E. (2003). *The television war.* [Online]. *American Journalism Review,* May. Available at: http://www.ajr.org/Article.asp?id=2988 [Accessed 12 December 2007].

Sharrock, J. (2008). *Am I a torturer? When Donald Rumsfeld approved 'harsh interrogation techniques,' it was grunts like Ben Allbright who did the dirty work.* [Online]. *Mother Jones,* March–April. Available at: http://findarticles.com/p/articles/mi_m1329/is_2_33/ai_n24376220/pg_1?tag=artBody;col1 [Accessed 6 January 2009].

Shaw, M. (2007). Western and terrorist ways of war. In S. Maltby & R. Keeble, eds *Communicating War: Memory, Media and Military.* Bury St Edmunds: Arima Publishing, pp. 130–140.

Shaw, M. (2002). Risk-transfer militarism, small massacres and the historic legitimacy of war. *International Relations,* 16(3), 343–359.

Shaw, M. (1993). *Civil Society and Media in Global Crisis.* London: St Martin's Press.

Show Me the Way to Aberystwyth. (2005). [song]. Creator: chrismoyles.net.

Sigal, L. (1973). *Reporters and Officials: The Organizations and Politics of Newsgathering.* Lexington, MA: D.C. Heath & Co.

Simpson, J. (2003). *The Wars Against Saddam: Taking the Hard Road To Baghdad.* London: Macmillan.

Singer, J.B. (2005). The political j-blogger: normalizing: a new media form to fit old norms and practices. *Journalism,* 6(2), 173–198.

Sipress, A. & Diaz, S. (2007). *A Casualty Of War: MySpace.* [Online]. Washingtonpost.com, 15 May. Available at: http://www.washingtonpost.

com/wp-dyn/content/article/2007/05/14/AR2007051400112. html?referrer=emailarticle [Accessed 7 August 2008].

Slackman, M. (2009). *Amid crackdown, Iran admits voting errors.* [Online]. *The New York Times,* 22 June. Available at: http://www.nytimes.com/2009/06/23/world/middleeast/23iran.html?_r=1&th&emc=th [Accessed 23 June 2009].

Smith-Spark, L. (2007). *US military takes Iraq war to YouTube.* [Online]. *BBC News Online,* 14 May. Available at: http://news.bbc.co.uk/1/hi/world/americas/6639401.stm [Accessed 20 August 2008].

Solomon, N. (2003). *A Lethal way to 'Dispatch' the News. MediaBeat.* [Online] Available at: www.fair.org [Accessed 27 February 2009].

Sontag, S. (2004). *What have we done?* [Online]. *Guardian,* 24 May. Available at: http://www.commondreams.org/views04/0524–09.htm [Accessed 7 August 2008].

—(2002). *On Photography.* London: Penguin.

Sooni. (2006). *Saddam's execution: right thing done the wrong way* [blog]. 31 December 2006. Available at: http://justsooni.blogspot.com/ [Accessed 7 August 2008].

Sourcewatch. (2008). *Abu Ghraib: photographic evidence of brutality.* [Online] Sourcewatch. Available at: http://www.sourcewatch.org/index.php?title=Abu_Ghraib:_Photographic_Evidence_of_Brutality [Accessed 17 August 2008].

Sousveillance Network. (2009). *Sousveillance network: surveying the emerging global sousveillance society.* [Online]. Available at: http://www.sousveillance.net/about/ [Accessed 7 September 2009].

Stansfield, G. (2006). *Divide and heal.* [Online]. *Prospect Magazine,* 22 May. Available at: http://www.prospect-magazine.co.uk [Accessed 11 December 2007].

Stanyer, J. (2004). Politics and the media: a crisis of trust? *Parliamentary Affairs,* 57(2), 420–434.

Stockman, F. (2005). *At last, Iraq finds a Web designation. Domain name .iq is set for Internet.* [Online]. *The Boston Globe,* 24 November. Available at: http://www.boston.com/news/world/middleeast/articles/ 2005/11/24/at_last_iraq_finds_a_web_designation/ [Accessed 24 July 2008].

Sulaiman, T. (2005). *Girl's rape 'filmed by teenagers on mobile'.* [Online]. *Timesonline,* 18 June. Available at: http://www.timesonline.co.uk/tol/news/uk/article534788.ece [Accessed 1 July 2008].

Suskind, R. (2006). *The One Percent Doctrine: Deep Inside America's Pursuit of Its Enemies since 9/11.* New York: Simon & Schuster.

Sylvester, J. & Huffman, S. (2004). The US embed program and Iraq War coverage. In Y. Passadeos, ed. *Mass Media in Transition: An International Compendium.* Oxford: Rowman & Littlefield, 317–336.

Taguba, A.M. (2004). *Taguba Report. Article 15–6 Investigation of the 800th Military Police Brigade.* [Online]. Available at: http://www.publicintegrity.org/articles/entry/505/ [Accessed 5 August 2008].

Tanner, A. (2005). *Ex-wife recalls her life with Abu Ghraib abuser.* [Online]. *Reuters,* 9 May. Available at: http://www.lookingglassnews.org/viewstory.php?storyid=452 [Accessed 8 August 2008].

Tatham, S. (2006). *Losing Arab Hearts and Minds: The Coalition, Al-Jazeera and Muslim Public Opinion.* London: C. Hurst & Co.

—(2005). *Al-Jazeera:* can it make it here? *British Journalism Review,* 16, 47–52.

Taylor, P.M. (2002). Information warfare and information intervention. In M. Price & M. Thompson, eds *Forging Peace: Intervention, Human Rights and the Management of Media Space.* Edinburgh: Edinburgh University Press, pp. 313–328.

—(1992). *War and the Media: Propaganda and Persuasion in the Gulf War.* Manchester: MUP.

Taylor, P. (1997). *Global Communications, International Affairs and the Media since 1945.* London: Routledge.

Teitelbaum, J. (2002). Dueling for Da'wa: State vs. Society on the Saudi Internet. *The Middle East Journal,* 56(6), 222–239. [Online]. English translation available at: www.al-bab.com/media/docs/saudi.htm. [Accessed 15 February 2010].

Telegraph. (2009). *Iran clamps down on Twitter in attempt to control images of election protests.* [Online]. Telegraph.co.uk, 17 June. Available at: http://www.telegraph.co.uk/news/worldnews/middleeast/iran/5558123/Iran-clamps-down-on-Twitter-in-attempt-to-control-images-of-election-protests.html [Accessed 1 November 2009].

The Aitken Report. (2008). *An investigation into cases of deliberate abuse and unlawful killing in Iraq in 2003 and 2004.* [Online]. Available at: http://www.mod.uk/DefenceInternet/AboutDefence/CorporatePublications/DoctrineOperationsandDiplomacyPublications/OperationsInIraq/TheAitkenReport.htm [Accessed 11 September 2009].

The Economic Times. (2008). *Bush's shoe-shoot duck becomes YouTube sensation!* [Online]. *The Economic Times,* 16 December. Available at: http://economictimes.indiatimes.com/Infotech/Internet_/Bushs_shoe-shoot_duck_becomes_YouTube_sensation/articleshow/3845594.cms [Accessed 16 December 2008].

The Economist. (2009a). *A special report on the Arab world: imposing freedom: Well, that didn't work.* [Online]. Economist.com, 23 July. Available at: http://www.economist.com/specialreports/displaystory.cfm?story_id=14027642 [Accessed 30 July 2009].

—(2009b). *How to stay in charge. Not just coercion, sham democracy too.* [Online]. Economist.com, 23 July. Available at: http://www.economist.com/specialreports/displaystory.cfm?story_id=14027720 [Accessed 30 July 2009].

The Economist. (2004). Move over, *Big Brother. The Economist,* 373, 31–34.

The Harris Poll. (2005). *Fewer Americans than Europeans Have trust in the media – press, radio and TV.* [Online]. The Harris Poll 4 (Published 13 January 2005). Available at: http://www.harrisinteractive.com/harris_poll/index.asp?PID=534 [Accessed 9 October 2009].

The Huffington Post. (2009). *Obama al-Arabiya interview: full text.* [Online]. *Huffington Post,* 26 January. Available at: http://www.huffingtonpost.com/2009/01/26/obama-al-arabiya-intervie_n_161127.html [Accessed 29 January 2009].

The Hutton Inquiry. (2004). *Report of the Inquiry into the Circumstances Surrounding the Death of Dr David Kelly C.M.G.* [Online]. (Published 28 January 2004). Available at: http://www.the-hutton-inquiry.org.uk/content/report/chapter01.htm [Accessed 12 March 2009].

The Independent. (2009). *Leading article: Obama is right on Abu Ghraib pictures.* [Online]. Independent.co.uk 15 *May.* Available at: http://www.independent.co.uk/opinion/leading-articles/leading-article-obama-is-right-on-abu-ghraib-pictures-1685168.html [Accessed 19 May 2009].

The Jawa Report. (2007). *Another Saddam Hussein dead video (ambulance).* [Online]. (Published 17 January 2007). Available at: http://mypetjawa.mu.nu/archives/186117.php [Accessed 11 January 2008].

The National Security Archive. (2005). *Return of the fallen.* [Online]. National Security Archive Electronic Briefing Book No. 152. Available at: http://www.gwu.edu/~nsarchiv/NSAEBB/NSAEBB152/index.htm [Accessed 4 October 2009].

Threadgold, T. & Mosdell, N. (2004). *Embedded reporting: lessons learned?* [Online]. BBC. Available at: http://www.publicservice.co.uk/pdf/dmj/25/DMJ25%200003%20Terr%E2%80%A6adgold%20ATL.pdf [Accessed 2 August 2007].

Townend, J. (2008). *'I am surprised by the lack of user-generated content', says Mumbai attack live-blogger.* [Online]. 27 November 2008. Available at: http://www.journalism.co.uk/2/articles/532930.php [Accessed 1 November 2009].

Tripp, C. (2007). *A History of Iraq.* 3rd edition. Cambridge: Cambridge University Press.

Tuchman, G. (1978). *Making The News: A Study in the Construction of Reality.* New York: The Free Press.

Tumber, H. (2004). Prisoners of news values? Journalists, professionalism, and identification in times of war. In S. Allan & B. Zelizer, eds *Reporting War: Journalism in Wartime*. London: Routledge, pp. 190–205.

Tumber, H. & Palmer, J. (2004). *The Media at War: The Iraq Crisis*. London: Sage.

Tweedie, N. (2007). *Outrage Mounts over 'Lynch Mob' Hanging*. [Online]. *Telegraph*, 3 January. Available at: http://www.telegraph.co.uk/ news/main.jhtml?xml=/news/2007/01/02/wiraq02.xml [Accessed 16 December 2007].

UK Defence Communications Strategy. (2007). *The Defence Communications Strategy*. [Online]. (Published 27 February 2007). Available at: http://ics.leeds.ac.uk/papers/vp01.cfm?outfit=pmt&requesttimeo ut=500&folder=34&paper=2884 [Accessed 12 September 2008].

UNHCR. (2007). *Statistics on Displaced Iraqis around the World*. [Online]. UNHCR: the UN Refugee Agency. Available at: http://www.unhcr. org/461f7cb92.html [Accessed 1 November 2009].

United Nations Development Program. (2009). *Arab human development report 2009: challenges to human security in the Arab countries*. [Online]. New York: United Nations Publications. Available at: http://hdr. undp.org/en/reports/regionalreports/featuredregionalreport/ name,3442,en.html [Accessed 12 November 2009].

—(2005). *Human development report 2005: international cooperation at a crossroads: Aid, trade and security in an unequal world*. [Online]. New York: United Nations Publications. Available at: http://hdr.undp. org/en/reports/global/hdr2005/ [Accessed 12 November 2009].

US Department of Commerce. (2004). *A nation online. Entering the broadband age*, [Online]. 6. Available at: http://www.ntia.doc.gov/ reports/anol/NationOnlineBroadband04.htm [Accessed 28 August 2008].

US Senate Armed Services Committee. (2008). *Inquiry into the treatment of detainees in US custody*. [Online]. United States Senate. (Published 20 November 2008). Available at: http://armed-services.senate. gov/Publications/Detainee%20Report%20Final_April%2022%20 2009.pdf [Accessed 19 May 2009].

US State Department. (2009). *United States Code*. [Online] (Published 5 January 2009). Available at: http://www.law.cornell.edu/uscode/ html/uscode18/usc_sec_18_00000921----000-.html [Accessed 1 November 2009].

USA Today. (2006). *Rumsfeld says extremists winning media war*. [Online]. *USA Today*, 17 February. Available at: http://www.usatoday.com/

news/washington/2006–02-17-rumsfeld-media_x.htm [Accessed 2 July 2008].

Vicky. (2003). *Comment on 'Friday sermon in Kadhmia mosque. Monday, 16-Jun-2003 00:00.' Where is Raed? the photographic supplement [I am working my way up to Pax TV]*. [Online]. By Salam Pax. 8 July 2003, 13:08. Available at: http://salampax.fotopages.com/?entry=445&back=http://salampax.fotopages.com/?page=0#CommentsTop [Accessed 29 June 2009].

Virilio, P. (2002 [1991]). *Desert Screen: War at the Speed of Light*. Trans. M. Degener . London: Continuum.

Wall, M. (2005). 'Blogs of war': weblogs as news. *Journalism*, 6(2), 153–172.

Walsh, J. (2006). *The Abu Ghraib files*. [Online]. Salon.com, 14 March. Available at: http://www.salon.com/news/abu_ghraib/2006/03/14/introduction/index.html [Accessed 8 August 2008].

Washington Post. (2006). *Chronology of Abu Ghraib*. [Online]. Washingtonpost.com, 17 February. Available at: http://www.washingtonpost.com/wp-srv/world/iraq/abughraib/timeline.html [Accessed 18 August 2008].

—(2004). *Abuse photos*. [Online]. Washingtonpost.com, 6 May. Available at: http://www.washingtonpost.com/wp-srv/flash/photo/world/2004–05-20_photos/index_frames.htm?startat=1&indexFile=world_2004–05-20_photos [Accessed 18 August 2008].

Weber, T. (2007). *BBC strikes Google-YouTube deal*. [Online]. *BBC News Online*, 2 March. Available at: http://news.bbc.co.uk/1/hi/business/6411017.stm [Accessed 17 September 2009].

Webtrends. (2009). *Yes, digital marketers can gain Obama campaign's data crunching advantage*. [Online] http://www.webtrends.com/About Webtrends/NewsRoom/NewsRoomArchive/2009/YesDigital MarketersCanGainObamaCampaignsDataCrunchingAdvantage. aspx?WT.rss=rss [Accessed 18 October 2009].

White, J., Davenport, C. & Higham, S. (2004). *The new images: videos amplify picture of violence*. [Online]. Washingtonpost.com, 21 May. Available at: http://www.washingtonpost.com/wp-dyn/articles/A43785–2004May20.html?nav=headlines [Accessed 18 August 2008].

White House. (2006). *The national security strategy of the United States of America, March*. [Online]. Available at: http://www.whitehouse.gov/nsc/nss/2006/nss2006.pdf [Accessed 11 January 2009].

—(2002). *The national security strategy of the United States, September*. [Online]. Available at: http://www.whitehouse.gov/nsc/nss.html [Accessed 11 January 2009].

Whitwell, T. (2008). Rogue elephant. *British Journalism Review*, 19(1), 57–62.

Wide angle. (2007). *Dishing democracy. Handbook: satellite television in the Arab world.* [Online]. PBS. Available at: http://www.pbs.org/wnet/wideangle/episodes/dishing-democracy/handbook-satellite-television-in-the-arab-world/1843/ [Accessed 20 April 2009].

Williams, G. (2004). Watchdogs or lapdogs? Media, politics and regulation: the US experience. In D. Miller, ed. *Tell Me Lies: Propaganda and Media Distortion on the Attack on Iraq.* London: Pluto, pp. 195–203.

Williams, K. (1992). Something more important than truth: ethical issues in war reporting. In A. Belsey & R. Chadwick, eds *Ethical Issues in Journalism and the Media.* London: Routledge, pp. 154–170.

Winseck, D. (1992). Gulf war in the global village: *CNN*, democracy and the information age. In J. Wasko & V. Mosco, eds *Democratic Communications in the Information Age.* Toronto: Garamond Press, pp. 60–74.

Woodward, B. (2008). *The War Within. A Secret White House History 2006–2008.* New York: Simon & Schuster.

—(2004). *Plan of Attack.* New York: Simon and Schuster.

Worth, R.F. (2009). *Defiance grows as Iran's leader sets vote review.* [Online]. *The New York Times*, 15 June. Available at: http://www.nytimes.com/2009/06/16/world/middleeast/16iran.html [Accessed 17 June 2009].

Wright, D.P. & Reese, T.R. (2008). *On Point II: Transition to the new campaign. The United States army in Operation Iraqi Freedom May 2003 – January 2005.* [Online]. Fort Leavenworth, Kansas: Combat Studies Institute Press, US Army Combined Arms Center. Available at: www.globalsecurity.org/military/library/.../onpoint/index.html [Accessed 1 August 2009].

Wright, R. & Graham, B. (2004). *Bush privately chides Rumsfeld.* [Online]. WashingtonPost.com, 6 May. Available at: http://www.washington-post.com/wp-dyn/articles/A5733-2004May5.html [Accessed 18 August 2008].

Yet another American. (2003). *Comment on 'New York Times House in Baghdad. Thursday, 26-Jun-2003 00:00.' Where is Raed? the photographic supplement [I am working my way up to Pax TV].* [Online]. By Salam Pax. 26 June 2003, 18:08. Available at: frohttp://salampax.fotopages.com/?entry=445&back=http://salampax.fotopages.com/?page=0#CommentsTop [Accessed 29 June 2009].

Yin, R.K. (2003). *Case Study Research: Design and Methods.* 3rd edition. California: Sage.

Zalewski, D. (2003). *A Baghdad blogger.* [Online]. *The New Yorker,* 31 March. Available at: http://www.newyorker.com/archive/2003/03/31/030331ta_talk_zalewski [Accessed 25 June 2009].

Zayani, M. & Ayish, M.I. (2006). Arab satellite television and crisis reporting: covering the fall of Baghdad. *International Communication Gazette,* 68(5–6), 473–497.

Zelizer, B. & Allan, S. (2002). *Journalism after September 11.* London: Routledge.

Zunes, S. (2006). The United States: belligerent hegemon. In R. Fawn & R. Hinnebusch, eds *The Iraq War: Causes and Consequences.* London: Lynne Rienner, pp. 21–36.

INDEX

Sousveillance, Media and Strategic Political Communication